Forbidden Homeland

STORY OF A DIASPORAN

Katia Tavitian Karageuzian

ISBN: 9798364494450

In Memory of

My Grandparents
Sarkis and Maryam Tavitian
Krikor and Yevnigeh Torossian

In Honor of

My Parents
Kevork and Manoushak Tavitian

In Dedication to

My Sons
Razmig and Raffi

In Solidarity

With All Marginalized Nations
And Victims of Genocide

Early Praise for *Forbidden Homeland*

"Forbidden Homeland immerses you in centuries of world-shaping history as its written pages become the rich landscape of a deeply personal journey…making you feel a part of it and reaching into your core. So it did to me. In her riveting odyssey to find the missing pieces of her own identity, Katia Tavitian Karageuzian takes the reader with her to uncover hidden truths and connect past with present. Dr. Karageuzian masterfully weaves her life's unexpected twists and turns, layered within stories of Armenian Genocide, Lebanese Civil War, immigration, and current world events, and paints a vivid, living mosaic of the unique and shared experiences of exile and resilience, loss and rebirth, discovering finally that even when forbidden our homeland, if we search, we will find home."

Ani Hovannisian Kevorkian, Filmmaker, *The Hidden Map*

"This is an amazing book which weaves seamlessly the fascinating story of her family life with the tragic history of the Armenian nation, all the while discovering by chance long-lost relatives scattered throughout the world after the Genocide of 1915."

Harut Sassounian, Publisher, *The California Courier newspaper*.

"Every migrant finding a haven in America has bittersweet memories of the Old Country to hold and cherish. Karageuzian's story stands out with the persistence of a dark shadow hovering over her picturesque description of a happy childhood interrupted by the terrors of Lebanese civil war. Halfway through her skillfully wrought narrative, the shadow closes in; she begins to untie the knots, and the narrative becomes the story of the Armenian Genocide through the lens of a third-generation survivor."

Rubina Peroomian, Ph.D. Genocide Scholar, Author

"I am sure this enticingly timely volume will be read with great interest by researchers, and all readers interested in the recent turbulent history of Lebanon, the Middle East and Armenia."
   Tatul Sonentz-Papazian, Editor of _"Hai Sird"_

"Part memoir, part history with revealing facts about Armenia, Katia's story reinforced my gratitude for being born in America and having the freedom of attending school without fear of bombs killing me or members of my family. This is a powerful story…"
   Kay Mouradian, Author, _My Mother's Voice_

Introduction

I WAS BORN IN BEAUTIFUL Beirut, Lebanon. As wonderful as life was in my earlier years, I could not help but notice certain curious oddities. For starters, we spoke Armenian at home, a language phonetically very different from the Arabic spoken in the rest of the country. My grandmother Maryam always wore black, and my other grandmother, Yevnigeh, lived in an interesting part of the city where everyone was Armenian. Eventually, I went through the rite of passage accorded to every Armenian child who reaches school age. I was told that Lebanon was not our true homeland and that our circumstances were unique due to a tragic event that befell my grandparents' generation. While the innocence of most children is shattered by such things as the realization that Santa Claus is not real, Armenian children need to also process the shocking disclosure that a certain nation had deported and murdered thousands of their ancestors, including children, just because of their race. The adults in my life did their best to make sure that the Armenian Genocide did not define our existence. Instead, they focused on upholding our heritage, being resilient, and moving forward. However, the unanswered questions lingered, hovering in the background of my life as the Lebanese civil war raged, until the early 1980s, when events that took place around me and incredible coincidences later in California, brought me face to face with my family's past as well as relatives I had known nothing about!

I started writing about my discoveries in a private memoir with the hopes that my children would read it someday. However, as I researched events to put my family's experiences into historical perspective, I found myself being led to a world of information previously unknown to me. Not only did I travel down my roots into Armenia's ancient history, but I stepped back into the crumbling Ottoman Empire and discovered why the Armenian Genocide had taken place in the first place, how it was executed and why, more than a century later, thousands of families like mine had yet to receive justice for the crimes they endured, the family inheritances they lost, and the ancestral lands they were cheated out of. I came out at the other end of my journey with the realization that my story did not belong to my family alone. It belonged to all of humanity as a living testimonial of not only the intergenerational consequences of crimes against humanity but also the consequences of impunity from them in a world where truth and justice are sacrificed in the name of geopolitics and national interests. Impunity that tragically only breeds more of the same crime, even now in the 21st century.

This journey would not have been possible without the destined involvement of my college friend Siranush and, most importantly, my father's collection of old family records and memorabilia, and his deep appreciation of past events, an interest that he has also instilled in me. Putting an Armenian experience onto paper is quite the endeavor, considering the timespan and complicated regional and international politics that have and continue to shape the Armenian destiny. I would not have been able to accomplish what I set out to do without the support and encouragement of family and friends, principally Maggie Mangassarian Goschin who has been a guiding light since the early stages of the book, the incomparable Dr. Rubina Piroomian and Mr. Harut Sassounian who have graciously assisted with content editing, my sister Betty Tavitian Kilaghbian and cousin Armig Adourian who carried me through the finish line, the amazingly talented Ani Hovannisian, all my colleagues in the education committee that I am currently part of, particularly, Dr. Kay Mouradian, Alice Petrossian, Zarik Hacopian, Arpi Krikorian, Dr. Carine Chorbajian, Sedda Antekelian, Laura Michael Gaboudian in addition to Nora Hovsepian, Prof. Vahram Shemmassian, Matthew Karanian, and Dr. Khatchig Mouradian. Most valuably, my family's story would not have had its colors and details were it not for the passionate accounts and corroboration of my parents Kevork and Manoushag Tavitian, my cousins Ilda, Vartoug, and Ari, and relatives in the United States, France, and Lebanon, particularly Uncle Vahak Tavitian and Mrs. Marie Bedoyan. A most precious gift has been the patient support of my husband Pierre and sons Razmig and Raffi, who graciously endured the long hours I spent at my computer. I had to involve my sister Betty's wonderful graphic talents in designing the cover of the book. I am thankful she has also put her stamp on this project, as this is as much her story as it is mine. The old typewriter is a symbol of the interviews, research, and self-education that shaped my journey and remain its most inspirational and cherished parts. The metal arms of the type bars symbolize all the atrocities, internal and external betrayals, and continuous wars and challenges, that have stricken and continue to strike the Armenian nation, which is represented by the Armenian tricolor flag in the ink ribbon. In its turn, the ink in the ribbon symbolizes the inextricable pull of our homeland that runs in our blood as diasporans. The fabric in the background of the cover is that of my dear grandmother Maryam's dowry bundle from the old country. The discovery of her story was the main driving force behind this book. Special thanks go to my patient editor Guadalupe G. Montano, who insisted on a light edit of the book to retain my authentic voice and what she referred to as my "strong passions." Her encouraging words and feedback as a non-Armenian were most meaningful.

This is the story of all marginalized nations subjected to crimes and wars, exiled from their homelands, or forced to migrate, whose destinies have been derailed by the blind ambition of rulers and leading nations engaged in the ongoing race for power. It is also a testament to bravery and resilience and the stubborn human will to live in freedom.

Table of Contents

Introduction · vii
Prologue · 1
The Man in the Photograph · · · · · · · · · · · · · · · · · 5
Where to Start? · 11
My Grandmother Maryam · · · · · · · · · · · · · · · · · · 19
1975, the Lebanese Civil War starts... · · · · · · · · · · 25
Years of War... · 29
Seven Days in Hell, 1978 · · · · · · · · · · · · · · · · · · 33
Schooling During War... · · · · · · · · · · · · · · · · · · · 39
Bourj Hammoud · 47
Odaroutioun, Diaspora · 55
River of Tears.... · 63
1983 · 67
My Grandmother Yevnigeh... · · · · · · · · · · · · · · · · 73
Not so Sweet a Birthday! · · · · · · · · · · · · · · · · · · · 85
Have a Nice Day! · 89
Pack Up Your Life! · 97
My Lebanon ·101
No Looking Back ·107
This is California! ·111
Life in America ·115
Where is Karabakh? ·119
1987: Another Armenian Tree! · · · · · · · · · · · · · · ·141
Malatya? ·143
Turkish Armenian Relatives? · · · · · · · · · · · · · · · ·147

They Are Dead, Dead.... ·151
Questions and More Questions ·181
Hit the Books ·187
The Treaty of Sevres and Justice for Armenians · · · · · · · · · 203
Those Who Stayed Behind · 223
Sovietization · 233
Wedding in the Mountains · 237
The Reawakening of the Monster · · · · · · · · · · · · · · · · · · · 245
Did You Know We Were Cousins? · · · · · · · · · · · · · · · · · · · 249
What Were Their Names? · 255
I Owe My Life to Turks?! · 263
Trip of a Lifetime · 267
Armenophobia with Impunity · 279
The U.S. Congress Recognizes the Armenian Genocide! · · · · 291
American Interests? · 303
2020, Annus Horribilis ·311
A Last Word · 337
Resources Used · 353

Prologue

WHAT IS CURRENTLY LEFT OF the State of Armenia is sandwiched between Turkey and Azerbaijan, two countries linked with historic ambitions of Pan-Turkism[1] that have been chipping away at the Armenian homeland for the past 100 years.

Armenia used to be much larger, an ancient nation of fascinating tales and cultural treasures spread over a plateau known throughout history as the Armenian Highlands. The Encyclopedia Britannica describes the Armenian Highlands as a "mountainous region of western Asia that lies mainly in Turkey, occupies all of [current day] Armenia, and includes southern Georgia, western Azerbaijan, and northwestern Iran covering almost 154,400 square miles." Often considered as a possible location of the Garden of Eden, it is believed to be the epicenter of the Iron Age.

Armenians call themselves *Hay* (pronounced [Hai]) and their country *Hayastan*, both words stemming from the name of their legendary patriarch Hayk, a descendant of Noah whose ark landed on Mount Ararat after the great flood mentioned in the Bible. The Iron Age Kingdom of Urartu or Ararat (in Hebrew), also known as the Kingdom of Van, rose in the 9th century BC around Lake Van in what is now Eastern Turkey. Urartu is mentioned along with Assyria and Babylon on the oldest map of the world, a piece of Babylonian clay tablet that dates back to between 700 and 500 BC. It shows the

---

1 A political movement that emerged in the late 1880s with the goal of uniting Turkish speaking peoples. It is related to the ideology of Pan-Turanism which envisioned the union of a wider region of Turk, Tatar and Uralic peoples.

river of Euphrates flowing down from the Armenian mountains and through Babylon (in today's Iraq).

The earliest internationally acknowledged record of *Armenia* and its people is in the Behistun Inscriptions of Darius of Persia, 517 BCE, which were recorded in three languages (cuneiforms), where Armenia is referred to as a neighboring country and is mentioned as Harminuya in Elamite, Arminia in Old Persian and Urartu in Babylonian. (Starting the 6th century BC, Urartu was referred to as Armenia). The name Armenia is mentioned on many Greco-Roman maps and in the works of renowned ancient geographers from as early as the 200s BCE[2], as well as those of medieval Islamic and Christian authors, Renaissance age, and modern era cartographers.

Recent studies have not only shown that the Armenians are indigenous to the Armenian Highlands, but that they have a distinct genetic isolate with almost no mixture with other populations since the end of the Bronze Age, 3,000 years ago.[3]

Genetics, archeological, and historical artifacts date Armenia to 7,000 years ago, with recorded history dating back 3,500 years, making it one of the oldest nations on earth. At its largest, the Armenian Kingdom under King Tigranes the Great (95 to 55 BC) expanded from the Mediterranean to the Caspian Sea, including most of current-day Azerbaijan, as well as Lebanon, Syria, and Judea at its southernmost tip. In 301 AD, Armenia became the first Christian nation in the world, with its apostolic church based on the teachings of apostles St. Bartholomew and St. Thaddeus, who had brought Christ's message to the region. Twelve years later, in 313, Rome accepted Christianity as its official religion.

---

2 Rouben Galichian, "A Brief History of the Maps of Armenia," accessed April 10, 2021 http://roubengalichian.com/2015/06/24/a-brief-history-of-the-maps-of-armenia/

3 Marc Haber, Massimo Mezzavilla, Yali Xue, David Comas, Paolo Gasparini, Pierre Zalloua, and Chris Tyler-Smith, (21 October 2015). Genetic evidence for an origin of the Armenians from Bronze Age mixing of multiple populations. *European Journal of Human Genetics* 24, no 6 (2015): 931–936. Our tests suggest that Armenians had no significant mixture with other populations in their recent history and have thus been genetically isolated since the end of the Bronze Age, 3000 years ago.

Although it has always kept its entity, situated in the crossing of major trade routes between Europe and Asia, Armenia has come under the rule of several regional empires, often divided geographically between them into what have become known as its Western and Eastern halves. Thus, Western Armenia was part of the Roman and Byzantine Empires and later the Ottoman Empire, while Eastern Armenia has been under the rule of Persians, Arabs, and Russians. Armenians continue to long for a united and free homeland.

The Man in the Photograph

It is October 2019. Wildfire season is upon us in Southern California. Crazy winds pick up around this time of the year, perpetuating fires that have become a staple of climate change.

I am at my parents' house. Everyone is resting after a hearty meal of *Mulukhieh* prepared by my mother's loving hands. *Mulukhieh*, royalty in Arabic, is a multilayered elaborate dish of chicken, rice, and pita chips covered with a stew of spinach, cilantro, garlic, lemon, and a topping of vinegar and onions. It is my favorite! Persian Armenians might be great at making *Ghormeh Sabzi*. We Lebanese Armenians, on the other hand, have picked up making *Mulukhieh*!

Lazy conversations overlapping with the sounds of a Western movie playing on the television make my mind wander. Almost thirty years ago, curious coincidences and discoveries led me to inquire about my family's background. People and events have since seemed to find their way to me as if guided by a mysterious energy. Yet, I was still yearning for a tangible connection with the past. I did not know what I was looking for, but something pushed me to keep on looking.

I decide to delve into my father's box of old family photos one more time. I grab it from the hallway closet and settle down on a couch, placing it gingerly on my lap. Here they were again, pictures that I had gone over many times prior. The amazing more than 100-year-old burial photograph of my father's uncle Napoleon, the family portraits taken during my father's visit to Malatya, photographs of unknown people that I always skip, and wedding pictures of several cousins during prosperous years in prewar Lebanon.

One picture of a wedding piques my interest the most. In it are most of the grandsons of my great-grandfather Garabed Tavitian and his brothers Manuel and Nishan. Twelve of them, to be exact, garbed in sixties refined suits next to equally elegant wives. The group oozes clan-like pride and sophistication far removed from the difficult predicament of the generation that preceded it. The photo is a testament to the resilience of the Armenian people, hard-working ethics, and drive to succeed. I continue on to pictures of my parents during their early courtship. Mother, with her natural red hair and stunning figure, and father, with his piercing blue eyes, made quite a handsome couple! Back to photos that I skipped. An old one of an unknown man with his wife and children; then pictures taken during holidays in Lebanon. I come back to Napoleon's burial picture. "My great-grandfather must have been well off to have commissioned this photograph back in the late 1910s," I think to myself. Why would he want to take a picture of his deceased son's funeral? Did he mean to send this picture somewhere as an announcement of his son's passing? I flip the photograph over. To my surprise, I discover that it is a postcard photo! There are no words written, however. Hmmm… I move on to more familiar current pictures of relatives and come back yet again to the beginning of the batch. And once again, the fading black and white photograph of the man with his wife and two children… This time I pause, dwelling on it for a moment. The man's eyes capture my attention. They look familiar. Possibly fair colored, piercing… hmm… "Who is this man, and why do we have this photo?" I ponder. Then I flip it around, wondering if it is also printed as a postcard. And lo and behold! Not only is it a postcard, but there is a handwritten message on it in Armenian! I proceed to read the beautiful cursive. "*Sireli kuyrs, ays ngareh geh nvirem kez ipr hishadag minchev mez disoutyan. Maryam Tavitiani, Maynuel Arpadjiani goghmaneh.*" "Dear sister, I gift you this picture as a souvenir until our reunion. To Maryam Tavitian, From

6

Maynuel Arpadjian" I am livid! I can't believe my eyes! I read the two lines once more. Maynuel Arpadjian! I flip the picture over again. I finally meet my grandmother's brother, who had stayed behind in Turkey. The brother and family she was separated from because of the Genocide. I finally know what he looked like! Maynuel, who was saved from death by his sister Elizabeth's Turkish husband, who took off for almost a year to look for his lost nephew Kegham, and who purchased his parents' home back from Turks who had broken in and settled in it. This was the connection I was searching for! The faraway fading call of the branch that was snapped, of Turkish and Armenian kilim rugs hanging from walls, of the last Armenian words written fluently and beautifully, of the signature that still bore the Armenian last name of a family that would soon be transformed in so many ways. Maynuel Arpadjian with his wife Vartuhi, his eldest son Bedros, named after his murdered father, and his son Krikor, possibly named after his killed younger brother. Knowing Bedros and Krikor's age places the picture around the year 1930, four years before Turkey's Surname Law that prompted the change of the last name Arpadjian. I realize that we will never know how many past generations of the family had carried the name Arpadjian. It has been replaced and gone, possibly forever. Little Krikor reminds me of his daughter, my newfound cousin Ilda. All the pieces are together now. I place the picture gently back into the box. I no longer sense the need to keep on looking for the unknown something. It has left me. I am at peace.

My grandmother Maryam's brother, Maynuel, with his wife and
two older children circa 1930. From my family's collection

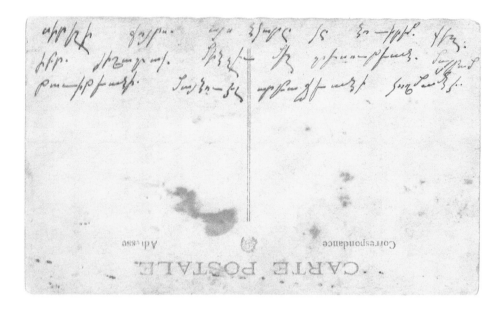

THE BACK OF THE SAME PHOTOGRAPH, WITH THE MESSAGE IN ARMENIAN CURSIVE, SIGNED MAYNUEL ARPADJIAN. A COUPLE OF YEARS LATER, THE TURKISH GOVERNMENT ENACTED THE SURNAME LAW, AND THE NAME ARPADJIAN WAS CHANGED TO A TURKISH NAME.

Where to Start?

ONE OF MY MOST CHERISHED possessions is a tiny Suisse Bank or *Credit Suisse* calendar organizer that I used as a diary in my last year in Lebanon. Bound in bright red leather, it fits in my palm and hums of memories as if it were a locked time capsule waiting to be opened. The number 1984 is etched in gold on the front cover. That year, 1984, was a most exciting year: the year I came to America! The red ribbon bookmark rests on the page with the most celebrated entry. It reads in Armenian, "It is 5:00 pm. We landed in California. My grandmother and uncle greeted us at LAX. My new life begins!" More than 30 years have passed since I wrote those words. In an ironic twist of fate, we had landed in the United States on Memorial Day, Monday, May 28 (and the Independence Day of the first Armenian Republic). I will always remember it as the day my family was given a new chance. The days following that fateful day became my reality. The days preceding it became part of someone else's life, someone I left in Lebanon on that beautiful Sunday morning. I was 16 years old.

Leaving Beirut, Lebanon, was the greatest adventure of my life! I flip the pages of my diary backward towards memories I have confined to the deepest recesses of my mind. I stop on Tuesday, March 6, a day seared in my memory that plays back as if it were yesterday! All I have to do is close my eyes, and my mind travels back in time and hovers over a long highway infested with back-to-back traffic stretching for miles on end. I see myself, a budding teenager with short dirty blond hair and quiet blue eyes, sitting on the left passenger seat behind the driver of a taxi. It was a slightly damp, crisp, beautiful morning. My parents and I had awakened very early. Excitement and eagerness were nibbling at our nerves. We had a most important appointment with destiny. After years of false hopes for the resolution of the Lebanese Civil War, horrific war experiences, and dashed dreams, my father had finally decided that we would immigrate to the United States, where my maternal uncle and grandmother were already settled. "I am doing this for my two girls," he would announce at gatherings. "Let them become the citizens of a big and powerful country. Peace will always elude the Middle East. This war has taken all my hard work and dreams away from me. Let my children, at least, have some hope for a bright future."

A year prior, in October of 1983, a suicide bomb at the Beirut U.S. Marine barracks had claimed the lives of over 200 Marines. Adding to our chagrin was the news that our Green Card applications were lost in that upheaval. All paperwork had to be resubmitted! We obliged, and five months later, we were finally on our way to the American Embassy in West Beirut for our immigration interview scheduled at 1:00 o'clock in the afternoon. There was only one main road leading from the Christian East Beirut to the Muslim West Beirut. It was guarded by militia from both sides of the conflict, and the flow of cars trickled through many checkpoints. The infamous Green Line that divided the Lebanese capital crossed through this highway.

Downtown Beirut, the epicenter of the Green Line where the first clashes of the civil war between Christian and Muslim Lebanese had erupted in 1975, had become a no man's land with streets of towering rubble amassed through years of constant shelling. The neighborhoods on both sides of the Green Line had endured the bloodiest periods of the war, and their residential buildings were tattered by the damage from bombings and sniper bullets. We lived in one of those neighborhoods on the Christian side of Beirut. Gemmayze was a mere 15-minute drive from the destroyed downtown and the dreaded Green Line. I still remember its old stone buildings with tall shuttered French windows, at once romantic and mysterious, the aged gurgling marble fountain at the foot of our street, the neighborhood butcher in his white, blood-stained apron, the large pieces of meat hanging from hooks amidst buzzing flies, the coffee and cigarette visits with our warm Lebanese neighbors and Feyrouz's[4] songs always playing in the background.

Further down the main street was the austere French Catholic *College Frères du Sacre Coeurs*, where my father had studied. Across the iron gates of the Sacre Coeurs was the large two-story bookstore *Librairie Samir.* In my teen years, it became my sanctuary. I looked forward to the rare quiet days when its doors were open. I remember venturing through deserted cobbled streets past brick wall fences covered with colorful bougainvillea vines down Gouraud Street to purchase the next book that was going to transport me to a world far away from the hellish one I was living in. Through the years of war, Gemmayze's newer buildings and its Ottoman and Colonial-era historic structures had all taken on a Swiss cheese look, and their inhabitants had moved to comparatively safer areas away from the Green Line. We stayed.

---

4 Feyrouz: One of the most popular and revered Lebanese singers

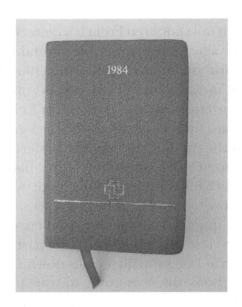

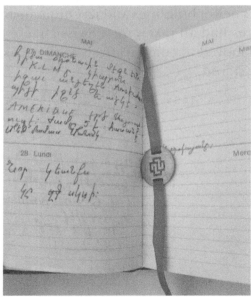

My 1984 Credit Suisse Calendar/Diary, and the Monday May 28th entry about our plane landing in America. It reads in Armenian: "My new life begins."

My childhood memories are connected to the different periods of the war. Since I was only seven years old when the Lebanese Civil War began, my recollection of the pre-war cosmopolitan Beirut, also dubbed the Paris of the Middle East, is very fuzzy. I remember, for example, walking once with my mother downtown to buy boots. I was very taken by the lights, the hustle and bustle, the taxis rounding the monument of Martyrs Square in *Sehet al Bourj* at the city center, shoppers being followed by porters carrying enormous loaded baskets on their backs with the thick leather handles pressed against their foreheads, and, oh, the aroma of delicious Falafel. We paid a surprise visit to my father's custom tailoring shop on the third floor of the Automatic Building. I was so giddy and secretly in awe of my father. His business was booming. Doctors, bankers, and politicians were regulars who came to be fitted into handmade suits crafted out of the best imported European fabrics. He had just hired additional tailors and had his store decorated in the latest 1970s Art Deco look, with trendy dark orange curtains and white laminate furniture with Formica trimmings. The sitting area was very chic. Tall windows overlooked a vibrant view of downtown Beirut with its souks, government buildings, mosques, and churches. Shelves were laden with yarns of fabric placed at a decorative diagonal angle. Further in was an area anchored by a large island where my father cut patterns and designed suits. Above was a loft where tailors who had become part of our family worked at sewing machines.

At my father's request, workers from café Idriss below delivered fresh baked sweets with bottles of cold 7UP. For me, that was such a great treat! My father shared the news of his recent successes and discussed the possibility of us moving into an apartment in the new construction sites further north in Beirut, across from the blue Mediterranean Sea. At 35, he was contemplating hiring a clothes designer and a store manager and going into semi-retirement!

My fondest memories, however, are of the summer days spent in the country. Beirut was unbearably hot and humid in the summer, and a good number of its residents rented vacation homes in the cooler mountains. Our summer apartment was on the third floor of a building in Dhour El Choueir, a picturesque village with thick pine tree forests and steep roads. We would wake with the roosters at every dawn and inhale the thick scent of pine trees, then rush to get fresh baked *Manaeesh* (baked flatbread with zaatar topping) from the baker's. Several of our relatives and friends with kids our age rented apartments in adjacent buildings and neighboring villages. I loved our visits with them on long lazy evenings, where our fathers would start singing old Armenian folk songs after a few glasses of Arak while we kids created a ruckus playing hide and seek. The barbeque would linger through the night, and the delightful Mezza appetizers would tease the senses. I especially looked forward to our way back home in the pitch dark. The bright stars in the sky were simply amazing.

My favorite time was during the Holiday of Martaklah; when all the villages took on an air of carnival, and the streets were lined with sweets and toy vendors. Strands of lights hung from all sides of the church at the *saha*, village center, and the villagers would walk to attend mass while singing hymns to the Virgin Mary. In Bolonia, north of our village, there was a restaurant with window openings covered only by thick red curtains where Armenian singers such as Antossyan and Adiss performed. Lazy summer afternoons were full of strolling enamored teenagers wearing bell-bottom pants and *minijupes* (French for miniskirts), humming the hit songs of these singers. Those were the good old days.

(Singer Adiss' hit)
Karoun Karoun Karoun eh, siroun siroun siroun eh
Ed ko sev sev atcherov, yar jan ints tou ayroum es

It is springtime, lovely time
With those black eyes of yours,
Honey, you are burning my soul

THE AUTOMATIC BUILDING, ON THE LEFT, IN PREWAR DOWNTOWN BEIRUT. OLD
BEIRUT (THE MUNICIPALITY OF BEIRUT 1960) OLDBEIRUT.COM, AUTHOR UNKNOWN

SEPTEMBER, 1993. THE AUTOMATIC BUILDING (LEFT) IN THE DESTROYED
DOWNTOWN BEIRUT (VEGETATION GROWING IN THE ABANDONED BUILDINGS)
PRIOR TO ITS DEMOLITION DURING THE RECONSTRUCTION OF DOWNTOWN
AFTER THE WAR. / ALAMY STOCK PHOTO (RIGHTS PURCHASED)

My Grandmother Maryam

ONE MORE PERSON LIVED WITH us in my early childhood years, and that was my father's mother, my nene Maryam.

I remember my grandmother always wearing black or dark-colored clothing. My grandfather Sarkis Tavitian, a heavy cigarette smoker, had succumbed to lung cancer two years prior to my parents' marriage. In the old tradition, widows wore mostly black out of respect for their husbands' memory. I do not know if my grandmother was still with us when the Lebanese Civil War started in 1975. I do, however, recall very clearly the day her doctor asked me to draw a sketch of his eyeglasses. My parents must have told him about my hobby of drawing. I concentrated and did my best to capture all the details of the spectacles he had placed in front of me on the dining table. Unbeknownst to me, my grandmother was taking her last breath in the room next door.

In the short time that I came to know her, I remember her as a frail-looking lady with distinctly smooth, ivory-like facial skin. In contrast to her fragile physical bearing, her piercing hazel blue eyes spoke of confident pride and eagle-like determination. To this day, I feel the deep pull of her love for me. Whenever I was in trouble with my mother, I ran to my grandmother and took refuge behind her skirt. She would defend me with her signature over-dramatized chastisement of my mom: "tserkeret godrin… atchkers gournan… yerpek chzarnes bzdigin," meaning "may your hands break and may I go blind and not ever see you hit this child." My father's paternal uncle Krikor and his family lived on the floor directly above us. My mother recalls hosting visitors all day long. My grandmother would apparently invite in every neighbor using the stairs and insist on a cup of coffee. She loved having people over.

Nene suffered from heart disease. My father made sure that she took her prophylactic antibiotic doses before visits to the dentist. She also suffered from another quiet problem that we all knew about but chose not to mention.

My grandmother would panic and become extremely concerned whenever a family member ran late. My father recalls mischievously how, on his way back in the wee hours of the morning from outings with friends, he would discover a whole group of alarmed neighbors gathered in the street around his worry-stricken mom. From afar, he could discern his uncle pacing in the middle of the crowd. His own father, on the other hand, had grown immune to his mother's worrying and would not bother joining the search party!

As a child whose young parents went out to enjoy the vibrant nightlife of pre-war Beirut, not only did I come to witness this behavior firsthand, but, in many ways, I became my grandmother's reliable secret confidante. At five, I did not know what to make of her reactions, but I somehow understood her pain. She did not have to explain it. I felt it just watching her. I remember vividly one chilly evening at our country home, where I was awakened by her pacing in front of my room. I slipped out of my bed, all too familiar with her need to have me for company. "Your mom and dad are so late!" she said, trying to control the anger in her voice. In order to not add to her alarm, I feigned nonchalance as if to imply that her extreme worrying fell within expected behavioral norms. I wanted to keep calm and stay strong for her. She proceeded to the balcony expecting me to follow her. I stood next to her on that chilly balcony. In her worry, she did not even notice that I was barefoot. Her dignified façade crumbled as the minutes passed, and her lamentations grew more desperate. "Dessar, pan me yeghan, yete meran intch bidi enenk. Katzin, ge dessnes. Katzin." "Something must have happened to them. What if they are dead? What are we going to do? It is so late. Something must have happened to them." Hitting her knees and rocking side to side, "Do you see? They are gone… gone…" Thinking back, I realize now how intense my grandmother's worrying must have been for her to seek comfort in the company of a five-year-old. Ultimately, of course, my parents would return, and I would slide back into bed, not making any fuss in order to uphold my grandmother's dignity. My poor grandma; if only we had cell phones back then…

ON MY CHRISTENING DAY, WITH MY PARENTS. FROM OUR FAMILY'S COLLECTION.

CUTTING MY BAPTISM CAKE, WITH MY NENE MARYAM
LOOKING ON. FROM OUR FAMILY'S COLLECTION.

MOM, DAD, BETTY AND I, ON THE BALCONY OF OUR COUNTRY APARTMENT
IN DHOUR EL CHOUEIR. FROM OUR FAMILY'S COLLECTION.

Dhour El Choueir, Lebanon, August, 1974, eight months prior to the start of the Lebanese civil war. My mother, Betty, and I pose for a picture on our friends' balcony across from our apartment. From our family's collection.

1975, the Lebanese Civil War starts...

ONE DAY IN THE SUMMER of 1975, my father was watching television at our country apartment when he turned pale as a sheet. The news coverage was of the damage inflicted in downtown following clashes between Muslim and Christian Lebanese. Firefighters were trying to put out flames at a store. At first, the footage was filled with heavy smoke and chaos, and then through the thinning smoke here and there, the sign over the store became more discernible. It read *Tavitian Frères* (Tavitian brothers in French). The fabric store that my grandfather Sarkis and his brother Krikor had opened and passed on to their sons was on television, burning. My father owned a share of that store. He later tried to take a mental inventory of a list of documents and the amount of cash kept in the store's safe, wondering what had happened to them. He was particularly concerned about the deed of a certain house in Turkey that his father had kept locked in that safe for so many years. He regretted not having brought it home for safe-keeping after his father's death. A few days later, the flames and destruction reached his shop too. The Automatic Building was also burning. Gone were the orders from renowned clients, visits and sweets from the restaurants below, and dreams of renting a newer and more lavish apartment.

The following summer was the last one we spent at our country house. The traffic on our way there was much lighter than the annual holiday madness we were accustomed to. A group of soldiers, the first ones we saw, stopped our car. They asked my father to give one of their wounded friends a ride home. The emaciated soldier sat next to my sister and me. He reeked of medicine and grimaced from pain once in a while without emitting any sound. His gaunt face was not shaven, and his drowsy eyes had a glassy look. He asked us to drop him off as we started climbing up Mount Lebanon. I looked back at him as our car drove off. Oh, how things had changed suddenly. I could sense my father's uneasiness, but I also understood that he had no choice but to agree to give the soldier a lift. We lingered in the country past our summer vacation that year, possibly to avoid the bombings in Beirut. It was almost November when we packed our belongings, covered our furniture with sheets, and locked our country apartment door for the last time. Not only had traveling around become unsafe, we simply could no longer afford a second residence.

We made it back to our apartment in Gemmayze, and soon the beautiful summer holidays spent in the country became distant memories of normal life. One day, my father was gone the entire morning, and my mother was starting to become concerned. I remember him finally showing up at our door, his eyes unusually bright in his soot-covered face and rolls of fabric hanging down his arms. Together with his friend Sako, they carried in all sorts of fabrics, unfinished client's orders, small furniture, and even the dark orange curtains I recognized. Later that evening, my father told us the heroic story of how he drove with his friend into the heart of Burj (downtown Beirut). When he was stopped by Lebanese Christian fighters, he pleaded with them to offer him and his friend cover so that they could run into the Automatic Building and check up on his store. He described to us with great suspense and a childish grin on his face how he ran under exchanged bullets, found his way up the stark, soot-covered building, turned the key, and walked into his store to find that the fire had started coming in from a window, had burned the edge of one curtain but was stopped by firefighters

26

just in time. Aside from a layer of ash flakes and the lingering smell of acrid burn, his place was virtually untouched.

In his customary positive attitude, my father told the story as if it was about a miracle, and all his troubles were now behind him. He set up shop in my late grandmother's bedroom and contacted some of his clients. His business, however, recovered only a small fraction of its previous volume. For the next seven years, we made do with whatever income it generated and lived mostly off of our savings. The customers would come during ceasefires, but they would mostly stay away because we lived in what became known as one of the most dangerous neighborhoods in Beirut.

THE TAVITIAN FRÈRES TAILOR SHOP AS IT TURNED UP IN A CENTERFOLD PICTURE IN JOSEPH C. CHAMI'S PHOTO COMPILATION BOOK *DAYS OF TRAGEDY LEBANON, LIBAN JOURS DE MISÈRE 75-76.* ARAB PRINTING PRESS JANUARY 1, 1977 (BOOK FROM MY FAMILY'S PRIVATE COLLECTION)

Years of War...

I recall very well the day the United States invaded Iraq in 2003. A live feed of Baghdad at night was playing on all TV stations. Operation Iraqi Freedom, with a campaign of shock and awe, was about to commence. I was alone in the living room, transfixed by the television, waiting, when a deep chill crept up my spine and took over my entire body. I looked deep into the image of the city lit by night lights. The news anchorman was babbling on about what was about to unfold as if it was some long-anticipated sitcom. I was not listening to his words. I did not care to hear about "weapons of mass destruction" and what President Bush, Colonel Powell, the tyrant Saddam Hussein, and this and that had to say. My heart was bleeding for the Iraqi children. They were living their last moments of innocence and normalcy. I sent prayers their way, wishing I could stop the senselessness that was about to unfold. When the shelling finally started and ferocious explosions lit up the night sky above the city, the anchorman started describing the different weapons that were being used with a zeal reminiscent of that of X-Box war game advertisers. The sounds of the bombing were nauseatingly familiar. I kept on staring at Baghdad, but all I was now seeing in my mind's eye was a young mother, smartly dressed in medium-heeled moccasins, crossing the street apprehensively, clutching the hands of her two young daughters as she rushed them to the school bus a block away before the bombing started again.

War is the debacle and failure of civilization. Those who relish in wars have not lived through one to know better.

I WAS EXPOSED TO WAR talk starting at age seven. Betty, my sister, was three. Conversations around the dinner table and in gatherings with our relatives and neighbors revolved around the latest political developments, assassinations, and weapons. At the start of the Lebanese Civil War, I heard the grownups laugh off the political unrest and say, "These Arabs are at each other's throat today, but watch and see how they will kiss and make up tomorrow." Soon, however, the residential neighborhoods became the targets of shelling, and destruction and death became part of daily living. Children competed in assembling the best collections of smashed bullets and bomb shrapnel. As the years wore on and the number of our neighbors dwindled, a dismal uncertainty and hopelessness settled in. A while back, my father's uncle and cousins who lived upstairs had moved to Ashrafieh, a neighborhood a few miles north of ours. Later, my aunt Ankine, in the building across from ours, settled in New York with her family. Betty and I were practically the only children left in our apartment building. Commodities that we took for granted slowly disappeared. Telephones became lifeless décor, electrical power was rationed according to an unpredictable schedule, and the ladies in the building planned for laundry once a week when water started flowing again from dried up faucets as if by some miracle. We placed a bucket next to each toilet and had to pour water in from a certain height to flush down our excrements in the absence of water pressure and functioning tanks. Candles and all sorts of kerosene lanterns became hot-ticket items at the stores. I studied in their light and became intimately familiar with the mechanism of a lantern and the feel of hot molten wax on my fingers. Petals of wax etched with my fingerprints surrounded my notebooks on the desk. In the mornings, I made a point of looking into the mirror to see how dark my nostrils looked in my pale face, then wiped the black soot clean from my nose and got ready for school.

Life became a helpless captive, caught in the cruelly unpredictable dance between regular glimmers of hope for peace and the despair brought by renewed fighting. We were happy when neighboring

Syria sent troops to reconcile the Muslims and Christians. Our hopes were dashed when it later became evident that Syria had, in fact, advanced into eastern Lebanon in order to occupy it. The Christian Phalangist fighters viewed the Palestinian refugees who had settled in the thousands in Southern Lebanon as a threat to Lebanon's security and political makeup. The Muslim Lebanese, on the other hand, felt a kinship with their Palestinian Muslim brethren, who were deported from their homeland by the Israelis. In March of 1978, Israel invaded Southern Lebanon in the Litani Operation, which was meant to wipe out Yasser Arafat's Palestine Liberation Organization (the PLO). The Christian side had high hopes that the growing power of the Palestinians would thus be eradicated. However, the operation failed, and Israel withdrew in June, following a UN resolution signed by the United States ordering it to do so. What ensued next is an experience that will forever remain seared in our memories.

Seven Days in Hell, 1978

I WAS 10 YEARS OLD. The scorching heat of summer had not settled in yet. Music was drifting out of a neighbor's window. We heard a familiar voice call out my mother's name from below: "Manoushag... Manoushag..." We all rushed out to the balcony. To our great surprise, my maternal aunt's husband, Hovanness, was standing there all by himself. That was quite unusual because our relatives, fearing the "Green Line," would visit us rarely and only on special occasions. "What are you doing here? Is everyone alright?" inquired my mother. Hovanness looked disturbed and in a great rush. "Pack your bags and come down quick... I will keep the taxi waiting... We are all heading to Anjar... I came to get you... There is talk about a serious retaliation against the Christians by the Palestinians and the Syrians because of their siding with the Israelis," he said frantically, beckoning us with inpatient hand waves. "Where will you stay?" asked dad. "At Hagop's house." My ever-skeptical father continued, "His house is small. How are we all going to fit in there?" "Who cares?" Hovanness dismissed the trivial concern, "we will manage something. My source is very reliable. Listen to me. They are going to start any day. Just come down." My parents looked at each other for a moment and mumbled some excuses. "Thanks for warning us, my brother," my father yelled. "Whatever it is they are going to do, we will stay and ride it out somehow. Who's going to go all the way to Anjar now? You go ahead and say hi to everyone." Hovanness was done persuading. "Be careful; may God be with you," he said and hurried along. We sat in silence in our living room, contemplating about, but not challenging, my dad's decision to stay on. In an attempt to alleviate our anxiety, my father feigned positivity and reasoned in a nonchalant tone, "No one knows anything. It is just a rumor. What if nothing happens? Why should we go all the way to Anjar and trouble Hagop in his crammed house? I don't feel comfortable doing that."

There was no music the following morning. As a matter of fact, an eerie silence had settled in, and many of our neighbors' cars were missing. I had taken up the hobby of crocheting and had a whole bag of different colored yarns and pattern samples. In order to ease my nerves and ignore the looming heaviness in the abandoned neighborhood, I distracted myself by starting a new crochet project.

Our city apartment building was five stories high; we lived on the fourth floor. The building was parted by open staircases in the middle, with two large apartment units on either side of each landing of stairs. The apartments on our side of the building had the same three-bedroom floor plan, with a foyer, a laundry room, a kitchen, a formal living and dining room open into each other, two baths, and balconies on all three sides of the unit. The apartments of the other half of the building had the even larger four-bedroom floor plan. At the time, the Armenian family who had replaced my father's relatives directly above us, a large Arab family in the apartment across from ours, and another Arab family on the second floor were the only ones, besides us, living on the upper floors of the building. We never knew about the comings and goings of the tenants on the ground floor. They mostly felt safe and rarely came out during bombings. In the course of the first three years of the war, we had become experts in guessing how far or how close a bomb would land based on the sound of its whistle. If the whistle lingered and was not too loud, the bomb had passed us and was heading further out. If the whistle was short and loud, then the bomb explosion was somewhere very close. Hearing any type of whistle meant that we were not at the eye of the target.

On the late summer day in 1978, when the first bomb fell, we heard no whistle. We only felt the sudden powerful tremble and the reverberating loud explosion in our heads, followed by the avalanche of broken pieces of glass pouring down the buildings. The sounds of gunshots near and far, and the firing of answering RPGs and tanks, were muffled by the barrage of incoming bombs. We knew this was not the random bombing we had become accustomed to. Panic-stricken, trembling, and wailing in fear, everyone stumbled down to the second floor, leaning against the side walls of the staircases and rushing at each exposed turn. Our Lebanese neighbors across from us, Mrs. Marie, her two daughters, one of her sons, her sister, two nieces, and another male relative, our Armenian neighbors upstairs, Mrs. Zabel and Mr. Harutyun and their grown children, my parents, Betty and I all crammed into the ten-by-ten foyer of our second-floor neighbors, a young Lebanese Arab couple who had a daughter my age. The relentless downpour of shells was horrifying. Bombs were grazing balconies, windows were exploding, pieces of chipped bricks were flying, and we all thought that it would be a matter of minutes before our building would sustain a direct hit and start crumbling down upon us. We were now inhaling air thick with dust and saturated with the smell of lead. The eerie stomach-churning, metallic smell of death that crept into the crevices of our brains and constricted the lining of our throats. I came to know that when death is close, so is God. Stripped from all pretenses and formalities, we were crying to God with abandon. "*Yesm el Salib! Ya yyadrah, ya dekhilik*!" "In the name of the cross! Mary mother of God be merciful" (in Arabic). My six-year-old sister and I were calling "*Hissus... Hissus...*," "Jesus....Jesus..." in Armenian. In all that commotion, one voice grew louder and angrier, to the point that it finally grabbed everyone's hushed attention. I was stunned to discover that it was my father's voice. He had made himself an impromptu commander and was yelling some sort of orders. "Listen to me, all of you. We have to make a decision fast. Do we stay here and wait to get killed, or do we take a chance and run to the underground parking structure of the new building behind us?" I could see their faces now. Pale, horrified... Mrs. Marie's lower lip trembling... all listening to my father. Fear had stolen their common sense, and this man was injecting some desperately needed reasoning and hope for survival into their numbed brains.

Next thing I knew, we were all huddled at the bottom of our building's staircase, and my father was sending our neighbors in twos, running to the underground parking garage of the new building. In true hero fashion, he ordered my mom, my sister, and me to run as fast as we could without looking back, while he stayed behind until the last person left. We were running in the street and around the side of our building as bombs were crashing nearby when I heard a loud commotion behind us. I looked back while running and saw a relative dragging Mrs. Marie by her arms. She had lost control of her legs. We all made it safely into the underground parking garage when a bomb landed near the entrance and splattered its shrapnel through the entrance onto the side wall.

In that new concrete-smelling garage, we passed the seven longest days of our lives. On the first day, my father, the ever-vigilant commander, had to break it to the ladies who had settled nicely on spread jackets that they were sitting under the exposed street above. The women bounced on their feet in frenzy and moved further into the middle of the garage, all of us uneasy about the possibility of a bomb landing in that spot of the street and right into our sanctuary. During what appeared to be breaks in the constant bombardment, the men would venture out and come back with some necessities. Blankets appeared, and sandwiches were made out of MaLing canned meat in freshly baked pita bread sold by one selfless baker who had decided that the neighborhood would not go breadless on his watch. At one point, everyone drove in their cars from the street outside and parked them in the garage so that we could sleep in them. Mrs. Marie's nephew was serving in the Christian Phalangist forces led by the charismatic young Bashir Gemayel, son of the founder of the Christian Kataeb Phalangist Party Pierre

Gemayel. He would drive in his military Jeep full of other young soldiers and bring us news of the fight. We learned from them that not too far from the building we were under, a bomb had made its way into another underground garage where neighbors were seeking shelter just like us. I heard from bits and pieces of hushed comments that the explosion had claimed everyone's life and that pieces of the victims' flesh were stuck on the walls.

One day, after a deluge of shells that were bringing down entire balconies off the side of buildings, Mrs. Marie's nephew skidded in with his Jeep to inform us that smoke was coming off the side of the top floor of our apartment building. The men jumped into the Jeep, and off they went to extinguish the fire in order to save the rest of the structure. They later described to us how a mattress in the top apartment had caught fire in a direct hit to the master bedroom. With the absence of water, they had to come up with creative ways to put out the fire. We relied on news from small battery-operated radios and survived on daily MaLing sandwiches. Towards the end of the week-long ordeal, my parents discovered a window with metal bars at the far end of the garage. Branches laden with crisp green leaves from an orange tree by the window had made their way in between the bars. We rejoiced at the site of this beautiful tree and picked from its fruit. Those were the most precious, delicious, aromatic citrus fruits we had ever eaten! They not only provided us with much-needed Vitamin C, but they also reminded us of the divine serenity and beauty of nature that stand in contrast to manmade destruction and ugliness. It was a simple yet meaningful bonding moment between my parents and us kids that awakened feelings of family unity and hope.

Seven days of atrocious and inhumane bombing of civilians finally came to an end in a ceasefire between the Christian Lebanese militia and the Syrians. We finally emerged from that underground parking structure, returned to our apartments, and lay in our beds.

Schooling During War...

IN THE HAZY MEMORIES OF my early childhood, school was an off-white colonial building with Roman columns jutting at the end of a row of palm trees. Marble stairs led to the entrance of the administration building. Tall French windows stood studiously on both sides of the door. I remember my first day there, however, very vividly. My Mother lingered at the door of the classroom, peeking in to see if I was faring well. Some of my classmates were wailing and clinging to their mothers' skirts. I had earnestly taken up the task of needle-poking a figure drawn on red construction paper. I turned and asked my mother to go on home. I was ready for school.

Nshan Palandjian Djemaran School, on Kantari Street in Beirut. Photo Varoujan, Biblioteque Orientale- USJ.

At "Paregentan" holiday, Elementary School, Nshan Palandjian Djemaran. I am on the second row, far left with braids. Mrs. Carmen seated in the middle behind second row students. Photo from personal collection.

I fell in love with *Nshan Palandjian Djemaran*. Its name alone warms my heart. I loved my preschool teachers, especially Ms. Carmen and Miss Zepur. (In the many fascinating occurrences in life, decades later, they would both teach my children in California!). Djemaran did more than teach. It instilled in its students a love for their nation and pride in their heritage. In that school, we were "the children of an invincible race." The mission of the school was to empower children academically and socially by encouraging performances and debates and enhancing self-worth by nurturing feelings of belonging. The highest caliber of the Armenian language was taught there.

I still remember the kindergarten school anthem:

Menk manougner hayotz azkin
We, the children of the Armenian nation
Dzakogh luysin hed ardvan
With the dawn of morning light
Mishd gensourakh yev jbdakin
Always happy and smiling
Guertank tbrotz sharan sharan
We head to school group by group
Mer sagarn eh teyev pokrig
Our lunchbox may be small
Payts mern eh gyankn ou Abakan
But the entire life and future are ours

It was at Djemaran that I learned how to recite the unique Armenian alphabet, which had emanated from a dream revelation to Mesrob Mashtots in the year 405 AD, and heard the story of St. Gregory the Illuminator who survived 13 years in the pit of Khor

Virab[5] dungeon at the foot of Mount Ararat and went on to convert Armenia from paganism to Christianity in year 301 AD.

I cherished all the Armenian traditions and holidays that prompted the instructors to teach beautiful Armenian songs and poems and to design elaborate hats and costumes for our performances, especially at *Paregentan*, the celebration of *Good Living*, where we would wear all types of masks. *Vartanants* Day was in honor of our legendary valiant hero Vartan Mamigonian, who, in defiance of the Persian King's order for Armenians to denounce Christianity, had marched his 66,000 men to face a 300,000-strong Persian army with elephants and tigers in the Battle of Avarayr in year 451 AD.

The names Levon Shant, Moushegh Ishkhan, and Nigol Aghpalian floated in my child's mind. I heard these names being mentioned in reverence on campus. I did not know who these professors were, but I was confident that many truths were going to be revealed to me when I reached higher grade levels. I cherished the quiet pride and confidence that exuded from the school and knew that this special place held within it something that my young mind did not have the capacity to decipher yet. Djemaran whispered in my ear the promise of uncovering truths that were meant to be passed on to me. I longed to join the ranks of Homenetmen, the Armenian General Athletic Union, and Scouts, which had a chapter next door to the school. I admired the scouting uniforms that my aunt Ankine's children, who also attended Djemaran, wore to their Sunday Homenetmen gatherings. The Scouts behaved like soldiers. They were taught to be tough and self-reliant while being loyal to their kin and devoted to the advancement of their community.

Homenetmen's motto of "Partsratzir, Partsratzour," "Elevate yourself and others with you," was about achieving your personal best physically and mentally while always staying cognizant of your

---

5 A monastery by the same name was later built at the site of the dungeon. Established in the 7th century Khor Virab monastery is located in the Ararat plain of Armenia near the closed border with Turkey. It is one of the most visited pilgrimage sites in Armenia.

heritage and striving to bring honor to your community. The Scouts were the army of a homeland stolen from us, an army realizing the honorable duty of gathering the flocks of a dispersed nation's children. "The Turk had stolen our land. The Turk had massacred our people. We will defy the Turk by not forgetting our unique language and passing it on to the generations that follow. As the first nation to adopt Christianity, we will uphold our religious beliefs and our age-old Christian hymns and prayers... We will make up for the thousands lost by marrying an Armenian and raising our children with Armenian values so that we may not go extinct as the Turk intended."

My bond with my friends was very special. There was so much to look forward to at Djemaran. And yet, it was not meant to be...

I had missed a couple of weeks of school because of a very bad case of chickenpox, but I managed to follow the extra-terrestrial-themed dance routine inspired by the book *Le Petit Prince* (the Small Prince) at my kindergarten graduation program. I also remembered to take a bow as I accepted my diploma from our principal, Mr. Hratch Dasnabedian. Little did I know that I was also bowing out of my Djemaran experience and of my aspirations of discovering more about the precious school. My parents registered my sister and me for the following year, but the Lebanese war erupted. It was 1975. My father grew concerned because the area where Djemaran was located became very unstable and dangerous. Reluctantly, he resolved to pull us out and enrolled us at *La Sainte Famille*, a French Catholic school in our neighborhood in Gemmayze. I longed for my friends. I felt left out. They were going to be taught the truths that I looked forward to uncovering in higher grades. Although at first, I felt a big void at La Sainte Famille, in time, I grew fond of its lax atmosphere and the kindness of the musically gifted nuns who could have walked out of the movie *The Sound of Music*. Two years passed, and my parents decided that we belonged in an Armenian school and enrolled us at the Catholic Armenian Nuns school of Hripsimiantz.

The education at Hripsimiantz was top-notch. We had to speak strictly Arabic or French at assigned hours. If a word in a language other than the one we were instructed to speak slipped from our mouths, we would end up with a copying assignment several pages long. We studied the Armenian, Arabic, and French languages simultaneously. Math and science were taught in French; geography and history were taught in Arabic. In addition to Armenian history, Bible studies class was also taught in Armenian, and introductory English was added to our curriculum in 9th grade. In no time at all, it became obvious to me that "Armenianness" was not as emphasized at this school as it was at Djemaran. The emphasis was placed mostly on discipline and academic achievement. The teachers were allowed to use the ruler to hit students, and the nuns enforced strict disciplinary rules. We wore Italian-made grey uniforms, matching navy-blue coats... even our socks had to match. Being over-friendly with boys was prohibited. As a matter of fact, I remember one ride to school where the boys and girls were segregated to the different sides of the bus. Once an all-girls school, Hripsimiantz had started accepting boys during the war. Anything having to do with discipline and academics seemed to take precedence over social development. Although I excelled in school, I found Hripsimiantz a bit stuffy, cold and intimidating. When the same jokes that made my friends at St. Famille laugh to tears incurred only ridicule and side glances, I became introspective and detached, much like a misplaced spectator.

Curiously, I came alive during recitals and end-of-year programs, activities that I had learned to celebrate at Djemaran. Unlike my more modest friends at Djemaran, many of my new classmates came from well-to-do privileged families. To console myself, I would dismiss them as shallow. In my heart, I belonged elsewhere. Years later, I came to appreciate the high academic standard at Hripsimiantz and the discipline it instilled in me. Back then, however, I would simply tolerate the dry and cold environment of the school, mentally separating myself from the French-speaking "brats." My mind would flutter to a certain "somewhere" that called upon me, a place that felt familiar, down to earth, and that made me feel warm in the heart. A place, however, that was still elusive and undefined to me.

At my graduation from Kindergarten at Nshan Plandjian Djemaran. Taking a bow next to Principal Hratch Dasnabedian. Photo from personal collection.

Bourj Hammoud

It wasn't long before I had figured out that my parents came from two varied backgrounds. My father's side of the family lived closer to the city center. They were a proud bunch who carried on as if they had descended from noble lineage. Many of them were successful fabric and garment business owners. Some had acquired sizeable inheritances. All were driven and ambitious. They were steadfast patriotic Armenians who also had Lebanese Arab friends. The majority chain-smoked and comparatively mixed more French into their Armenian. The fact that the Tavitian name was respected in the community and political and church leaders frequented their homes made them a bit elitist. Stories were told about how the Tavitians were great fabric merchants in pre-Genocide Turkey and how they had escaped with tins of English gold coins. Spirited discussions that on many an occasion escalated into heated debates and outright arguments were common at family gatherings. I remember evenings when we all sat around my aunt's table, drinking tea and munching on Armenian string cheese, pickled Labne, and deli meats. My aunt was a great cook and quite the hostess. Conversations lingered until midnight and covered recent disputes with certain acquaintances, current political affairs, and jokes about Beshara, the mini-market owner on our street. Ladies would yell requests from their balconies and lower a basket at the end of a rope for him to put the products in. We would all make fun of the toilet paper and detergent preferences of this or that neighbor in addition to Beshara's elaborate arguments trying to substitute with brands he carried. My father's generation comprised thirteen male and three female first- and second-cousins, all from his father's side. Most of these cousins had, in turn, married and had children of their own. Back then, I really did not know how all the members of my father's big clan were related to each other. I know now that they are the descendants of my great-grandfather Garabed and his two brothers, Manuel and Nishan.

And then there was my mother's side of the family... from Bourj Hammoud.

Every time I think of Bourj Hammoud, my heart swells with warmth, and I can't help but smile. I get visions of its narrow streets, hanging balconies that seemed to pour into the living rooms of the neighbors across, meshes of cable dangling from poles, noisy livelihood, and sweet familiarity. When the hungry and destitute survivors of the Armenian Genocide arrived in Beirut from their death marches through the Syrian Desert of Der el Zor in 1915, the accommodating Lebanese allowed them to construct shacks in the marshes of the eastern banks of the Beirut River. Under the leadership of Armenian Catholic priest Paul Ariss, the shacks were slowly replaced by two- to four-story buildings, and the municipality of Bourj Hammoud was eventually founded. Mostly inhabited by Armenians, Bourj Hammoud, with its 2.5 km square spread, became one of the most densely populated cities in the Middle East. The streets were named after cities in modern-day Armenia, such as Yerevan, and Armenian rivers, such as Arax (also known as Araz). Many were named after cities in historic Western Armenia from where the majority of the Bourj Hammoud residents hailed, such as Sis, Marash, Adana, and Cilicia.

Many a time during the war, we escaped the bombings at Gemmayze and found refuge at Bourj Hammoud. My maternal grandfather, Krikor Torossian, had built a two-story building across from Shamlian Tatiguian School. I never came to meet him. When I was a year old, he passed away at the age of 48 from a massive hemorrhagic stroke. The unpretentiousness and community feel of Bourj Hammoud fascinated me. My mother, her siblings, and their tenants' children had grown up together as if they were one big extended family. My grandmother was very close to the tenants' wives. You could never tell that she was the landlady of the building. I could sense that the pain of losing my grandfather was still very raw because my mother's family would talk about him in sparse, pain-impregnated conversations. They had placed a large portrait of him in his officer's uniform in a prominent place in the living room. The way he was described to us children left no doubt that he was revered by his family. His story made him a legend of sorts in our minds. The only other pictures of him that I had seen were those in my parents' wedding album and my christening pictures. He towered over my uncles, who were pretty tall themselves. The large features of his face were subdued by the calm and depth of the look in his eyes. His parents outlived him by several years. By the time I was eight, his mother had passed away, and my grandmother was caring for his ailing father, Karekin.

Great-Grandpa Karekin Agha was a mysterious man. My mother tells stories of him standing at the entrance of their building with a wooden stick, threatening the girls not to leave home alone. For a while there, they had apparently let him run one of the shops as a general store. The ladies of the neighborhood would make purchases and ask him to add the tab on their accounts, of which he never kept a record. One of his eyes was shut closed as a result of an injury he had sustained while helping a friend in construction. On days when we stayed at my grandmother's, my curiosity would make me linger around his day bed. He would mix words in Turkish and Greek. He pronounced my name as a very unflattering "Kakia" because of his missing teeth. I did not mind because of the tenderness in his smile. The once sturdy oil merchant was now an incontinent elderly with dementia. On one occasion, I noticed him talking to himself, lamenting about something with a hurt that rocked him back and forth. The grownups were whispering about how his mind was failing him. I inched closer and observed apprehensively from the corner of my eye, almost hoping I could ease his pain. I wondered how deeply torn he must have been about outliving his only son. The rocking became more pronounced, and he whimpered in Turkish with his open toothless mouth: "Why did I do it? Why? She begged me. She begged me to spare her and her child's life... Why did I do it?" I jumped back at this strange confession and never stopped wondering about it.

Living in Bourj Hammoud was like cohabiting with a thousand people. Everyone knew everyone. Many were known by nicknames that often were in Turkish. Individuals would be referred to by an adjective followed by their first names, such as Topal Toros (wobbling Toros), Havgitdji Levon (Levon the egg seller), Keor Stepan (blind Stepan), and so on. People were boisterous and carried on animated conversations. At times, Bourj Hammoud gave me the illusion of a live comedy show where the characters were oblivious to the fact that they were downright funny. The architecture and build of the homes were like afterthoughts fitting and squeezing into available space. Most balconies and windows were uneven; the entries to the buildings were intimately accessible from the narrow streets, and sidewalks were either nonexistent or acutely narrow with cars parked on them. The neighborhoods were undoubtedly modest, yet the inhabitants had a surreal sense of dignity and high esteem that manifested in things as simple as beautifully planted pots on the edge of balconies, immaculately clean apartments, and eyebrow-raising beautifully decorated trendy stores next to hole-in-the wall restaurants. A whole community, with churches, schools, and centers, had risen from muddy marshes, thanks to the will of an exiled people who fought to survive by rebuilding a new home to identify with. Streets were named after places in the old country in a stubborn effort to keep the past alive. Men would assemble around small tables to play backgammon in front of minimarkets filled with freshly pressed assortments of pickles, barrels of varieties of olives next to varieties of detergents and soap. And oh yes, the food! There was the two-level corner restaurant Zankou[6] with its finger-licking good rotisserie chicken, Falafel Arax, and its amazing sandwiches, and, to top it off, Sarkis Pastry with its delicious desserts. But my favorite was *Keghk*, a sesame-crusted bread that looked like a handbag and was sold at stands. I have been craving it ever since leaving Lebanon! The traffic was particularly noisy in Bourj Hammoud. There was no need to turn on the radio because international hits, as well as the latest Armenian music, were blasted from passing cars. Wedding party car processions were announced with rhythmical belligerent honking, and there was no shortage of disputes culminating at times into fist-fights between drivers competing for space in the narrow streets.

When I was really young, my mind did not question the existence of Bourj Hammoud. I accepted it for what it was: the Armenian area in Lebanon, where to my delight, everyone spoke Armenian and where my beautiful grandmother Yevnigeh barbequed Kebab for us on the landing of the stairs on the second floor. But as I grew older, my maturing mind wanted to grasp the strange phenomena of this area which was inhabited exclusively by a single ethnic minority hailing from Transcaucasia within a majority Middle Eastern Arab country. I started noting interesting dynamics that I had not previously taken into account. There was an accepted governing structure that somehow kept order in Bourj Hammoud. Different chapters, or *gomideh*s of mostly the Armenian Revolutionary Federation, otherwise known as the Tashnak party (one of the three major Armenian political parties in the Diaspora), oversaw disputes, supported cultural, educational, and welfare organizations, and made sure that the area stayed cohesive and aligned with the Armenian community's stance in the country. The majority of the residents of Bourj Hammoud were the descendants of the most destitute refugees and orphans of the Armenian Genocide. Just like the rest of the

---

6 Zankou Chicken is currently a restaurant chain in Southern California. The original one was in Bourj Hammoud, Lebanon. The family that owned it moved to California and opened its first location in Hollywood, California.

Armenian settlers in Lebanon, these first-generation refugees had not only lost relatives, spouses, and children in the Genocide, but they were also stripped of everything they had owned, from homes, businesses, bank accounts, inheritances to lands. Given a second chance at life, they had first prioritized shelter and basic survival needs. They had gone to great lengths to pass on to their children the Armenian language and as much of the history of Armenia that they could reassemble, as well as snippets of shocking survival and eyewitness accounts of atrocities they had endured at the hands of the Ottoman Turks. This shared fate and a communal quest for survival and the upholding of their identity had created a strong bond of compatriotism among the residents of Bourj Hammoud. Although they came to develop a unique heavy Arabic accent, made fun of by both Arab Lebanese and self-deprecating Armenian comedians, the ghetto they lived in allowed them to congregate and keep their national identity, a task that would prove more challenging in larger countries where assimilation is part of the social system. With the passing of time, as they had settled more into the country that allowed them religious and economic freedom as well as a chance to prosper, they had stopped considering their circumstance as "temporary exile" and had come to view Lebanon as their second homeland. However, the simmering bitterness over the injustice and black fate that had befallen their people lay just under the surface. These feelings would evolve into militant activism.

A STREET IN BOURJ HAMMOUD. PHOTO © ARA MADZOUNIAN, REPRINTED WITH PERMISSION FROM *BIRDS NEST, A PHOTOGRAPHIC ESSAY OF BOURJ HAMMOUD.*

Odaroutioun, Diaspora

I DO NOT RECALL WHAT year it was. All I remember is that it was sum-
mertime. Our apartment building in Gemmayze had emptied some
more, and a heavy bombardment of our neighborhood was under
way. In the heat of the moment, my father ordered us to run to our
car so that we may flee to Bourj Hammoud. I remember running to
our beloved Buick Skylark, with its body of pale yellow and black top,
parked against a building. As I was running along with my family, my
breathing heavy in my ears, my eyes were zooming in on the shrapnel
holes on its entire exposed side. My father started the engine and
was yelling at the top of his lungs for us to jump in. Miraculously,
the wheels were somehow spared, and, to our relief, our car took
off. Our Buick meandered through the streets of Gemmayze as
the sniper bullets whizzed overhead and exploding shells rocked
the ground. In what seemed to take an eternity, we made it onto
Jsr Beirut, the bridge that ran over the Beirut River in Nahr. Bourj
Hammoud spread ahead of us, our safe haven. As we reached the
other side of the bridge and were about to sigh with relief, a bomb
fell to our right among transportation buses parked alongside the
river bank. The shock made my father lose control of the wheel.
Our car jerked to the right, then to the left, and somehow found
its way through one of the narrow streets of Bourj Hammoud. We
noticed an unusual tranquility. As we drove further down the street,
some individuals started emerging from buildings on both sides.
My father stopped our car, which was now surrounded by a whole
group of men. I noticed the weapons in their arms. *"Parev Unger"*

(Hello friend), said an older man. *"Amenkt lav ek?"* "Is everyone alright?" A young man on my side of the street was eyeing Betty and me. *"Lavek oriortner? Chour gouzek?"* "Are you alright, ladies? Would you like some water?" As I nodded, he produced a bottle of refreshing water. The attention we received from this beautiful Armenian young man was so endearing to us. We continued on further into Bourj Hammoud and arrived at my grandmother's building in *Nor Marash* (New Marash). Again, the neighborhood was eerily quiet. I recognized my mother's cousins in the street. My mother's maternal uncle and his family lived in the building next door. They rushed towards us as we found the strength to maneuver our tensed bodies out of our car. I was smiling at them, wondering absentmindedly why my legs felt so heavy. They were not smiling back. They looked very concerned and inquired if we were alright. I followed the trail of their perturbed looks down my pants, and that is when I noticed the thin lines of blood at the sides and back of my trousers. We all had them. In our rush to escape, we had lunged onto the car seats without realizing that we were sitting on the shattered pieces of glass from our Buick's blown-out windows.

All I know is that I slept very well that night, wrapped in the warm blanket that was Bourj Hammoud. Was that how it felt like, being in your motherland?

It is safe to say that Bourj Hammoud was generally spared during the Lebanese Civil War. This was mostly because of the official neutral position that the Lebanese Armenian community had taken with regard to the dispute between the opposing parties of the war. The Armenian community's neutrality and refusal to openly side with the Christian Phalangist forces would, unfortunately, sour relations between the Armenian political parties and Christian Lebanese forces, who from time to time would bomb the Armenian neighborhoods in retaliation and threaten to kick Armenians out with sayings such as *"Ermen meskiin, tahtel skkiin;* Armenians are meek, under the knife!" Graffiti would appear on the walls at the outskirts of Bourj Hamoud's neighborhoods, threatening to kick "the Armenians out of the country naked like the day they had arrived." However, with continuous concessions and diplomacy, the Armenians would succeed in patching things up and leaving Bourj Hammoud and other Armenian-populated areas such as Anjar in the Bekaa Valley out of armed conflict.

Nevertheless, the Tashnak party did not want to take a chance by letting its guard down. There were nightly scheduled patrols in Bourj Hammoud neighborhoods and makeshift barracks on the outskirts. My mother's younger brother had already migrated to the United States. Her older brother and cousins were deployed to shifts standing guard at night. In the evenings, we would hear groups of men assembled in front of buildings. On nights when professional Armenian singers were on duty, the men were treated to free impromptu concerts. Singers Harout Pamboukjian and Paul Baghdadlian, in their trendy afro hairstyle and thick gold chains with the Tashnak insignia, were regulars. One of the 1980s hits by Paul Baghdadlian (song and lyrics), *Odaroutioun* (Diaspora or Foreign Lands) had become the staple of those times. Whenever I listen to it now, all I have to do is close my eyes, and it transports me back to the streets of Bourj Hammoud.

Odaroutioun	Diaspora
Odaroutioun ayskan darov,	Diaspora, for this many years
Goulam garodov, garodov,	I cry with longing, longing
Mer khntirn al loudzvi shoudov,	May our cause resolve soon
Hampereh hokis, hampereh.	Be patient my love, be patient
Heratsel em hayrenikes,	I am far from my homeland
pajanvel em undanikes,	Separated from my family
Pajanvel em ungerneres,	Separated from my compatriots
Anshoushd or muh bid' miyanank,	Of course, one day we'll reunite
Hampereh hokis, hampereh.	Be patient my soul, be patient

Srdis mechuh gah mee grag,	There is a fire in my heart
Gayreh sirds ammen jamanag,	It burns all the time
Hayrenikes chgar namag,	No letter has come from my homeland
Hampereh hokis, hampereh.	Be patient my soul, be patient
Mayrig gertnoom, asdvadz vga,	Mother, God as my witness
Hedaysou ints tatar chga,	No rest for me from this point on
Vad char toorkuh togh imana,	The mean bad Turk should understand
Hayuh gabri oo guh mna,	Armenians have survived and will live
Arar ashkharh togh imana,	The whole world should hear
Hayeh mishd gha, guh mna	Armenians exist and will continue to exist
Yergir mounink menk Hayasdan	We have our own country, Armenia
Inchou abrink odaroutyan	Why live in the Diaspora?
Ays e houyseh katch hayoutian	This is the hope of all Armenians
Hampereh Hokis, Hampereh	Be patient my love, be patient

"We have our own country, Armenia. Why live on foreign land in the Diaspora?" The lyrics of this song reverberated from apartments and windows on lazy afternoons. They spoke to everyone's soul…

Days passed, and things returned to normal: music, vendors on bicycles, the bells of the *St. Karasoun Manoug* church, incorrigibly flirtatious boys, grandpas playing backgammon, the bustling Arax Street, plays at the Melkonian Hall, fresh-smelling laundry hanging from lines, tantalizingly sweet aroma wafting from bakeries, neighbors cracking seeds on balconies… all kinds of seeds, sunflower, melon, pumpkin seeds, seeds, and more seeds. Power came on and off randomly, so we could not watch our television shows regularly. The personal computer and the cell phone were still years from being invented… We only had pure human interaction over several coffee breaks a day that was a thousand times more connecting than today's Internet. And then, once again, mayhem! Gunfire and shelling in the distance... The streets were cleared in an instant. You could only hear the huffing of men running about. Somehow, they were all armed again.

We were next door, at the ground level of my mother's uncle's building. His wife, Anna *Kergin* (Aunt Anna), was a very articulate lady who prided herself on her exquisite talent for reciting lengthy poems written by pre- and post-Genocide era Armenian poets such as Siamanto, Taniel Varoujan, and Silva Kapoutikyan. She had a heart of gold, but, as customary, she was monopolizing an ongoing conversation. As the ladies carried on about this and that, I walked to the door and peeked out into the corridor leading to the entrance of the building. To my astonishment, there were several young men in uncoordinated military uniforms lined up against the walls holding rifles. Among them were my uncle Albert and my mother's cousins, Kevork and Garo. I noticed that they had also armed my father. They were all peering out into the street as if waiting for some kind of a signal. My father noticed me and beckoned me to get back in. "What is going on, Dad?" I inquired. "The Kurds might attack," he said, then bellowed angrily, "I said go back in!" Somehow, in a few hours' time, the conflict dissipated, and there was no attack.

I later found out that there were Kurds living right beyond the outskirts of Bourj Hammoud. Whenever the Lebanese Christian Phalangists attacked them, the Kurds would threaten to attack Bourj Hammoud in return. The idea of Kurds invading the Armenian neighborhoods awoke deep-seated anxieties emanating from not-so-distant memories of vicious massacres of Armenians perpetrated by the Kurds in Turkey during the Genocide. The Gomideh did its best to fend off any Kurdish threat. Sandbag barricades were strategically set up to give the impression that Bourj Hammoud was heavily guarded, and evening patrols were intensified. Of course, like elsewhere in the country, tensions eventually died down, and the vigilance eased following long stretches of an absence of gunfighting.

And so, the Armenians lived in a country that was not theirs. The original refugees had entrusted to the world the duty of bringing

Turkey to justice while they struggled to survive, looked for lost kin, and patched up their tattered lives by building new communities in foreign lands. The whole world knew what the Turks had done. Of course, they will be held accountable! But the world had long moved on and all but forgotten about the Armenian Genocide. The cold war between America and Russia was in full force, and Turkey, taking advantage of the power-play at hand, had cozied up to the United States, negotiating perks in return for its strategic alliance. In 1920, the little that remained of Armenia was annexed by the USSR. In their efforts to strip the country of its cultural identity and any aspirations for independence, the Russians had exiled all nationalist Armenians to Siberia, in particular those belonging to the Tashnak party. They had banned worship, closed churches, and forced the Armenians to conform to the Soviet citizen's mold within the communist regime, where equal wages were equally small and impossible to live on. The new "*Daguits*" (under the table) concept of dealing and wheeling slowly became part and parcel of survival in Armenia. Since all communication was screened by the authorities, everything was done in secrecy or code. If a relative wanted you to stay away from the dreadful life in Armenia, he would write you a letter recommending you to "visit a certain relative before coming." That certain relative would be mentioned because he or she was dead, and the intended message would be that "you'd rather be dead than come to Armenia."

Singing Armenian patriotic hymns about the loss of homeland and heroic resistance by freedom fighters was also forbidden in the new Soviet Armenian Republic. In the Diaspora, however, they became cherished cultural treasures used to propagate our history and keep the memory of our martyrs and heroes alive. They were sung by the exiled survivors of the Genocide who carried them to faraway lands all over the world. Generations would learn lyrics about Adana, Cilicia, Van, Kars, and Mush, ancestral venerated lands and villages that they will never come to see. They would memorize popular songs about *General Antranik, Kevork Tchavush, Serop*

Akhpuyr, and many other valiant fighters who sacrificed their lives to protect their people. The Diaspora Armenians fought to retain the character, memory, traditions, and history of their ancient people as best as their limited resources could allow. While the Armenians in Armenia embarked on a centrally imposed metamorphosis of identity, those living in the Diaspora congregated and clung to the sting of the Genocide as their sacred collective connection to their homeland. And of survivors who somehow stayed behind in Turkey, no one knew much…

River of Tears....

ON AN AFTERNOON IN 1980, a lone explosion tore the silence at Gemmayze. It was right around the time when my father was due to return from work. A high school friend who owned a garment factory had offered him a job as a supervisor. After a moment's realization, my mother, Betty, and I ran to the radio, frantically scrambling for any news about the explosion. Sure enough, the all-dreaded news alert came on, and it was announced that a car had exploded in neighboring Ashrafieh, on the same road that father took on his way back home! Dread descended like a white ghost on our faces. The newscast continued informing that an assassination attempt on Phalangist leader Bashir Gemayel had instead claimed the life of his eighteen-month-old daughter Maya who was being driven home by his chauffeur. This was the second attempt on his life. Moments dragged like snails… Desperation and gloom pinned and suffocated us like invisible boulders. What to do? Whom to reach out to? And then, the familiar, reassuring sound of dad's key in the door made us release a collective sigh of relief. He looked livid. He knew we would be worried sick. As if in a daze, he explained how he had become embroiled in a conversation with a colleague and ended up leaving work a few moments later than usual. Moments that had saved his life!

Bashir was the youngest son of the founder of the *Kataeb* Christian Phalangist Party, Pierre Gemayel. The Gemayels were one of the elite Lebanese feudal families who competed with each other for power. The charismatic Bashir, who had studied law in the United

States, climbed ranks in the Phalangist party, first as a militia commander notorious for ferocious fighting, which had produced many important victories, and later as the leader of the Lebanese Forces, the military wing of the coalition of several Christian Maronite political parties. He was against the assistance of the Syrians, whose eventual occupation of eastern Lebanon he had foreseen from the start. He was also against Israeli occupation, even though Israel and the United States had supported him and assisted his forces against the PLO. He wanted Lebanon to belong to the Lebanese, and in many ways, this became his undoing. In August 1982, Israel invaded Southern Lebanon in an effort to oust the PLO. The intensely overpowering sound of diving fighter jets and the earth-shattering crashes of bombs were terrifying. Gemmayze is one of the most southern points of the Christian side of Beirut. We heard the sound of the jets and wondered how much louder and more terrifying they must have been for the residents of the areas being attacked. The consensus is that Bashir had stopped cooperating with the Israelis against the PLO. He started broadcasting speeches regularly on the radio, calling for Christians and Muslims to come together and defend their nation against foreign intrusion. His message resonated like the ring of a newly minted bell rising from the ashes of the war-torn country. In an era where Facebook and Twitter were not conceived yet, these radio addresses made people congregate and spend hours dissecting and replaying quotes that inevitably became his staples. The clever observations he made and his articulate assessment of the different facets of the country's political state were eye-opening; their intention nothing short of starting a revolution. His message was also openly defiant of all domestic and foreign powers. In a brazenly bodacious move that caused a mob scene, he shocked everyone one day by suddenly appearing in the midst of his notorious enemies in one of the most fanatical Muslim areas of West Beirut, telling everyone that it was time to unite. Muslims and Christians alike started believing in a new kind of Lebanon. He placed his bid as the only candidate in the presidential elections, and on August 23, 1982, he was elected president. On September 14, 1982, in the afternoon, I was in our dining room, reading yet another Barbara Cartland romance novel I had just bought at Librairie Samir when an explosion was heard. After visiting his sister the nun, Bashir had gone to the Phalangist headquarters in Ashrafieh to give his farewell speech before his inauguration as president when a bomb exploded, claiming his life as well as 26 other Phalangists. He would later be identified by his sister's well-wishing letter in his shirt pocket.

To say that all hope was sucked out of Lebanon on that day is an understatement. The Phalangists were quick to assume that Palestinian militants had a hand in Bashir's assassination, although eventual evidence would point at a Syrian involvement. Our neighborhoods drowned in sadness and tears, only to be doubly shocked a few days later when gruesome pictures of massacred women, children, and men in the Palestinian refugee camps of Sabra and Shatilla were telecast. In a vengeful retaliatory move, the Phalangists had massacred the residents of those two refugee camps under the watchful eyes of the Israelis who had surrounded the region after PLO forces had withdrawn from it. We were back to square one.

And the dream that was Bashir, who at age 36 was set to become the youngest Lebanese President, was not to be...

1983

Summer of 1983 was a special one. Things had gotten quieter with the Israelis occupying Southern Lebanon. My mother's older brother, Albert, was about to get married, and my younger uncle was set to come from the United States to be his best man. The concept of jet-setting was in its infancy back then. Travels and travelers still held a revered status in our lives. So it was that my cousins and I were counting the days until we got to see our uncle, whom we had missed so much. We had so many questions to ask him about America. Everything American was "cool" for us. Our favorite movie was *Grease*. We had watched it at least a dozen times and could recite all the lines by heart. We were hooked on television series such as Dallas and Dynasty; the twists and turns in their plots perpetuated many debates and discussions with equally intrigued neighbors and friends. The wedding reception was both elegant and fun. It was a truly happy time for us. I still laugh when I remember how my uncle, who had grown accustomed to driving in orderly traffic in America, was confused and flustered by the chaotic anarchy in the streets of Beirut.

Another novelty in our lives was the men's boutique store that my father had opened in Bourj Hammoud. It was on a narrow neighborhood street across from Nouga Pastry. My father was once more in good spirits, and we seemed to be easing into comfortable normalcy. I long for those days when we had the luxury of spending hours at each other's homes. On one of those cozy sweet days, we had gathered at my grandmother's apartment in Bourj Hammoud to help my uncle pack when the doorbell rang. "Mommie…! The door-bell!" I hollered. That was the nickname we used for Yevnigeh, my maternal grandmother. Mommie, my mother, and my aunt were in-side, earnestly debating how to distribute my uncle's clothes into his suitcases and what gifts to send to acquaintances settled in America. When I called for my grandmother a second time, she asked me to open the door myself. By now, all the tenants in the building had moved out or had left the country. A year prior, my older uncle had expanded my grandmother's apartment by opening it up onto the vacant one next door. Since our family gatherings most often turned into sleepovers, the newly renovated spacious apartment suited our needs very well. Many a New Year's Eve was spent around a long table spread out in what used to be the hallway in my grandparents' original apartment. My grandmother would barbecue her Kebab at the open landing of the stairs, then let chestnuts roast in the fire while we dined and wined until midnight. Gunshots would then an-nounce the arrival of the New Year and rain bullets on the rooftops.

The shadow behind the glass panel of the door moved left and right impatiently as I grew near. I opened the door. The young man standing in front of me had the most remarkably expressionless dark eyes set deep in their sockets. They looked as if they were gazing at a faraway horizon. He was holding up dry-cleaned suits and pants covered in plastic bags. "Dry-cleaned clothes for Mrs. Yevnigeh," he said in Armenian. "Merci," I said, taking the bag from him. And off he went as I closed the door behind him.

The day my uncle Manoug left for America was very sad. We were all lined up at the airport, tears streaming down our cheeks, waving long after the plane had taken off. Everyone was much more emotional in those days, mainly because of life's uncertainty. We wondered if we would ever see him again. A few weeks later, on July 27, 1983, havoc rose in the neighborhoods of Bourj Hammoud. Everyone was glued to their television. Video coverage of the Turkish Embassy in Lisbon, Portugal, played on the screens. Smoke was ris-ing from the Turkish ambassador's compound next door. Five young

Armenian men from our humble Bourj Hammoud neighborhoods had raided the compound! It was so strange to hear the words being used in the coverage: "Turkish Embassy Raid by Armenian Gunmen." Our Armenian… us… we? We had never heard the word "Armenian" being uttered by any international news media before. It was surreal! Feelings of excitement and pride for the fact that the word "Armenian" was being mentioned on foreign news were clashing with the seriousness of what was unfolding. A Special Forces squad of the Portuguese police was gingerly approaching the building when the picture on the screen shook as explosives inside the building were detonated. When it was all done, the wife of a Turkish Diplomat, a Portuguese Policeman, and the five young Armenian men were killed. It was announced on the news that a certain "Armenian Revolutionary Army" claimed responsibility. The five young men had all along planned on taking their own lives. A typewritten letter turned in to The Associated Press office in Lisbon said, "We have decided to blow up this building and remain under the collapse. This is not suicide, nor an expression of insanity, but rather our sacrifice to the altar of freedom." The group said that the attack was carried out to raise awareness of the 1915 Armenian Genocide that went unpunished.

The bodies of Setrak, 19, Ara, 20, Sarkis, 21, Simon, 21, and Vatche, 19, were later returned to Beirut and buried in the Armenian National Cemetery in Bourj Hammoud. They became known as the *Lisbon Five*, who paid the ultimate price in order to bring the story of the horrendous crimes committed against our people onto the world stage, a world that had decided to sweep it under the rug. In the fog of my confounded mind, I heard my father mention examples of assassinations and terror committed during many leading nations' struggle for independence as well as paramilitary groups like the Irish Republican Army. But I felt that, deep inside, he also was in turmoil, saddened by our people's desperate plight. We, the first nation to adopt Christianity, hard-working, peace-loving, creative, and innovative people who had contributed so much of our blood and sweat to Ottoman Turkey and continued contributing to the prosperity of all societies that took us in, had come to this; communities used, abused, stripped of all possessions, and tossed to the winds. Traumatized not only by the barbaric, undignified, and dehumanizing ways our families were treated but also by the deafening betrayal and stunning dismissal of justice by the Allied nations who had fought against the Turkish Ottoman Empire and had borne witness to the atrocities it committed against all its Christian minorities. And yet, they had chosen Turkey, a nation born out of crime that promised them strategic geopolitical alliances. Choosing Turkey meant ignoring the Armenian Genocide and trampling over the rights of the massacred victims and their families. They had already moved on and written us off. This was the choice of the powerful modern-day nations, who ironically promoted themselves as forefront defenders of human rights and justice for all. In truth, they were the defenders of their interests alone.

I remember how we all remained seated in my grandmother's living room that afternoon in dumbfounded silence, trying to process the unnecessary tragic loss of life we had just witnessed on television. While we did not condone their actions, our hearts bled for the five fanaticized Armenian young men. They came from poor families and lived humble lives. They had most likely not even visited what was left of Armenia. They had not seen much, period. And yet, they had decided to cut their young lives short so that the world took notice of their nation's cause. Days later, my grandmother was sitting pensively with her lips pressed together, as was her habit when something upset her. After a while, she finally spoke up to tell the grownups how a certain lady was so terribly devastated by the loss of her son, who was one of the Lisbon Five. She said: "*Kheghdjeh Manougin hakousdnere hos perav... moreh namag me tskereh vor ir masin tchi mdahokvih*" "The poor fellow dropped off Manoug's clothes here a few days prior to leaving the country. He left his mother a letter saying that he will be traveling and for her not to worry about him..." No one was paying attention to me, but I suddenly had an urgent need to get my grandmother's attention. The words were scrambling to get out of my mouth and took a few seconds to burst out of my lips. "Mommie," I called excitedly, "the same young man I opened the door for?" "Shh Shh," she quieted me, touching her finger to her mouth, "don't tell anyone of that. Just forget about it." When my grandmother Yevnigeh told you to do something, you did it. So it was that out of respect for her, I put that tidbit aside and never mentioned it to anyone again. No God-fearing person would want to associate themselves with an act of violence, an act that the rest of the world described as terrorism and of which only we understood the true etiology. Protests, revolutions, and terrorism are the languages of the unheard, the oppressed, and the desperate. The so-called "Armenian Revolutionary Army" militant movement proved to be short-lived and was dismantled not long after.[7] Only time would tell if those young men succeeded in pushing the conversation about the Armenian Genocide to the forefront.

To this day, whenever I see the famous banner of the Lisbon Five with the Armenian Revolutionary Federation insignia in the middle, I recall that fateful afternoon...and those sad dark eyes.

A few months later, in October, a suicide bomber claimed the lives of 200 Marines at the Beirut U.S. Marine barracks. News outlets on television replayed footage of surviving Marines walking around in sleepwear, dazed and in shock, trying to save colleagues from under piles of rubble. We received communication from the U.S. embassy instructing us to resubmit our Green Card applications; the bombing had apparently thrown a wrench in office paperwork. My father who, after struggling for years with the idea of uprooting our family, had finally decided that we should emigrate to the U.S., rushed to have the paperwork filled out and sent in again.

---

7 Several members are said to have been assassinated by the Turkish Intelligence.

My Grandmother Yevnigeh...

Just a small tangent.

IN 2010, I STARTED NOTICING that my grandmother Yevnigeh was losing her mental sharpness; after all, she was 86 years old. Mommie was the keenest, smartest, and strongest woman I knew. It was hard for me to imagine her succumbing to old age. I had always known her as a well-centered, positive grounding force. I loved her staple fried cheese *boeregs*![8] None of us could emulate her steady finger-pinching technique that produced a crust design so uniform that the boeregs looked as if they had come out of a machine! She was a natural beauty, with a straight chiseled nose, high cheeks, and almond-shaped hazel eyes. Even in the humblest of surroundings, an effortless innate elegance together with a quiet strength gave her the aura of a queen. When we misbehaved as children, all she had to do was look us in the eye and utter some measured words, and we knew to obey.

So it was that on the rare occasion when she was staying at our house that I decided to sit down with her and ask her to tell me a little about her youth and how she met my grandfather. Being the private lady that she was, I was fully anticipating her shrugging off my request. To my surprise, she welcomed the attention. Her eyes lit up, and she happily obliged.

---

8 Savory pie of thin dough with cheese stuffing baked or fried.

Née Yevnigeh Bchakjian, she was the third of seven children: five girls and two boys. She told me how much she loved attending school as a young girl. Every morning, she would walk a distance of about four miles from the Trad (one of the original Armenian refugee camps in Lebanon) to the city high school in Ashrafieh. Her eyes twinkled with mischief as she informed me about her academic competitiveness. She would strive to surpass her classmates and rank first in her class. In the afternoons, she would run down the famous Ashrafieh stairs to catch a ride behind their neighbor's wagon. As if reliving those moments, she recounted with animated gestures and excitement how she would time herself and knew exactly which step to jump from to land swiftly into the back of the wagon. Their neighbor, an oil merchant, would be on his way back home around the same time. "When we made it home," she said, "I would run into the house and get the horse's hay that my mother would have prepared in order to repay our neighbor in some way." "Well..." she lowered her voice, "this neighbor's son apparently liked me."

"Your grandfather, Krikor (Torossian), was an only child. His aspiration was to become a soldier. At 17, he enlisted in the Lebanese French army[9] by lying about his age and withholding the fact that he was an only child. He even claimed to have two sisters!" She went on to say that when her parents refused his offer of marriage, stating that they did not wish upon their daughter the life of an army wife, he threatened to kidnap her! Her parents, fearing embarrassment within the community, ended up relenting. She became engaged to Krikor at the age of 16. They stayed engaged for two years while he completed different military assignments. They were poor at first. She described how she convinced my grandfather to purchase a rug for the floor because it was too cold in the house. Later, when their finances improved, they built a two-story building in Bourj Hammoud. Her voice lowered to a whisper as she timidly described my grandfather. He was quite tall. He had a white horse, which was

---

9 For a period following WWI, Lebanon was placed under a French mandate (1923-1946).

his most prized companion. He would entertain the neighbors by slapping the side of the animal and jumping over it from the sides as it galloped in a startled frenzy. He reached the rank of *Adjudant-Chef* in the army (the equivalent of Lieutenant Commander). His French was impeccable. He trained generals but did not qualify to become one himself because of his inadequacy in Arabic writing. He was part of the French *Légion étrangère* forces during WWII and had fought in the Palestinian Israeli war of 1948 and the battles during the 1958 Lebanese riots. He was stationed as an artillery officer in the Lebanese army at the southern border city of Naqoura. During one war, he saw his horse on the ground crying. It was severely injured, so he shot the animal in order to halt its suffering. He went missing in action twice, the second time for several months. Each time, army representatives informed my grandmother about his MIA status. She would wear black, thinking he was dead, and then he would show up at the door.

I wanted her to elaborate more about what had happened to my grandfather while he was missing in action the second time around. She told me that he was injured in one leg with his boot melted into his flesh. He escaped a sure amputation by dragging himself for miles until he collapsed. He did not recall where. A Sunni Muslim couple took him in and remedied his leg with homeopathic medicine. He stayed with them for a long time while he healed. "Do you see how there are such nice people in the world? Thanks be to God!" "Yes…" she said, her mind traveling to the distant past. "They even tried to assassinate him." "What?!" I exclaimed. "My Manoug had a fever, and I had laid him next to the window when a bomb exploded below!" "He ended up with pieces of glass stuck on his tepid face. Apparently, the news was rushed to Krikor because next thing we know, ho hooo, he came with his entire squad in army trucks to check up on us!" That image in her memory drew a mischievous smile on her lips even after all these years. I knew from my parents that my grandfather was quite the athletic type. He enjoyed swimming in the ocean at night and was also an avid hunter. My father fondly recalls bird hunting trips where my grandfather would teach him techniques that landed correct shooting angles. My grandfather was decorated with several medals. According to my mother, he was a generous soul. Having no siblings, he relished inviting relatives to large gatherings. But he also loved quiet moments, where he would have a drink on the balcony while reading a French novel. He retired from the army in 1967 and continued as a trainer of the cadets in the Lebanese army. A year or so later, the unthinkable happened. He had a major hemorrhagic stroke which took his life. His last words were a complaint about a massive headache.

As if on cue, the question that I always longed to ask my grand-mother pushed from its confinement in the rear of my memory and jumped to the forefront of my mind. My eyes widened. I could barely contain myself. I massaged the words carefully in my mouth and thought twice about how to inquire about great-grandfather Karekin Torossian's strange lamentations. Mommie was a very matter-of-fact, sharp-minded, private lady. She hated gossipers, complainers, and whiners and did not like dwelling on sad stories or serious topics for too long. When a subject bothered her, she would be visibly shaken and start reciting her prayers. She prayed constantly for all of us. We have never once heard her complain or even open up about how she felt about losing her husband at a young age or what challenges and difficulties she had to overcome when she was on her own, caring for her ailing in-laws and overseeing the tenants. She seemed to barricade herself from negativity and hopelessness. If she saw someone depressed or brooding about, she would say, "*Hadeh nayim, yerest lva, Park Asdoudzo eseh, on aratch*!" "Come on now, wash your face, give thanks to the Lord and move on forward!" After my grandfather's death, she had become a born-again Christian and had found solace in the Armenian Protestant church and Jesus Christ. A plaque with her favorite quote from Jesus hung in her Bourj Hammoud dining room and later on top of her bed in California: "*Mi vakhnar, kanzi yes hedt em*," "Do not be afraid, for I am with you!" Pushing the envelope with inquiries about family secrets could very well cause her to shut down and change the subject, so I had to make every effort to exude a nonchalant carefree demeanor in order not to give her an inkling of the serious topic coming up. And here it went.

"Mommie, how did [great-grandpa] Karekin dede and [great-grandma] Yeghisapet dudu[10] meet? Mom tells me they were adorable together." Mommie did not notice any hidden agenda: "They pointed out Yeghisapet from afar and told Dede, "You see that girl in pink? She is your betrothed." He did not see her again until their wedding night." "Oh, so they had an arranged marriage?" "Karekin dede was an orphan," continued Mommie, "and Yeghisapet, who was from Hadjin, had come to Adana to live with her uncle's family. Back then, the townspeople set up Armenian couples together." "So who was Karekin dede referring to when he used to cry about a lady and her child?" I asked, feeling my heart beating in my throat. When she did not say anything, I continued: "He would cry that he should have spared their lives..." After seconds that seemed like an eternity, my grandmother answered in her low gossipy tone, a tone that came out during the very rare occasions where she spilled secrets. "Karekin dede, just like both sides of my family, was from Adana. He came from a big family. They were eight boys. During the Adana massacre[11], six of his brothers were killed along with his mother and father. He was the youngest. He was hiding behind something, and no one saw him. When things calmed down, he found his eldest brother, Kevork. In the frenzy of the massacre, his brother had lost part of his left ear to an ax and was thrown in a well along with other Armenians. He had survived, lying under a pile of dead people; may God rest their souls! Having lost the rest

---

10   Dudu was the equivalent of "grandmother" in the Hadjin Armenian dialect of great grandma Yeghisapet.
11   During the 1909 Countercoup of Sultan Abdul Hamid, anti-Armenian pogroms took place in the city of Adana 20,000-30,000 Armenians were killed by Ottoman Muslims. Raymond H. Kévorkian, "The Cilician Massacres, April 1909" in *Armenian Cilicia*, eds. Richard G. Hovannisian and Simon Payaslian. UCLA Armenian History and Culture Series: Historic Armenian Cities and Provinces, 7. Costa Mesa, California: Mazda Publishers, 2008, pp. 339-69.

of their family, the two boys wandered the streets for a while and were later taken up by a gang of Armenian *fedayees* (paramilitary). They stayed with those men. They were called the *Chakhejeh* group, defending the Armenian community from up in the hills... and it seems that they took part in some vengeful killings of Turks and Kurds. Towards the end of his life, he kept on lamenting about an incident he deeply regretted."

I had heard what I wanted to hear. Now, I had to make a smooth transition to a more positive topic before my grandmother became annoyed and closed up. "Mom says that Karekin dede and Yeghisapet dudu spoke Greek with each other whenever they did not want to share a topic..." I continued swiftly. "During the Genocide," Mommie explained, "the newlywed Karekin and Yeghisapet escaped by ship to Greece, lived there for some time, and had your Dede there, and afterward, they all settled in Lebanon." I sensed that Mommie was getting tired, so I retreated to our mundane daily topics. But ooh... in my mind, I was stunned by these revelations. Karekin dede had witnessed his parents and six siblings get killed. Did he have to identify their bodies? As a mom, I could not imagine having eight children, strapping boys, full of promise... and losing six of them... how many grandchildren would those six boys have born to their parents had they lived? What careers or businesses would they have ventured in? Who were they? What did they look like? These uncles that my grandfather never came to know.

The Adana massacre of 1909 took place amidst the chaos of a countercoup by supporters of Sultan Abdul Hamid II against the Young Turks' Committee of Union and Progress (CUP) that had toppled him in 1908. The Armenians had supported the CUP because it had reinstated the Constitutional system that was meant to give equal rights to minorities. The more fanatical and conservative element within the Muslim population, however, was offended that infidel Armenians were going to be elevated to their level and were wary of the technological advances that Armenians were adopting. Feelings of nationalism had come to a boiling point with a countercoup by sympathizers of the Sultan. The mobs that were unleashed on the Adana Armenian population also included nationalist CUP members. Previously the center of the Armenian Kingdom of Cilicia (1080-1375), the Adana district is said to have been the area most heavily populated by Armenians. Estimates place its pre-WWI Armenian population above 200,000, with some towns being completely Armenian[12].

The massacre was unconscionably heinous and resulted in the complete destruction of half of the Armenian quarter in Adana and cost the lives of 20,000-30,000 Armenians.[13] The same Sultan had previously ordered massacres across the six Armenian *vilayets* (occupied Armenian provinces) from 1894 to 1896. They came to be known as the Hamidian massacres, where upwards of 300,000 Armenians were slaughtered. These massacres preceded what is known as the Armenian Genocide of 1915-1923, which cost another million and a half lives. How scary it must have been to live and raise a family in a country where your kind was brutally pursued and killed with impunity! How sad for Karekin dede to have grown up as a wandering orphan. And the Muslim lady and her son who kept on haunting him… my heart went out to them, too.

I so regret having cut my inquiries short that afternoon. I thought that I would have another opportunity to ask my grandmother about her side of the family. She had said that both sides of her own family were also from Adana. Unfortunately, that opportunity never presented itself. In 2012, we admitted my grandmother into Ararat, the Armenian retirement home in the San Fernando Valley of Los Angeles. To our surprise, being surrounded by folk from her generation blew a second wind into her. As if by miracle, her mind returned to its sharpness. She would help in the kitchen with chopping vegetables for Tabbouleh salad and win "Resident of the

---

12 The American mission in Adana estimated 195,200, but Armenian estimates were closer to 400,000. "The Pre-War Population of Cilicia," Bodl. MS Toynbee 44, Stats.

13 Rouben Paul Adalian, *Historical Dictionary of Armenia* (Lanham, MD: Scarecrow Press, 2010), s.v. "Adana Massacre."

Month" awards. She even wondered why they did not offer English classes there! Her prayers were so eloquent that the administration asked her to offer the daily table blessing in the cafeteria. I found her there one day when I visited. She introduced me proudly as her grandchild to the other ladies at her table. When she repeated it a second time, a bitter senior on the table yelled, "So what!" My grandmother mumbled something under her nose in disgust. She showed off how she drove her "car," maneuvering her wheelchair back to her room. When I told her that our house was very close to Ararat Home and that I would be visiting her often, she lit up and asked me to give her directions. She said she could come visit me in her wheelchair! I could barely contain myself. The look in her eyes told me that the prospect of driving her wheelchair to my house sounded very plausible to her, as if she were once again the young girl who flew down the Ashrafieh steps. She asked us not to disclose the fact that she was in a retirement home to our acquaintances. Her pride would not allow it.

My grandmother passed away in the early morning hours of Saturday, August 30, 2014. The staff at Ararat Home was shaken. When she had complained about not feeling well, the nurses had offered her medication. She had refused and asked for her bible instead. "It happened so fast," they said; they could not notify us in time. Holding on to her bible tightly, my grandmother had uttered "Jesus" three times and released her spirit into the hands of her beloved Savior. We were devastated that she had died alone. Why didn't she wait for us? We wanted to say goodbye. She had been the anchor of our family. She made us all feel safer and stronger with her presence alone. Who was going to pray for us now? I will always miss the way she greeted me with arms wide open, calling me *"Katias, Katias"* "my Katia, my Katia!" Her name, misspelled in her passport on her way to America, was continuously mispronounced by non-Armenians as "Younika" instead of Yevnigeh. She was indeed unique. I miss her dearly.

20 - *Le transport des cadavres hors de la ville, à Adana, en avril 1909.*
CPA, coll. M. Paboudjian.

THE PRINT ON THIS PHOTO FROM 1909 READS (TRANSLATED FROM FRENCH): THE
TRANSPORT OF THE CADAVERS (MASSACRED ARMENIANS) OUT OF THE CITY OF ADANA,
APRIL 1909. MY GREAT-GRANDFATHER KAREKIN'S PARENTS AND SIX OF HIS SIBLINGS
WERE KILLED DURING THOSE MASSACRES. SOURCE: ARTAXIAD, CC BY-SA 3.0
<HTTP://CREATIVECOMMONS.ORG/LICENSES/BY-SA/3.0/>, VIA WIKIMEDIA COMMONS

THIS PICTURE FROM THE ADANA MASSACRE IS DESCRIBED AS DEPICTING BODIES
RETRIEVED FROM A WELL. IT MAKES ME WONDER IF KAREKIN DEDE'S BROTHER
WAS THROWN IN THE SAME WELL AS THE VICTIMS IN THE PICTURE. SOURCE: THE
ARMENIAN GENOCIDE, ARTE FRANCE, THE CIE DES PHARES ET BALISES COPYRIGHT:
ARTAXIAD CREATIVE COMMONS ATTRIBUTION-SHARE ALIKE 3.0 UNPORTE

MY GRANDFATHER KRIKOR: IN THE PHOTO ON THE RIGHT, FROM HIS EARLIER
MILITARY YEARS (STANDING ON THE LEFT), AND WITH ONE OF HIS UNITS IN THE
LEFT PHOTO (MIDDLE WITH HAT). PHOTOS FROM OUR FAMILY COLLECTION.

MY MATERNAL GRANDPARENTS KRIKOR AND YEVNIGEH TOROSSIAN
STANDING. MY MOTHER IN THE MIDDLE OF THE FRONT ROW WITH HER
SIBLINGS AND HER PATERNAL GRANDPARENTS KAREKIN AND YEGHISAPET
TOROSSIAN. PHOTO FROM OUR FAMILY'S COLLECTION.

Not so Sweet a Birthday!

Back to 1984.

ON JANUARY 29, AND FOR the first time in a long time, my relatives came over to celebrate my sixteenth birthday. We had grown lax with the long stretch of ceasefire. The New Year presented renewed hope. My mother made her new specialty, double fudge chocolate cake, into the shape of the number 16. I received many books and journals as gifts, which delighted me. I would soon fill their pages with cutouts of historic people and places that fascinated me, in addition to many poems I wrote in French. As a teenager, I was testing the waters of more mature levels of thinking and inquisition. I was excited about the unraveling changes in my life and the promise of new possibilities. Predictably, this normalcy of life was short-lived, and our world came crashing down again a week later, on February 8, when a most-harrowing bombing claimed the panes of all our windows. Barely had we run out of the door when a small explosive opened a hole in our kitchen wall and wreaked havoc within. We were huddled once again on the second floor of our building. Nearby, a loud upheaval was followed by desperate cries of anguish. We found out that a neighbor's son had gone to check the area where a bomb had just landed, only to be killed by a second one that crashed in the same spot a few moments later. My father made sure to shield us from seeing any dead bodies as we once again defied destiny, ran to the street, jumped into our car, and headed to Bourj Hammoud. This time we stayed there for good. In March, the schools closed because of the constant shelling. I had started writing about the events occurring in my life on the pages of a small 1984 Credit Suisse calendar organizer that my father had given me at the beginning of the year. He had received it along with other New Year's calendars and promotional material. My maternal aunt and her family had also moved to my grandmother's apartment. Together, we experienced firsthand all that living in Bourj Hammoud entailed. This was a dream come true for me. Finally, I was one with the mysterious force that pulled me to Bourj Hammoud. I was one with my people. The short time we lived there proved to be the most eventful and memorable time of my young life.

I will never forget the inspiring sermons of the energetic Pastor Djambazian at the Protestant Church of Shamlian Tatikian School across from our building or the mass held at candlelight on a day with no electricity at St. Karasoun Manoug Church. Our community's resolve in the dark powerless church suffused by burning incense bonded us with an unspoken dignified togetherness. For the first time in my life, I observed Lent as well as other traditional Armenian religious practices, a feat that warmed my heart. I came to cherish the day-to-day activities, the hustle and bustle of the community. I will always remember the orange vintage BMW that all the neighbors' boys seemed to share. Every other week, its hood was up, and the boys were frantically tending to its ongoing mechanical problems, attracting the coveted attention of the neighborhood's young girls. Soon it was Easter, and the ladies were rushing to the bakeries to turn in their orders of Cheoreg[14] and traditional Armenian Easter cookies. The sweet smell inundated the streets! We knew by then that we were expected at the American Embassy on March 6 for our Green Card interview. I started polishing up my English, which was introduced at our school in 9th grade (the year prior). My cousins and I kept on watching the movie Grease and

---

14 Armenian sweet Easter brioche

blasting Beatles and Michael Jackson songs. We had already started to "Americanize" ourselves! Around that time, I received the sweetest belated birthday card from my grandmother Yevnigeh who had left several months prior to join my younger uncle in California. Meanwhile, my father was conducting his research on traveling safely to and from the American Embassy in West Beirut. The road to the West side of Beirut was a very perilous one. Through the years, many unlucky Lebanese citizens and foreigners were kidnapped or shot dead trying to cross the Green Line. To this end, several meetings were held at my grandmother's flat, where some leading figures in the community and well-informed neighbors came to advise my father. What derived from all this research was the following plan: an Armenian named Goruyn, which translates to "lion cub" in English, had made it his specialty to transport folks back and forth to both sides of divided Beirut. True to his name, Goruyn was a short-statured slender man with rippling muscles, a nervous energy, and reddish-brown eyes that burned with focus in his sun-tanned face. Since my sister was younger than 16, she was exempt from the interview. I, however, had to attend. And so it was that we awoke early on March 6ʻ ready to meet destiny face to face.

Have a Nice Day!

GORUYN'S TAXI PULLED UP IN front of our door early in the morning.
Everyone in the household wished us well. Goruyn gave us two
distinct instructions: to abide by his orders and, if questioned by
armed militia, to say that we were Armenians visiting a friend in
West Beirut. Off we went. The spring air was damp and crisp. As
a matter of fact, I remember thinking that it was a truly beautiful
morning. Diverse and contradictory feelings were churning in our
stomachs. This could prove to be the beginning of the rest of our
lives or a tragic ending. I was sitting behind Goruyn in the back
passenger seat. My mother was sitting next to me, a white knit-
ted jacket draped over her left arm, strategically hiding our Green
Card paperwork underneath. My father, seated next to Goruyn,
was uncharacteristically quiet. An hour into our travel, we made it
into the long stretch notorious for standstill traffic. We were now
advancing a few feet every 10 minutes. I kept on playing "we are
Armenians visiting a friend" in the back of my mind. The fact that
Armenians had stayed neutral in the war was supposed to shield
us from any sectarian hatred. The voice in my head continued in a
self-conversation: "We are Armenians… Armenians… Then why the
heck are we in Lebanon? Why are we in this dreaded country that
I love so much? If we are Armenian, shouldn't we be in Armenia?
Why are we subjected to the possibility of being shot at or kidnapped
by Syrians, Palestinians, etc.? Why aren't we in Armenia? Is there
an Armenia? It is in the Soviet Union. Where is the Armenia of my
grandparents?"

Further on, we started hearing the immortalized speeches of Bashir, the assassinated darling leader of the Christian Phalangists, being played through loudspeakers. We could see a huge billboard of his picture placed on top of a building. Up ahead, the Christian militia checkpoint was inundated with numerous cars and their impatient travelers. The traffic came to a complete halt. We were not moving at all. An hour went by, and my father expressed concern about possibly missing our appointment at the American Embassy. We finally made the drastic decision to cross the Phalangist checkpoint on foot. Goruyn assured us that, no matter what, he would meet us at the U.S. embassy to bring us back. So the three of us started walking on the side of the road. As we neared the Christian Phalangist checkpoint, Bashir's voice resonated louder. I looked up at his charismatic face on the billboard. "Where are you heading?" asked a militia. My father recited our rehearsed explanation. "Go, may God be with you," said the soldier. We continued on through an empty stretch. We were now in Muslim territory. Crossing the "Green Line" on foot had apparently become part of the norm because several taxis were on hand on the other side to assist folk in continuing on their journey. My father rented one. This time, I was seated behind an Arab Muslim taxi driver, a complete stranger who smelled of sweat. My heart was beating in my throat, and I was swallowing nervously every so often. I could also feel my parents' nervousness. From my vantage point, I could not see my father's face, so I focused instead on his left hand resting on his knee. My father was a leftie. That robust hand had cut so many clothing patterns and drawn so many figures to entertain my sister and me. It was the same hand I looked at one day when my father, in his desperate attempt to protect us during a bombing, had lain a blanket over us and spread himself on top of it to shield us. All I could see through an opening of the blanket was his strong left hand and his clean square nails.

Our taxi slowed down as we were nearing another checkpoint. This time, it was a group of Murabitoun Sunni militia soldiers who seemed to be cracking a joke amongst them. Our taxi driver looked over, hoping to make eye contact with one of the armed men and get authorization to proceed safely. Behind him, I was also looking apprehensively in their direction. One of the soldiers took notice of our taxi, threw away the match he had lit his cigarette with, and motioned us forward with his head. Our taxi driver waved at him in recognition of his gesture and drove on forward. His mind at ease, he was focusing ahead. My eyes, however, remained on the armed group. Another soldier in sunglasses turned his gaze towards our car as he was finishing a sentence to his colleague. Oblivious of the previous soldier's gesture to us, he thought our car was proceeding without being checked and yelled, "Waeef!" "Stop!" Given the green light to proceed just moments prior, our driver was perplexed and did not stop the car fast enough, which prompted the soldier in the glasses to charge his upheld gun and move toward us. When he finally processed what was happening, our driver braked hard, and the car came to a screeching halt.

One of the gunmen walked around the front of our car and opened the door on my father's side. The soldier wearing sunglasses, on the other hand, was coming right at me. Every step he took made my heart rate quadruple, and when he stood in front of my window, I stopped breathing. He leaned in and rested his elbows on the edge of the window, the gun hanging from his shoulder protruding through the window and hovering inches over my lap. I overheard my father being ordered to get out of the car. Next, I heard them order him to open the trunk in the back. The cowering taxi driver was hunched forward, mumbling all sorts of sweet nonsense to calm the situation down. Visions of my father being shot dead rolled behind my eyes. For the first and only time in my life, my limbs went numb, and then a paralysis claimed all four of my extremities. The stiffness was so strenuous on my muscles that my cranium, neck, and jaw bones started aching. I was experiencing a new level of terror. The soldier on my side approached his face within a few inches of mine. I could see my terrified reflection in his dark-tinted aviator sunglasses. My eyes processed the words *Ray Ban*. I was terrified of the prospect of him ordering me out and my paralyzed body failing me. He looked at my mother. "Passports," he said. My mother handed him our passports. "Where are you heading, ma'am?" My mom responded in an incredibly calm voice: "Ermen[15]...We are Armenian, just visiting a friend at the hospital." The soldier held my mother's passport in front of my nose. He looked at her picture and then stared into my eyes. I thought to myself, "what if he says I am not the person in the picture and pulls me out of the car?" At that moment, I knew what being completely powerless meant. My limbs and arms stiff and unresponsive, I felt as if I was succumbing to the final moments of my life. Time stood painfully still for what seemed an eternity. My trance was suddenly broken with the sound of the trunk shutting and my father returning to his seat. The soldier next to me handed the passports back to my mother and pulled himself and his gun out of the window with a last look at me. I will forever wonder why he terrorized me so and what his hidden gaze looked like. He motioned our driver forward with his hand. Destiny had decided that it was not our time to go. Had my mother's jacket slipped in her attempt at getting our passports out of her purse and had our American Green Card documents been exposed, we would have found ourselves in a very precarious situation. Any affiliation with the America they hated would have given these soldiers incentive to harm us if they so wished.

Not long after, shaken by the incident, our driver stopped the car under a tree and asked us to get another taxi. Traffic had become sparse, and a distant sound of explosions was growing persistently louder. There were only two taxis on the side of the road, and we moved into one of them. Although finally cooperating, my body felt sore as if it had undergone a strenuous exercise session. All pretexts thrown aside, my father asked the driver to take us to the American Embassy. We were soon on one of the most beautiful

---

15 "Ermen" is "Armenians" in Arabic.

highways running up the coast of the blue Mediterranean. My father pointed out a once-elegant, now bullet and bomb-torn building. "Hotel Alcazar, where we were married," he said. My mother, who I am sure was absolutely mortified by what had transpired at the last checkpoint, was feigning normalcy for my sake: "Oh yes... It was so beautiful when we got married." "It was on Christmas Day," she added.

"These sidewalks used to be packed with people," reminisced my father, "Eh, where did you go, Lebanon?" he lamented. The setting was bizarrely eerie: on one side, a wide sidewalk with a metal railing running the length of the coast with waves crashing beneath, and on the other side, the ghastly sight of mostly dilapidated buildings. The few cars we saw were speeding away. A large compound surrounded by thick barbwire was looming ahead. The taxi driver dropped us off at the security gate. Once inside, we were guided by a worker to the vicinity of the ambassador's office. He told us that someone would be with us shortly, and then we were virtually forgotten. The bombing in the far was creeping closer and louder. There was a hustle and bustle in the hallways. Folks were rushing about. No one was paying attention to the three individuals sitting on the bench. One of the workers finally did a double-take, reversed his steps backward, and inquired, "Who are you, and what are you doing here? They are bombing outside!" With further scrutiny, he added, "Are you Armenian?"

He was a tall man with large eyes and thick black hair. My father divulged with excitement that we had been waiting and that our Green Card interview appointment was 20 minutes ago! The worker's name was Peter, a little unusual for an Armenian. "Oh, *you* are Peter!" my father exclaimed in Armenian, establishing spontaneous kinship and trust. His response made us conclude that he was previously told that an Armenian named Peter worked at the American Embassy. Peter raised his voice: "What interview? They are about to air-lift the ambassador by helicopter! Can't you hear the bombing?" My father's face became livid. "Peter, you know how hard it was for us to get here? Do something! We need to get interviewed now!" he demanded, the general in him on full alert. "Wait here," said Peter after taking a deep breath. He rushed towards a set of doors and disappeared inside. A few moments later, he reappeared: "Come on in," he said. And so it was that we walked in to face destiny.

The whole affair lasted just a few minutes and is pretty much a blur in my mind. I remember that the ambassador was very nervous about the bombing. He was gathering his belongings and wanted to leave as soon as possible. He asked us to raise our right hands. "Will you be good citizens in America?" he asked. He inquired about my father's line of work and asked if there was a tailor in America who was sponsoring him. With my father's affirmative response, the ambassador swore us in, congratulated us, and flew out of the room. Peter told us that they were evacuating the workers, and he suggested we come back another day for the Green Card certificates. At this, my father's eyes became downright murderous. A bulging vessel was throbbing on one side of his forehead. Barely containing his cool, he articulated, "Peter, we will not leave here until we get our Green Cards." Peter succumbed to my father's unshakable resolve. "Ok, let me see what I can do," he said. He conjured up an Armenian female employee to the task of producing the paperwork. Things were typed, corrected, retyped... and, finally, the pieces of paper that our future depended on were placed in our hands. "Is this really happening?" I remember asking myself. "May God be with you," said Peter. My father could not thank him enough.

As the employees rushed towards a van, we headed out a door, disoriented and lost. "Not this way!" yelled a Marine. No sooner had he uttered those words that about a dozen German Shepherds were ferociously running our way. We backed up and closed the door behind us just in time! A couple of Marines finally approached us and guided us to the exit. The last Marine opening a metal door in the fenced wall was a vision to uphold. He was the first Black man that I had ever seen in my life! A giant with massive muscles, he nodded his head and uttered the following words in his James Earl

Jones voice: "Have a nice day!" All three of us responded, "Thank You!" giddy with our use of the English language. The irony of the situation was glaring. We were being wished a "nice day" while we were heading towards the bombing! The gate closed behind us. We braced ourselves for what lay ahead.

As we proceeded, we noticed that we were the only ones on the street: my father, mother, and I, dressed in our Sunday best, walking all by ourselves. Our footsteps could be heard on the deserted sidewalk as splashing waves rose to peek at us. A big smoke cloud could be seen behind the buildings in the distance, explosions ringing closer. There is no limit to the risks our instinct for survival propels us to take when we are faced with persecution, death, or a hopeless existence. From running across monitored borders, hiding in car trunks like sardines, sailing in inflatable boats with sharks lurking in the waters to walking on a deserted street in front of a backdrop of a city being bombed, humans will just about do anything in order to live. We kept a steady pace. The sounds of explosions grew louder. The sidewalk seemed to run forever. No cars were lining it. None, except for one we discerned from afar, a single parked car with a lone figure leaning against it. Goruyn!

I cannot put into words the relief we felt as we saw him! It was as if the stars were finally starting to align for us! For me, the only way to describe that slender human being with nervous energy and crazy courage, that unassuming individual leading the humble existence of a taxi driver, is by conjuring up the words "A Giant among Men!" For us, Goruyn, the lion cub, was a true-life hero! He sprung forward as he saw us, motioning us into the car. No sooner were we in than he instructed my mother and me to crouch on the floor in the back. As the car made its way into a neighborhood, he floored the gas pedal. Our car flew at incredible speed as explosions rumbled all around and bullets flew overhead. "Duck your heads!" my father kept on yelling.

Soon enough, we switched to normal speed and then slowed considerably. The sounds of explosions were now muffled by the distance of miles. I raised my head to peek through the window and saw several French soldiers looking in Goruyn's direction with admiration in their eyes. In those days, United Nations troops were placed in different areas around the Green Line dividing Beirut in the hopes of keeping the peace. They were often the victims of indiscriminate shelling. Slowly, we made our way back to Bourj Hammoud. The ordeal we had just gone through was quickly forgotten as the realization that we were future legal immigrants to the United States sank in. Our joy was limitless! True hope had finally sprung in our midst. Hope given to us by unforgettable individuals to whom we owed so much! Individuals that we, unfortunately, failed to thank in a decent fashion due to the circumstances we were in. "Thank you to the American ambassador, to the nameless Armenian female worker who typed our documents at the embassy. Thank you to generous soul Peter! Thank you to Goruyn, who will live in our hearts forever!"

Pack Up Your Life!

THE NEXT MONTHS WERE DEDICATED to packing and liquidating all our possessions in Lebanon. My father sold his store in Bourj Hammoud as well as our home furnishings for rock-bottom prices. According to my diary, we traveled seven times to our apartment in Gemmayze to transport our belongings. A couple of years prior, we had sold our Buick and purchased a brand new silver Peugeot, which we put to great use during those last trips home. We hired a packing company to box our housewares, rugs, wool comforters, memorabilia, and the framed pictures of my grandparents Sarkis and Maryam. The apartment on the ground floor of the Bourj Hammoud building filled up with boxes. My father and I went together on the last trip to our apartment. The final memory I carry of our home is of the curtains on the broken windows flying with the breeze as my father went on and on about how priceless some treasured items he had saved from our attic were. He had unfolded a double-sided sewn piece with bright purple fabric in the top piece and retrieved a strange-looking narrow metal barrel with intricate carvings. He said it was his mother's "dowry bundle" from the old country and recounted some sort of a meaningful story about his father having paid 40 gold coins for that piece of metal. I, on the other hand, was trying to absorb the aura of the house in which I, my sister, and my father before us were raised. I lingered at the custom-made built-in entertainment center in our living room and thought back on the plans my father was making all those years ago about moving us to a brand new apartment across the Mediterranean. He was now leaving behind everything he had worked a lifetime to build: the two stores in the destroyed downtown Beirut, a strip of land in the countryside, and a pile of dashed hopes and dreams. They will be lost forever. As I was trying to unlock the trunk of our car to place our last items inside, a bullet flew right above my head and hit the wall of the building behind me. My hand started shaking, and I imagined a sniper toying with us from afar, a very good possibility given the number of snipers captured in the high-rise buildings over the years, some of whom were later dragged behind cars in retaliation. We hopped in our car and drove away from our home for the last time.

Back at Bourj Hammoud, we spent the days planning ahead for our trip. We were allowed eight bags in total. All our boxed home items were going to be shipped to California a few days prior to our departure. We needed to have plenty of cash on hand in order to bribe the border patrol workers and the checkpoint militia to spare our bags from inspection, which often amounted to confiscation of valuables. I spent the days on the balcony reading my English dictionary book while, around me, life in Bourj Hammoud proceeded as usual. We went to school for the last time to get our report cards and attestation letters confirming that we were students there. My classmates came over for a goodbye visit. As I held the picture frame and Snoopy doll they brought me as mementos, I realized that as budding teenagers, we were finally developing closer bonds. Alas, I would not be with them on future trips to the beach and afternoon shopping ventures.

The last item we sold was our Peugeot. We stood staring behind it as its new owner drove it away, feeling vulnerable, as if naked. The numbered days we had left in Lebanon flew by all too quickly, and the day to leave was soon upon us: Saturday, May 26. We labeled and numbered all eight of our suitcases: Tavitian 1, Tavitian 2, etc. My mother had sewn our jewelry inside makeshift fabric belts that we wore under our clothing. Wearing them all on our bodies would attract attention, and packing them in bags was risky. "This is what

our ancestors did when they left Turkey," said my mother as she
wrapped the belts around us. Once again, I shrugged off that piece
of information, my teenager's mind not interested in nostalgia. I
slipped on the red and white polka dot dress that I had picked for
our trip to America and munched on freshly baked Manaeesh. The
last authentic Lebanese Manaeesh I would eat for a long time!

Despite the early hour and the chilly air, a crowd of well-wishers
was forming downstairs. It seemed as if the entire "village" had come
to bid us farewell. We went over our paperwork, making sure we were
not missing any documents. Around us, family members were making it their business to oversee our every move. My mother's cousins
were busy bringing down our numerous suitcases without us needing to ask them. In true Armenian fashion, a nervous commotion
was brewing. Once on the street, we found ourselves surrounded by
friends, family, and neighbors. More neighbors were hanging from
balconies all over, waving at us and yelling good wishes. The car that
was going to take us to a bus station was parked to the side. Here it
was: the moment to say goodbye to Bourj Hammoud, to Lebanon,
and to my childhood. I took a deep breath, fighting back tears, and
started hugging everyone down the row. Once situated in the car, I
scanned every face and zoomed in on as many details of the picture
facing me in order to take in as much as I could. If I could have
stopped time or frozen a moment, it would have been my last glance
of Bourj Hammoud: the crowd waving at us in the middle of the
street, with the humble buildings in the background, their laundry
lines and the electrical wires mish-mashing between them. Here
they were, descendants of genocide survivors who had followed the
trajectory of their destiny from faraway Western Armenia (today's
eastern and southeastern Turkey) to the Syrian Desert to Aleppo to
Lebanon… and now to America. The tears started streaming down
my cheeks uncontrollably. It felt as if I was being snatched from the
bosom of my people, my landless resilient people. Little did we know
that many in that crowd would soon follow our example and move to
different parts of the world. At that moment, however, I remember

feeling close to my mother's clan. Based on my limited experience in life, they represented the definition of being Armenian. I did not know then about the surprise curve ball my father's side of the family would be swirling in my direction.

My Lebanon

THE TEARS CONTINUED FLOWING AS the car drove through streets first familiar and then increasingly unknown to us. The scene of our relatives and neighbors waving goodbye in the warm cocoon of that Armenian neighborhood, with its familiar smells, names, and crooked buildings, kept on playing over and over in the back of my eyes. I could not help it. Eventually, the scene went still as if transformed into the cover of a book that one day I hoped to reopen. We made it to the bus station. A crowd of citizens leaving the country like us were ready to embark on a traveling bus heading to Syria. The war was at its peak in 1984. The heavily damaged airport in Beirut was closed. The most pursued option was traveling to neighboring Syria by bus and flying from there. Instead of crossing the country in a straight line into Syria next door, these buses had to travel northbound along the length of Lebanon, past the city of Tripoli, then turn eastbound into Syria and down towards the capital of Damascus. Travelers had to endure this long journey in order to avoid the areas heavily armed by the Syrian forces in central Lebanon. We placed all eight of our suitcases in the cargo of the Pullman and sat in our seats along with the other passengers.

As the bus started its journey, the excitement of travel intertwined with our apprehensions of what lay ahead. One minute, we were stopping at a convenience store for a snack. The next minute, we were slowing down at a checkpoint, hearts palpitating, praying that our bribes would be good enough and our bags left alone. As we traveled the miles, familiar sights of damaged buildings hurried before us. Here and there, we saw the sign for some national monument or archeological site. This prompted my parents to tell us about all the lovely Lebanese locales they had visited when they were newly engaged. Betty and I had come to recognize this as our parents' futile attempt to normalize our circumstances. My father went on to tell us about his daring diving adventure at the rock of Raouche, where he ended up knocking his head on a rock many feet underwater but made it back up safely. My mother said she will always cherish the picture they took at the fountain of Beit El Deen Palace. And, oh, how about the Roman temple of Baalbek and that restaurant where watermelons were cracked in the cold water of a stream flowing down from Mount Sannine? As we passed the coastal city of Jounieh, they went on to describe the Shrine of Our Lady of Lebanon, *Notre Dame de Liban.* One of the most known shrines in the world to honor the Virgin Mary, it was erected in 1907 at the top of a hill in the village of Harissa. The beautiful white statue with the serene face and soft eyes looks down towards Beirut with her palms open. My father reminisced about how they used to take the *telepherique* (gondola lift) from the coastal town of Jounieh to where the statue stood in Harissa. "This is what is so special with Lebanon," he went on to say. "You can be at the blue Mediterranean Sea, and in 10 minutes, you can rise to the mountains." We were called back to the reality at hand when, in a few miles, we came up to yet another checkpoint. Armed men came onto the bus, supposedly checking us out, but mostly to intimidate us so that we paid them well. Halfway into our trip, we were munching on sandwiches as the radio in the bus played one of the 1984 Lebanese hits. Ironically enough, it was about a trip on a bus. It was sung by Lebanon's darling singer Fayrouz: "*A Hadir il-Bostah*"... It went like this.

'Aa Hadir al-Bosta

The bus song

Lyrics & Music: Ziad Rahbani

By the roar of the bus we traveled / from the village of Him-laya to the village of Tannurin / and I remembered you, Alia / and remembered your eyes / and God forgive you, Alia / what beautiful eyes you have.

On our way to the mountains from the heat we almost died / some ate lettuce others munched on figs / one had his wife with him, and God / how ugly his wife was / lucky are the passengers on their way / to Tannurin / they take everything in stride / but they don't know, Alia / what beautiful eyes you have.

Way up we went and we hadn't even / paid our fare / some-times we calmed down the rattling door / sometimes we calmed the passengers / the guy found out his wife was getting dizzy / I wouldn't put it past him / to let her go up alone / and if you could only see your eyes, Alia / how beautiful they are, your eyes / Driver if you'd just close that window / the air, O driver / the air will make us catch cold / the air O driver.

That song, to me, summed up what Lebanon was: an old country with impressively rich history, where Jesus had performed his first miracle by turning water to wine at a wedding in the village of Canaan, and where amazing Phoenician and Roman ruins transport you back to lost civilizations. Similar to Western Armenia, Lebanon was ruled by the Ottoman Empire for several hundred years starting in the early 1500s and had come under a French mandate in 1923 at the end of World War I. From 1915 to 1918, during the Armenian Genocide, the Turks had also starved to death almost half of the Christian Maronite population of Lebanon (estimated 200,000 killed) by means of land blockade of crops, confiscations of supplies, and cutting down of trees for fuel for the Turkish army. May 6 is observed in Lebanon as Martyrs Day, and a square of the same name in downtown Beirut is dedicated to the memory of those victims. In 1943, Lebanon gained its independence from the French.

The one single trait that defines being Lebanese most is "resilience," bordering dare devilishness. It is the attitude of being in the now and throwing your cares to the wind that has helped Lebanese survive the many tragedies and upheavals they have faced. Known as the Paris of the Middle East, Beirut was and remains a glamorous city with an unmatched nightlife. Lebanese live with the romantic mantra of *Savoir Vivre*. They rebuild and keep on going with elegance, education, and enjoyment. They face adversity with unrestrained defiance, self-effacement, and finding humor in everything. They are aware of their ancient history yet know how not to take themselves too seriously. In addition to Arabic, most are fluent in French and English, and regardless of their circumstances, they uphold an exquisite taste in architecture and fashion. Almost in denial of the ever-looming violent feudal system they live in, the general public tends to look forward, never back, weary of passions igniting when one looks back to past disputes. Even in the toughest years of war, Lebanese were always chic, in step with the latest trends in Europe, and were building the hippest nightclubs and resorts. It took a couple of days of a ceasefire to get them to party and live it up again! Bikinis and cocktails on the Mediterranean, cigarettes and coffee, three kisses on the cheeks, and *Chéris* galore!

We were now leaving Lebanon and entering Syria. The terrain changed. The scenery of blue sea on the left and green hills on the right was replaced by dry empty desert.

No Looking Back

"POOR LEBANON! *LEBNAN EL AKHDAR* (Lebanon the Green in Arabic)…" said my father in an emotionally charged mocking tone as we moved into Syria after the final and most time-consuming checkpoint. He now had a sorry distant look on his face, his eyes looking down. I knew it was hard on him: losing everything he had built… losing the memory of the Lebanon he once knew. My mother looked at him from the side of her eyes, containing herself and quietly willing him not to lose his composure. Our bus was now going full speed. The dry wind from the windows was wreaking havoc with everyone's hair. The terrain was barren, and a yellowish hue of dust was lurking all around. We were heading south towards Damascus. Hours passed.

Our travel was no longer interrupted by checkpoints. I kept on squinting through the dust. Glimpses of one-story structures slowly morphed into those of more visible buildings, and finally, we were in a city. The same yellow dust was lingering in the streets. From fellow travelers, we found out that we were traveling through a desert dust storm. Our bus halted in front of the hotel at which we had made reservations. The driver got into a long discussion with a hotel manager. It dragged forever. Betty and I were on our feet, stretching. We were all exhausted from the eight-hour trip and were anxious to get some rest. Our driver came back and announced that there were no rooms available due to some political figures who booked last-minute for a conference. He was going to take us to another hotel. Arguing was a moot point. Everyone took back their seats.

Soon enough, we and our eight suitcases were dropped in front of Hotel Al Bustan. My parents hurried up the stairs to book us a room.

"Betty, do you feel like we are being watched?" I asked, the hair on the back of my neck sensing a certain lurking presence. "Yes, I was going to ask you the same thing," Betty whispered. As we looked around, the figure of a young man emerged from the cloud of dust. He was wearing a burgundy silk shirt, with gold threads running vertically down the fabric. He started circling us, looking at our suitcases and reading the name and number on the tags out loud. "Tavitian 1, Tavitian 2…" I looked around, hoping my parents would resurface soon. The shadowy figures of two women wearing headscarves hurried by. The young man was staring us in the eyes now. "Come on, bring the bags," called my mom suddenly. "It's about time you guys came back!" I responded agitated, and started maneuvering two bags at the same time. In the lobby of the hotel, the emotions and fatigue of the day started weighing on us. When we finally made it to our room, we cracked up in laughter as we saw our reflections in the mirror. Our frizzy hair spread like fans around our faces. We looked ridiculous! We received static shocks from everything we touched, even from the water while washing! Later we went back to the lobby area for some fries. That was all the kitchen could offer at that hour. My father bought a bag of tangy green plums, *djenerik*, from a vendor in front of the hotel. We had to make it to the airport on time the next morning. We also had to allow time for a possible checking of our bags. My father made arrangements for a taxi and a U-Haul type of cargo trailer that would hold all of our luggage. We could not sleep all night long. The idea of not waking up on time terrified us. Scary thoughts crossed my mind as I struggled to sleep. What if the taxi driver does not take us to the airport and kidnaps us instead? What if the checking of our eight bags takes so long that we miss our flight?

"Wake up and get dressed fast," my mom instructed. I woke up, amazed that I had actually dozed off. How many hours had passed? It was still dark out as we placed our bags in the trailer and sat in the taxi. As we drove down the quiet highway lit by tall street lights, I started realizing for the first time that the prospect of living a normal life in a safe normal country could actually be in our destiny. My soul lit up with that overwhelmingly positive revelation. The ever-present specter of death had crushed all possibilities in my life up to that point. Now, standing so close to the sweet dream of life, liberty, and pursuit of happiness, I wanted it all! My parents were carrying on as friendly of a conversation as they could muster with the driver. We made it to the airport. The driver asked for additional money. My father paid without hesitating, and we hurried inside the building. The moment of truth was here: "checking in of the luggage." We watched with horror as an airport employee took everything apart in the suitcase of a lady traveling with her daughter. I looked at our eight bags, fearing the worst. Our turn came. One, two, three, four bags were taken in without being inspected. The employee tapped on the fifth bag. "Open," he ordered my dad. We were praying in our heads that it was not the one stuffed with our small antique rugs. My father's wrist bobby pin holder popped out. "I am a tailor," my father explained. "*Badna nkhsrak zaken khayo,* then we are losing you, brother," the man said and motioned to my dad to reclose the bag. And that was it! I do not remember anything else but holding my breath and gripping the armrests as our KLM took off. The take-off felt like going through a resurrection! We rose into the air inching away from that God-forsaken place that hadn't known peace in so long. We were out. We were saved. No Looking Back!

This is California!

WE FLEW FOR THE BETTER part of the day. We did not mind. We were enjoying every minute of our flight. Years of stress and worry were melting away with every mile as we allowed our itinerary to carry us through. I remember layovers in Cyprus and Amsterdam as if they were parts of a dream. In an ironic twist of fate, we landed in the United States on Memorial Day, Monday, May 28, a day we will remember forever. When the plane finally parked, we had to walk through never-ending hallways to the immigration line at LAX. The process seemed to take forever! Paperwork, more questions, hundreds of people... We were exhausted. When we finally made it out of the terminal, we were greeted by my grandmother Yevnigeh, my uncle Manoug, and a cousin of my father's who had immigrated to the United States with his family a few months prior. My grandmother's expression of relief and pure joy was priceless! I miss her warm hugs! She gave us plenty of those on that day. She started briefing us about California. Everything she could inform us about came pouring out of her mouth. LAX was huge! It was a reflection of the vast country and the large city we were in.

The dry warm air that hit us was a novelty to our system, very different from Beirut's more humid air. We divided our eight bags among my uncle's car and a small minivan my father's cousin had brought. We were soon on the freeway. The view through the window was of an industrious area of mostly two- to three-story buildings and some high-rises in the distance. For the first time in my life, I saw wooden houses. Their size and shape reminded me of the plastic Monopoly houses. The city spread for miles on end, miles of flat terrain with some hills in the far. The structure and engineering of the many intertwining freeways impressed me the most. However, it was the palm trees and the green manicured lawns that screamed California! While driving, my uncle started telling us about how he had first settled in Hollywood (in an area now known as Little Armenia). At times, he was so lonely that he would stand on freeway overpasses and count the passing cars for hours. As we drove, we observed folks in the street dressed extremely casually by Lebanese standards, even some in pajama bottoms and bare feet! We exclaimed out loud about this because, back then in Lebanon, even going down to the grocery store below our building warranted getting dressed in serious clothes, even heels for my mother.

For every observation we made, my uncle and grandmother responded, "This is California!" We finally made it to Hazeltine Ave, Van Nuys. We were looking around in amazement. Everything was new to us. The swimming pool in the open courtyard in the middle of the complex, the cleanliness, the very well-tended landscape, and the sheer orderly way of things amazed us. There was something not so obvious at first that was very different from my life in Lebanon. It took me several hours to realize what it was. It finally hit me! The one major difference was the quiet I was experiencing. The quiet tranquility of the place. Folks following traffic rules with no traffic officers in sight and passengers going about their business, making sure to keep their personal space and not look you in the eye. No one said, "Hello!" No one was yelling and talking with animated gestures. There were no more honking cars, yelling merchants, wheeling and dealing consumers, laundry hanging on balconies, chaotic traffic with nonfunctioning traffic lights, trash bags piled high on street corners, and the sound of gunshots in the background. None of that. Just an omnipresent quiet. It was as if the whole city was on a tranquilizer.

My uncle was visibly elated to be surrounded by family after years of living alone! He had many plans for us. We were going to visit Disneyland, Sea World, the San Diego Zoo… The topics of conversation jumped to more serious subjects like finding a job for my father, getting a driver's license, and enrolling my sister and me in public school. Quite late at night, we finally surrendered to a deep slumber in my uncle's one-bedroom apartment. Every inch of my body seemed to release itself into the open skies of California, devoid of any tension, worry, apprehension… I was in a fully safe haven… until the first explosion shook the ground underneath me.

My slumber was so deep that it prevented me from opening my eyes. The walls and windows shook with a second and a third explosion. Another bombardment… They are bombing us… I knew I had to get up and start running down the stairs to our second-story neighbors' apartment, but my body was not cooperating. Why wasn't I hearing Mrs. Marie? She is usually the first one to lead the way, along with her daughters. Certain neighbors will take their Valium tablets and light up their cigarettes as always, I am sure. Another explosion… where is everybody? I finally was able to force my eyes open. My mother was standing at the entrance of the bedroom with my grandmother. "It hardly rains in California," I heard my uncle say, "let alone a thunderstorm!" But on the eve of Memorial Day, May 28, 1984, there was a thunderstorm with lightning and pouring rain in Southern California. I decided that it was a good omen for a new life full of opportunity and prosperity. And with God's grace, that is how it turned out to be!

Life in America

IN 1984, RONALD REAGAN WAS the president of the United States, and the Olympics were taking place in Los Angeles! As a matter of fact, we watched from the sidewalk as the Olympic Torch was carried through our very own street! Moments that stand out in my mind from that summer are Mary Lou Retton landing her perfect 10 on the vault and the family picture we took in front of the Sleeping Beauty castle at magical Disneyland. Most Americans had heard of Lebanon but were not familiar with "Armenian" as an ethnicity or the existence of a country called Armenia. We lived on Burbank Boulevard in Van Nuys in a ground-floor duplex apartment. Our landlord, who lived above us on the top floor, came to check up on us often. He always wore the brightest colored t-shirts and shorts and looked as if he was on his way to play golf. He harbored a puzzled curiosity towards us. When we bought our television, he came to congratulate us and asked, "Are you excited about your new color TV?" We had to explain to him that we had color television back in Lebanon. He looked perplexed and incredulous about our answer! We did not feel the need to elaborate that our current residence was half the size of our apartment in Beirut and that of our vacation house in the mountains. Doing so would rehash our past, which we were adamant about leaving behind.

We assimilated into the American way of life in no time. Soon, we were hooked on daytime TV soap opera shows and Dryer's ice cream. My mother mastered the use of the building laundry room, from collecting quarters to picking times when the other tenants were at work. She prided herself on her expertise in coordinating this chore. For my part, I could not wait to start school and have my own "Grease" experience. When we presented to Ulysses S. Grant High School with my Hripsimiantz report card, the counselor had only one question. "You studied Armenian, French, and Arabic literature and grammar, math and science in French, geography, and history in Arabic, Armenian history, Bible Study in Armenian, and had an introductory course of English. Nine subject matters in one year. Four languages at the same time?!" "Yes," I responded. After pondering about what courses to enroll me in, the counselor produced a list that contained the following: AP French, AP Chemistry, English Literature, Geometry, Health... Needless to say, I had no idea what *AP* stood for.

The first day at school was a total culture shock, and my language barrier a crushing handicap! The few English words I had learned in Sir's (that's how we called our English teacher at Hripsimiantz) class were refusing to come to me, so I used French in asking strangers to help me locate my classes. "Whaat?" they responded disparagingly until I produced my list of classes. A lad with a tricolor Mohawk hairdo plunked down next to me in math class. In the hallway corners, couples were making out, and I was the only one lacking eyeliner and mascara. "Oh, if only the Hripsimiantz nuns could see this!!" I thought, passing a couple embroiled in a wet French kiss! AP French, on the other hand, proved to be an easy "A" class. My French was superior to that of the teacher, who ended up passing some of her teaching duties onto me to keep me occupied. My brain, accustomed to the rigorous academics at home, absorbed the lone English language in no time. The easy-going culture and the concept of picking classes that matched your abilities, ranging from English as second language to remedial to honors and AP fascinated me. In Lebanon, you had one choice in every high school subject, and it was quite the equivalent of the AP (advanced placement) level in the United States!

I truly enjoyed Ulysses S. Grant High School! It played a large role in reshaping my life. I morphed from a quiet introspect teenager to an articulate student who presided over the French and Armenian clubs and was elected "Miss Friendship!" Succeeding in school was important to me. It meant taking advantage of the amazing opportunities that the United States offered to every citizen regardless of their background and financial standing. It meant grasping at the "bright future" that my father had hoped for us when he decided to leave Lebanon.

My drive to succeed in school paid off as I graduated with high honors.

The fact that Grant High School had a pretty sizeable Armenian student population also helped with my transition into American schooling. It is there that I met, for the first time, Armenian immigrants from countries other than Lebanon who spoke the Eastern Armenian dialect, such as the ones who hailed from Iran and Armenia, compared to the Western Armenian dialect that Lebanese and Turkish Armenians used. During recess, a bond reminiscent of the one that glued the Armenians of Bourj Hammoud would manifest itself under the "Armenian tree" in the schoolyard. This big shaded tree was known on campus to belong to the Armenian students. It is where we gathered to reinvent the communities that we had left behind in the countries we immigrated from and to uphold the memory of the original villages that our grandparents came from. We were the embodiment of William Saroyan's famous poem about Armenians:

"I should like to see any power of the world destroy this race, this small tribe of unimportant people, whose wars have all been fought and lost, whose structures have crumbled, literature is unread, music is unheard, and prayers are no more answered. Go ahead, destroy Armenia. See if you can do it. Send them into the desert without bread or water. Burn their homes and churches. Then see if they will not laugh, sing and pray again."

Where is Karabakh?

Late 1980s early 1990s, California.

THE COLD WAR BETWEEN THE United States and the Soviet Union had reached its pinnacle and seemed to be thawing. The Soviet Union was suffering from a stagnant economy and a bureaucratic system dominated by Russian old men bent on keeping the existing soviet economic structure and the corruption that went with it. President Reagan had proposed a Strategic Arms Reduction Treaty for both parties to reduce the stockpile of nuclear weapons they had been amassing. Hoping to revive the Russian economy, President of the Soviet Union, Mikhail Gorbachev, launched *Perestroika,* political and economic restructuring, and *Glasnost,* an era of transparency and openness. This was the closest a Russian leader came to acquiescing to Western-style governance and open-market economy. Seizing on this rapprochement, on June 12, 1987, President Reagan gave his now-famous speech in front of Germany's Berlin Wall that separated Communist East Germany from West Germany.[16] We watched on the evening news the clip where he delivered the following daring message: "Secretary General Gorbachev, if you seek peace- if you

---

16 After WWII, defeated Germany was divided into four occupation zones: the United States, Britain and France occupied West Germany and the Soviet Union occupied East Germany. In 1949, West Germany became the Federal Republic of Germany and East Germany became the Communist German Democratic Republic. The Berlin Wall was constructed in 1961 to reduce the flood of refugees from East Germany into West Germany. In 1990, East and West Germany reunited and formed one independent country.

seek prosperity for the Soviet Union and Eastern Europe- if you seek liberalization: come here, to this gate. Mr. Gorbachev, open this gate. Mr. Gorbachev, tear down this wall."

The reforms that Gorbachev introduced for a semi-open market economy, however, created chaos and brought the Soviet Union to the brink of collapse. Democratization and the inclusion of the people in the political process, freedom of speech and of the press opened the flood gates to Soviet-era grievances. Gorbachev declined to intervene militarily as different Soviet republics abandoned the Marxist-Leninist governing system. We followed in world news as SSR Armenia, similarly to other Soviet republics, started calling for independence. That we were living through uniquely historic times for our homeland was not lost on us. From the ancient Syrian cities to the humble neighborhoods of Bourj Hammoud, Europe, and the far away Americas, Armenians all over the world had held onto the dream of a united independent Armenia, and it seemed that part of it, the Soviet Republic of Armenia (Eastern Armenia), was about to step into the light of freedom!

For the first time in my life, I started hearing about Nagorno-Karabakh on the news. I had no previous knowledge of this region or its significance in Armenian history, but as most Armenians, I was gripped by horrific images of burned and dismembered Armenians in state-sponsored pogroms in Azerbaijan and masses with raised fists demanding independence. During the Soviet era, the Russians had apparently transferred the regions of Nakhichevan[17] and Karabakh from Armenia to Azerbaijan. Nakhichevan, with a population of 40% Armenian at takeover, was made into an "exclave of Azerbaijan", separated from the rest of Azerbaijan by Zangezur or Syunik, the southern province of Armenia. Since Karabakh's population was predominantly Armenian, the Soviets had made it instead into a self-governing Armenian "minority enclave" within SSR Azerbaijan.

---

17 Nakhichevan: in Armenian tradition, Nakh (first) and Ichevan (settled), is the region where Noah had settled with his family, when they came down from Mount Ararat where his ark had landed.

It was known as the "Autonomous Oblast of Nagorno-Karabakh." Now that the Soviet Union was collapsing, the Armenians wanted Karabakh returned. We all followed this story which was covered extensively by the American media. Hundreds of thousands of Armenians were fleeing from Azerbaijan. Packed helicopters kept on airlifting distraught civilians, some with physical signs of the beatings and torture they had endured, most with only the shirts on their backs. The enclave of Nagorno-Karabakh was blockaded and was being shelled viciously by the Azeri forces. The sporadic information that got out was of misery and an alarming shortage of food, medicine, and essentials. Some Armenians from the Diaspora left to join the defense movement of Karabakh, which did not even have an official army. In response to Karabakh's wish to secede from the Soviet Union, the Azeri government had threatened to strip the authority of the enclave's autonomous government in order to annex the region once and for all. This had mobilized the Karabakh Armenians, who foresaw a fate similar to that of the Armenians of Nakhichevan awaiting them. Ever since taking it over, the Azeris had pursued a systemic campaign of emptying Nakhichevan of all trace of Armenian existence. Its Armenian population had declined dramatically, as more and more migrated to Armenia next door.

In 1988, in an extraordinary joint session, the councils of Nagorno-Karabakh appealed to the Supreme Council of SSR Azerbaijan with the enclave's wish to peacefully secede from SSR Azerbaijan and to the Supreme Council of SSR Armenia on their wish to be joined to SSR Armenia. Armenia agreed; Azerbaijan refused. A petition bearing thousands of signatures was also sent to Moscow, urging the Russian government to approve this request based on legal norms, only to be rejected. Political experts surmised that the Armenians had either jumped the gun with Gorbachev's reforms which backfired on them because the latter did not want Karabakh to set a precedent for other enclaves in the Soviet Union or that the Russians did not want to lose their leverage with oil-exporting Azerbaijan. In retaliation to Karabakh's peaceful appeal to be returned to Armenia, a large group of Azeris had marched onto the Armenian village of Askeran, destroying everything in their path and instigating a first physical clash with Armenians. Violent anti-Armenian pogroms had broken out next in the Azeri cities of Sumgait, and Kirovabad (name given to historically Armenian Gandzak during the Soviet era; today's Ganja for Azeris). Reminiscent of the Hamidian and Adana pogroms in Ottoman Turkey, angry mobs armed with metal rods, knives, and hammers, holding lists of Armenian addresses and chanting about cleansing Azerbaijan of Armenians had attacked, looted, and destroyed Armenian homes and businesses. They beat, raped, tortured, burned alive, mutilated, and threw off of balconies women, men, and children, killing and injuring thousands, while local police and authorities looked on. As ethnic tensions mounted, a massive migration of Armenians from Azerbaijan and of Azerbaijanis from Armenia began.

On November 9, 1989, the Berlin Wall came tumbling down, ushering the fall of the Iron Curtain[18]. As Americans, we celebrated America's victory in the Cold War. A month later in December, the Supreme Soviets of SSR Armenia and Nagorno-Karabakh made a joint proclamation of the unification of Karabakh with Armenia in accordance with the Soviet Constitution's law of self-determination. Our cautious optimism was crushed when the declaration was followed by the brutal "Black January" pogroms against the Armenians of Baku, the capital of Azerbaijan. For seven days, raging mobs subjected the residents of the Armenian district to extreme forms of cruelty and violence, with no intervention by the police or fire fighters. Ninety civilians were murdered, and the Armenian Orthodox Church was vandalized and burned. Some Azeris hid their Armenian neighbors until Russian armed troops were finally sent to stop the carnage and usher the Armenians out of the city.

---

18   The Iron Curtain was a symbolic political boundary that separated the Eastern Soviet bloc of Europe from the West after WWII, and lasted until the decline of Communism in 1989.

The Supreme Soviet of the USSR did not react favorably to Armenia and Nagorno-Karabakh's reunification proclamation. Instead, having resigned to the reality of the collapse of the Soviet Union, the Russian government created a legal framework for secession by democratic vote for Soviet republics and autonomous oblasts formed during the Soviet era, such as Nagorno-Karabakh. Article 3 of the 1990 law said the following: *In a Union republic which includes within its structure autonomous republics, autonomous oblasts, or autonomous okrugs, the referendum is held separately for each autonomous formation. The people of autonomous republics and autonomous formations retain the right to decide independently the question of remaining within the USSR or within the seceding Union republic, and also to raise the question of their own state-legal status In a Union republic on whose territory there are places densely populated by ethnic groups constituting a majority of the population of the locality in question, the results of the voting in these localities are recorded separately when the results of the referendum are being determined.*[19] The Autonomous Oblast of Nagorno-Karabakh elected to follow the secession framework in deciding its status and prepared to cast its democratic vote on a referendum for independence. Azerbaijan, however, continued fighting tooth and nail to keep Karabakh to itself, and Moscow chose not to enforce its own law and ignored the people's will. In fact, the secession law seemed to have been crafted to prolong the political entanglements of Soviet era oblasts.

The exact number of victims killed in the anti-Armenian pogroms of Azerbaijan is still unknown. In the ensued upheaval, communities were swiftly expelled, and families were not allowed to see their killed loved ones or even give them a proper burial. Hundreds of thousands of Armenians left Azerbaijan in total shock. American news was sympathetic to the plight of the Armenians. In fact, the United States hailed Karabakh's challenge to the Soviet

---

19 Law on Secession from the USSR, *Seventeen Moments in Soviet History: An On-Line Archive of Primary Sources*, accessed April 10, 2021, http://soviet-history.msu.edu/1991–2/shevarnadze-resigns/shevarnadze-resigns-texts/law-on-secession-from-the-ussr/

Union and welcomed its leadership in instigating democratic movements throughout the Soviet Union. Coverage of the conflict left no doubt in my mind that America was at the side of Karabakh's heroic independence movement.

Intrigued, I started researching about Karabakh in between school exams. I found out that most of Azerbaijan was once part of the Kingdom of Armenia (321 BC to 428 AD),[20] which at its peak stretched from the Mediterranean in the south to the Caspian Sea in the northeast. Karabakh is situated on the eastern edge of the Armenian Highlands. Throughout written history, it has been consistently inhabited by indigenous Armenians. It falls within historic Artsakh, which along with adjacent Utik on its east, were the 10th and 12th provinces of the Kingdom of Armenia. Ancient historians and geographers such as Strabo, Pliny the Elder, Claudius Ptolemy, Plutarch, and Dio Cassius have all mentioned Artsakh (or Urtekhini) as a province of Armenia "abundant with horses" (as described by Strabo). Armenian King Tigranes the Great (reign 95-55 BC) has built four cities in his name, Tigranakert, and one of those cities is in Artsakh's Askeran province. In 387 AD, Greater Armenia collapsed, and Artsakh became part of the Eastern Armenian Kingdom. The ancestors of current-day Azeris, the nomadic Oghuz Turks, started migrating to the region of the Caucasus centuries later during the 11th century Turkic invasions from the Steppes of Central Asia. While Seljuk Turks proceeded to head westbound where their leader Alp Aslan sacked the Armenian city of Ani in the Byzantine Empire[21] and slaughtered its population, spearheading events that eventually launched the formation of the Ottoman Empire, the Oghuz Turkic tribes that hailed from the Altai Mountains of Central Asia settled instead in northwestern Persia, and in the triangular region between the Kura and Araz rivers on the east of Artsakh and below

---

20 The Kingdom of Armenia lasted from 321 BC to 428 AD through the successive reigns of three royal dynasties: Orontid (321 BC – 200 BC), Artaxiad (189 BC -12 AD) and Arsacid (52 AD – 428 AD)

21 The Byzantine Empire ruled over Western Armenia

current day Albania, most of which comprised of territories lost by the ancient Armenian Kingdom. In the 12th century, the Armenian Principality of Khachen ruled Artsakh. Also known as the Kingdom of Artsakh, Khachen included the entirety of Artsakh as well as additional territories to its west (Syunik), south and north, in addition to parts of Utik including its central city of Gandzak (now Ganja). The Armenian princes known as *Meliks* led a semi-autonomous and often independent existence. The Persian Empire which came to rule over the entire Caucasus (including the Eastern Armenian Kingdom, Georgia and Dagestan), treated Artsakh's Meliks well in the hopes of deterring them from siding with the Russians. The newly arriving nomadic Oghuz Turks mixed with the local Medians, an ancient Iranian people, and lived among Caucasian Albanians, Armenians, Kurds, Jews, Talish, Tats, and Lezgins. In time, as their numbers grew, they infiltrated[22] the Persian armed forces and eventually the governing class, and started Turkifying the locals. The area where they settled became known as the Persian satrapy of Arran (Aghuank in Armenian) or Shirvan, where local Turk and Persian *Khans* (governors), who answered to the Persian Emperor or *Shah,* came to rule over *khanates* (districts or provinces). By the 14th century, the Persians started referring to Artsakh as *Karabakh* (Kara, black in Turkish, and Bakh, garden in Persian, although some experts think Karabakh means "Large Garden" in the old Persian Pahlavi language). The principality of Khachen collapsed in the 15th century and was divided into five Melikdoms: Gulistan, Jraberd, Khachen, Varanda, and Dizak. In contrast to how the Artsakh Armenian Melikdoms were left alone, in 1604, during the Ottoman-Persian wars in the plains of Ararat (in Eastern Armenia), Safavid Persian emperor Shah Abbas I followed a scorched-earth strategy to prevent the advancing Ottoman army from resupplying itself. He had entire Armenian towns and farms in the Ararat valley, parts of Yerevan, and surrounding regions set ablaze and ordered

---

22 RoubenGalichian.com. Karabagh (Artsakh) in Old Maps, 2018

upwards of 300,000 Armenians to accompany his army back to Persia. Almost half of the refugees died of starvation or drowned while crossing the Araz River. Those who survived were settled in the Isfahan region of northern Persia. Abbas' strategy worked, and he regained control over all of his Armenian territories at a great cost to the Armenians, who, for the first time, had a demographically lower presence in Armenia.[23] In order to retain the Armenian lands, the Shah moved Muslims to Yerevan and built several mosques there. It was not until the 18th century when the Oghuz Turks of Arran started infiltrating Karabakh by exploiting divisions amongst the Armenian Meliks of Khachen, and developing alliances with some of them. This coincided with the formation of the Karabakh khanate in 1748 under Iranian suzerainty. The Oghuz Turks started to also settle in larger numbers in Armenia's Nakhichevan region, as well as within Yerevan (Armenia's capital). Through the years, in their effort to adopt Karabakh as their own and mask its ownership, they assigned the historic Armenian names of Artsakh's towns and villages phonetically similar-sounding alternate names. Shusha (Shushi in Armenian) was derived from the name of the nearby ancient Armenian village of Shosh. Armenian Karvachar became Kalbajar, Gandzak (derived from the Armenian word *Gantz*, treasure) became Ganja, and so on.

The Persians and Russians went into a full scale war in 1804. In 1813, they signed the Gulistan Peace Treaty by which Persia ceded Dagestan, Eastern Georgia, parts of Northern Armenia, Karabakh and Arran to Russia. In their mountainous hideaway, the Armenian Meliks of Karabakh continued to be left alone, while the Oghuz Turks in Arran had to adapt to Russian rule. The Russians added the description "*Nagorno*" (mountainous) to Karabakh's name, making it Nagorno-Karabakh. Artsakh's five Melikdoms were ultimately dissolved in 1822 when the Russian Empire abolished ethnic feudal entities. With the 1828 Treaty of Turkmenchay, the Persian

---

23 Hewsen, Robert H. (2001). *Armenia: A Historical Atlas.* The University of Chicago Press. p. 168. ISBN 0-226-33228-4.

Empire ceded its remaining holdings in the Caucasus north of the Araz River to the Russians, namely the Nakhichevan and Yerevan Khanates which made up Eastern Armenia. A small number of the Armenians settled in Iran by Shah Abbas repatriated to Armenia and Karabakh (Azerbaijan takes this out of context to claim that Armenians of Artsakh have all come from Iran!).

According to an official Russian survey in 1836, the population in Nagorno-Karabakh was 96.7% Armenian.[24] Taking advantage of the First Russian Revolution in 1905, the Oghuz Turks, who were locally known as Caucasian "Tatars," started massacring the indigenous Armenians in earnest in Arran and Nakhichevan in order to take over those territories. Their policy of ethnic cleansing of the Armenians mirrored that of their Turkish brethren in Western Armenia. As a preemptive security measure against Turks bent on annihilating them and taking over their lands, the Armenians of Eastern Armenia, in turn, started harassing the Tatars settled in Yerevan as well as their southern province of Zangezur, forcing many to leave. Clashes and wars continued between the Armenians and Tatars, as the Tatars tried to take control of Nakhichevan, Zangezur and Karabakh. The takeover of these three southern Armenian provinces was strongly pursued by Ottoman Turkey in its goal of linking itself territorially to Arran. While control over Nakhichevan reverted back and forth between the Armenians and Tatars, all attempts by the Tatars and Turks at taking over Zangezur/Syunik (province between Nakhichevan and Karabakh) continued to be met by fierce resistance by the Armenians (under the command of General Antranik Ozanian and Garegin Njdeh).

Towards the end of WWI, taking advantage of the chaos created by the 1917 Russian Bolshevik Revolution, most Transcaucasian nationalities in Arran committed ethnic cleansing and vied to gain control over the yet-to-be-defined area. As the Russian Empire

---

24 George Bournoutian, "The Politics of Demography: Misuse of Sources on the Armenian Population of Mountainous Karabakh," *Journal of the Society for Armenian Studies* 9 (1996–1997): 99–103.

collapsed, the territories it was holding started breaking away. In May of 1918, the Eastern Armenians, overwhelmed by an influx of destitute refugees fleeing the genocide perpetrated by the Ottoman Turks in Western Armenia, drove back an all-out invasion by the Turkish army and announced the independence of the first Republic of Armenia. (The Turkish leadership's intention was to wipe out the remainder of Armenia and march all the way to Baku). At the same time, with the leadership and assistance of the Ottoman Young Turk regime and the cooperation of the Bolsheviks, the Tatars in Arran established a new country, and for its name, they borrowed the name "Azerbaijan" from the Iranian provinces to the south of the Araz River. The motive behind the choice of the name "Azerbaijan" could have been to link the artificially forming country ethnographically to the region by assigning to it the long history of the Persian provinces of the same name (Iran was not receptive to this choice of name because it could implicate future territorial claims to its East and West Azerbaijan provinces where large numbers of Tatars had settled). This naming technique was similar in its intention to that of the naming of villages and towns in Artsakh with Turkish names that sounded like their original Armenian ones in order to blur their history and ethnic origin. Arran was simply overtaken by/handed over to the local Muslim Tatar Turk population, a circumstance that has perpetuated a national identity crisis in Azerbaijan, as its leadership resorts to creative history revisionism and the destruction of ancient cultural monuments of older indigenous people, in particular in historic Artsakh and Utik, in order to lay claim to those regions. While it identifies as Turkic, the Azeri leadership borrows Persian history and advertises it as its own, then switches to Turkic history when it suits its political needs. The fact remains, however, that there was no country or nation of Azerbaijan in the history of the world prior to 1918.

At the time of announcing its May 1918 independence, Azerbaijan did not even have an established central leadership governing its yet-to-be-defined territories. It had two competing governments: a

Musavat government in Ganja affiliated with the Ottoman Young Turks that had spearheaded the idea of a Turkic independent state in Arran and a Bolshevik government in Baku made up of Armenians and Russians that favored good relations with the central government in Moscow. It is also important to note that the newly established Republic of Azerbaijan contained neither Nakhichevan nor Karabakh with its surrounding lowlands. While Nakhichevan was undoubtedly part of the 1918 Republic of Armenia, the region of Karabakh was referred to as "historic Armenian lands in the Caucasus" by the Treaty of Sevres and the League of Nations, with the only outstanding issue being the finalization of Armenia's eastern borders with Georgia and Azerbaijan (at no time did the League of Nations recognize Nakhichevan and Karabakh as part of Azerbaijan). A few months later, in September of 1918, while the Russians were distracted with their civil war, Enver Pasha, the exiled minister of defense of the embattled Ottoman Empire and one of the architects of the Armenian Genocide (in Western Armenia), rushed his Army of Islam to Ganja. From there, together with his local Tatar Turk allies, he attacked Baku; where they massacred 30,000 Armenians, and captured the city to make it Azerbaijan's new capital.[25] Baku, a city built by Armenians, whose Armenian historic name was Alti-Bagavan, a district within Paytakaran, the 15th province of the ancient Armenian Kingdom, was a predominantly Christian city with a large Armenian community who dominated the oil industry and, along with the Russians, constituted the city's financial elite. Taking advantage of the uncertainty and political turmoil perpetuated by the collapse of the Russian Empire, Turkey and Azerbaijan coordinated their efforts to snatch as much land from the Armenians as possible. In 1919, another 10,000 or so Armenians were massacred by the Tatars in Nakhichevan, and Azerbaijan's government announced its intent to annex Karabakh, declaring it "a contested area," even when its population was predominantly Armenian. This

---

25 Baku became the capital of Azerbaijan in 1920.

was a bold, crafty strategic move that put the wheels of Karabakh's conquest into motion by casting doubt on its history and ownership. Instead of "contested," Karabakh was rather "desired" by Azerbaijan not only for its strategic elevation, pastures, gold, and other mineral resources, but also because it brought Azerbaijan one step closer to acquiring Armenia's Zangezur and Nakhichevan provinces to form a land connection with Turkey. A country that came into existence in 1918, that had "no lands to its name" prior to that at any time in human history, could not, logically, have had "historic" territorial claims, particularly over lands of ancient nations with established histories. However, with the Russian Empire collapsing, it was an opportune time for the Tatars to grab as much land as they could while they "defined" their country's borders.

Overriding the Armenian National Council of Karabakh that governed the area, the British, who, at the end of WWI had stationed some troops in the region in order to study its prospects of oil and other natural resources, in a surprising move, approved the appointment of Tatar (Azeri) Khosrov Bey Sultanov as "provisional governor" to oversee Karabakh until the scheduled Paris Peace Conference that was to decide its ownership based on its ethnic composition prior to the war (they even convinced Armenian reinforcement troupes that arrived in Karabakh from Zangezur to retreat in order not to adversely affect the outcome of the peace conference!). The Armenian National Council of Karabakh decried Sultanov's appointment, asserting its right to its homeland. The Armenians explained to the British that their lives would be in danger under the Tatars (Azeris) who had joined forces with Ottoman Turks to subject them to all sorts of abuses and outright massacres. On February 24, 1920, a Special Commission of the Paris Peace Conference published its proposal about Armenia's borders with Azerbaijan and Georgia. It recommended that in the event the three countries did not reach an agreement of their own, the Supreme Allied powers should decide, by arbitration, the borders between them. Since the League of Nations had already de facto recognized Armenia a month prior in

January, 1920, when it officially recognized the Armenian government and invited an Armenian delegation to partake in the Paris Peace Conference, Karabakh, including the surrounding regions of Kashatagh (Lachin), Karvachar, Shahumyan, and Agdam were all de jure included in the State of Armenia as presented by the Armenian delegation. The Special Commission's recommendation was approved by the council of the League of Nations and included in the Treaty of Sevres as Article 92.

In response to the Armenian National Council's refusal to acknowledge his authority, governor Sultanov blockaded Shushi, then Karabakh's capital, Armenian cultural center, and most prosperous city, and Tatars started taunting Armenians living in its outskirts with regular attacks, terrorizing the locals and killing hundreds of villagers until the Armenians rose up in March of 1920 in an attempt to throw out the Tatar forces from their city and stop the killings. Similarly to the Ottomans, who infringed upon the basic human rights of the native Armenians then labeled their self-defense as "rebellion," the Tatar Turk citizens, incited by calls for Jihad by governor Sultanov, joined their armed forces and a battalion of irregulars and proceeded to destroy the entire Armenian quarter of Shushi to squash what they called an "Armenian revolt." Thousands of Armenian structures, including schools, libraries, churches, homes, and businesses, were set on fire and destroyed, women were raped and shot, the Bishop's head was cut, placed on a spike, and paraded through the streets, and wells were filled with the mutilated bodies of killed Armenians. Outwardly, the British condemned Sultanov's criminal actions, but on the ground, they had withdrawn from the vicinity and allowed him free reign. Hoping for a change in demographics (the population was clearly majority Armenian), the British had stalled the decision over Karabakh in order to assist the Azeris in annexing it. The consensus was that by supporting the Azeris, the British were hoping to take over the country's oil export from the Bolsheviks. This was quite a departure from the support they had provided the Armenians at the conclusion of WWI. Many written eyewitness accounts, including those of Near East Fund American nurses working in Shushi, attest to the massacre that ended up claiming the lives of close to 20,000 Armenians (almost the entire Armenian population of the city). Thus, in its aggressive bid to claim Karabakh, the Azeri leadership transformed its capital, Shushi, into a majority Tatar Turk populated city, bearing its alternate Azeri name of Shusha.

While the massacre was taking place in Shushi, the Russian Red Army penetrated Baku. In April of 1920, the Armenian National Council of Karabakh convened and announced officially that Karabakh was part of the Republic of Armenia. At the same time, the Tatars surrendered to the Russians, and their two year old country became part of the Soviet Union as the Socialist Soviet Republic of Azerbaijan. The Russian Bolsheviks cooperated with the idea of a new state called Azerbaijan, not only to pacify the Ottomans who were determined to form a second Turkic nation, but also with the objective of joining it as a "country" to the Union of Soviet Socialist Republics (USSR) that they were forming as leaders of the future Communist Party.

The following was the chain of events that catapulted into the ongoing conflict over Karabakh. In August of 1920, the fallen Ottoman Empire and the victorious Allies signed the Treaty of Sevres. With U.S. President Woodrow Wilson's arbitral award, the Armenian state, recognized by the League of Nations, contained 3 of its Turkish vilayets, access to the Black Sea at Trabizon, in addition to Eastern Armenia. On November 30, 1920, SSR Azerbaijan declared the end of all territorial disputes with Armenia and acknowledged Nakhichevan, Zangezur and Karabakh as legally belonging to Armenia (Azerbaijan did this!). The Russian leadership had acknowledged the territories of the Republic of Armenia as they were recognized by the League of Nations and had announced them as such to the newly formed SSR Azerbaijan, a decision the League of Nations welcomed. Experts think that this gesture could have also been Russia's way of luring the Armenians into joining the USSR. The following month, in December of 1920, attacked by both Turkey and Russia, Armenia itself surrendered to the invading Bolshevik army and reluctantly became part of the USSR. With the March 1921 Moscow Treaty (also known as the Treaty of Brotherhood between then Turkish Grand National Assembly under Ataturk and the Russian Bolshevik regime under Lenin) and the Kars Treaty that followed, Ataturk bartered for more lands from Armenia and the Soviets obliged. Territories of the 1918 Republic of Armenia: Kars, Ardahan, Ani and our holy Mount Ararat, were thus passed to Turkey, and Nakhichevan was transferred to Azerbaijan. Armenian leaders along with the British who were assisting them were kicked out of Nakhichevan. These treaties gave the pretense of legitimacy to the unlawful trading of Armenian lands between the Turks and Russians while Armenia was under Soviet occupation and coerced with the threat of force to concede. With the Russians faltering on their promises, the Armenian leadership strived to secure Karabakh. In June of 1921, the Russians, Armenians, and Azeris signed agreements that officially recognized Karabakh as part of Armenia. A month later, on July 4, 1921, the Caucasian Bureau of the Central Committee of the Russian Communist Party, in turn, announced that Karabakh belonged to Armenia. However, the following day, on July 5, 1921, Joseph Stalin, who was then the Soviet Union's People's Commissar of Nationalities, decided unilaterally to award Karabakh to SSR Azerbaijan (while the province of Zangezur between Nakhichevan and Karabakh would remain in Armenian hands geographically separating the new autonomous Azeri territory of Nakhichevan from mainland Azerbaijan).[26] This was an unprecedented and undemocratic decision wherein a representative of a political party of a third country went against the official agreement between two other countries, undid the agreement on his own, and decided the fate of a disputed territory without involving the party losing the territory. More importantly, this decision

---

26 Robert Service, *Stalin: A Biography* (Cambridge, MA: Harvard University Press, 2006), 204.

was unconstitutional even within the Russian government system because it was not debated or voted on by the Communist Party Bureau. The Armenians simply had no say in the transfer of these lands, and when they protested, they were told that the new borders were finalized as such. The Bolsheviks, aspiring to the bigger ambition of annexing Turkey to the USSR, had fallen for Turkish President Ataturk's anti-"Western Imperialism" rhetoric and caved into awarding the two Armenian regions to Azerbaijan at his insistence. Since Armenia was absorbed by the Soviet Union and no longer within the jurisdiction of international law, the League of Nations that was mandated to determine its borders with Azerbaijan, was kept out of the affair. Weak and occupied, Armenia could not fight against the usurpation of its territories. In defiance to the Treaty of Sevres and the League of Nations, the lands of Armenia were thus divided among Turkey, Russia (as SSR Armenia) and SSR Azerbaijan (a northern section of Armenia, Javakhk, passed to SSR Georgia). In its official response, the United States refused to recognize the borders redrawn by the Bolsheviks and denounced the USSR as illegitimate because it was formed under duress and without the free consent of the nations involved. The legal admissibility of the Treaties of Moscow and Kars (and therefore the legality of the current borders created by them) remains a point of contention, considering their cosigners were not recognized by the League of Nations at the time of their signing. Additionally, none of the signatories of the 1921 Kars Treaty that established the current border between Turkey and Armenia and the parties involved in the transfer of Nakhichevan and Karabakh to Azerbaijan exist today. The Grand National Assembly of Turkey, SSR Armenia, SSR Azerbaijan, the Russian Soviet Federative Republic, and the USSR have all been dissolved. (Following the fall of the Soviet Union, the governments of Russia, Georgia and Azerbaijan officially accepted the Treaty of Kars).

In 1923, against the raised objections of the Armenians, Karabakh was further dismembered. Its lowlands in the north, and those lining the eastern border of current-day Armenia, including the regions of Karvachar, Kashatagh (Lachin), Varanda, and others, were absorbed by SSR Azerbaijan, and a smaller mountainous Karabakh, with a 96% Christian Armenian population, as a compromise, was made into a self-ruled "autonomous oblast" within SSR Azerbaijan, a majority Muslim country with genocidal history and intent against Armenians. Reduced in size, and now engulfed entirely by "Azeri" land, Karabakh was effectively severed from Armenia, with the Lachin corridor being the narrowest area of land separating it from mainland Armenia. This was a staple move of Stalin's Divide and Conquer policy, which has implanted time bombs of ethnic conflicts that keep on erupting in the region. (Ethnic groups were intentionally intermingled in hopes of deterring nationalism and creating a mixed population for the USSR). The arrangement not only allowed Azerbaijan to displace and ethnically cleanse the Armenians from Karabakh's lowland regions, but it also provided an opportunity to, over time, harass and drive the Armenians out of the enclave of Nagorno-Karabakh proper, and settle Azeris in their place.

Despite the authority they were given to govern the oblast within SSR Azerbaijan, in the years that followed, in the 1930s as well as 1945, 1965, 1967 and 1977, the Armenians of Nagorno-Karabakh kept on filing petitions with the communist regime to rejoin Armenia to no avail. In fact, the individuals who advocated for the petitions were often times imprisoned. Even with all of his concessions, Stalin failed to annex Turkey to the Soviet Union, and Ataturk ended up keeping the entirety of Western Armenia (territory awarded to the Armenians by U.S. President Woodrow Wilson), as well as the regions he had snatched from the first Armenian Republic. As the regional economic and political dynamics were shifting, the Western Allies decided not to fight to keep the Armenian lands for the Armenians. The fact that no "independent" Armenian administration has officially acknowledged the Soviet era borders continues to be a thorn in the side of Turkey and Azerbaijan who strive to cement their ownership of all the Armenian lands they have gained thanks to the Soviet regime.

In the 1930s, the Soviets created and officially adopted the new ethnonym of "Azerbaijani/Azeri," whereas the Tatar Turks, along with all the different tribes in Azerbaijan, were now referred to as Azeris in order to attach an official ethnicity to the newly created nation. Since the entire region belonged to the Soviets, accuracy in history and truthfulness were not critical to the Russians. Sovietization of republics involved the creation of a suitable history to link the people to the land. Therefore, the Azeris came up with a history for their country that borrows mostly from the days of Iranian rule, presenting it as "Azeri" rule, making indigenous peoples' culture and traditions their own, and glossing over the fact that the land's tribes were simply Turkified by the masses of Seljuk and Oghuz Turks who migrated to the Caucasus.

Seventy years passed in relative peace under Soviet control while the Azerbaijani government launched an intensive campaign of settling Azeris in Nagorno-Karabakh, its surrounding areas, as well as the new Azeri exclave of Nakhichevan. Heydar Aliyev, current Azeri President Ilham Aliyev's father, will later be quoted in a 2002 interview: "At the same time, I tried to change the demography there... By doing this and other things, I tried to increase the number of Azeris there and reduce the number of the Armenians in Nagorno-Karabakh. Those who worked in Nagorno-Karabakh at the time know about it."[27] The "other things" refer to the intentional neglect of the infrastructure in the Armenian-populated villages, the confiscation of farms and cattle, the pillage of precious museum artifacts proving that Karabakh was ancient Armenian land, the closing of schools, unfair labor practices, sabotaging of industrial development, erasure of Armenian history and the name Artsakh from books and publications, changing the names

---

27 "Aliyev Admits Azerbaijan Worked to Boost Number of Azeris in Artsakh," *Horizon*, December 16, 2020, https://horizonweekly.ca/en/aliyev-admits-azerbaijan-worked-to-boost-number-of-azeris-in-artsakh/.

of historic Armenian figures to Turkish sounding names and referring to them as Turks, promoting Armenian cultural heritage as
Azeri, harassment of Armenians and the settlement of Azeris in their
homes, all designed to push the Armenians into leaving the area.
Armenians who complained were either imprisoned by Baku or sent
to Siberia. By 1989, when Karabakh petitioned to secede from the
USSR, its Armenian population had dropped from 96% to 76%,
while its Azeri population had increased to 23%. Nevertheless, the
designation of "autonomous enclave" had by and large protected
the Armenians of Karabakh and allowed them to hold key governing positions and teach Armenian in their schools. By contrast,
the Azeris had successfully driven most of the Armenians out of
Nakhichevan.[28]

Fast forward to the early 1990s, when Karabakh Armenians were
receiving pushback from the same Soviet Regime that had put out
the legal framework of secession that they were meticulously following. The Azerbaijani and Russian authorities and their media
collaborated to cover up and keep the details of the violent pogroms
against the Armenians from the world as Azerbaijan escalated the
propaganda about its compromised "territorial integrity," a mis-
representation of what was, in fact, the liberation movement of
Karabakh from illegal Soviet Azeri occupation.

As fascinated as I became with the erupting Karabakh conflict,
during the same time frame, a life-changing event ended up divert-
ing my attention to the opposite direction, to the depths of Western
Armenia.

---

28   The last Armenians left Nakhichevan in 1999. By 2006, Azerbaijan had destroyed all Armenian cultural, historic structures, ancient churches and cemetaries in
Nakhichevan, leaving no trace of Armenian existence in the area.

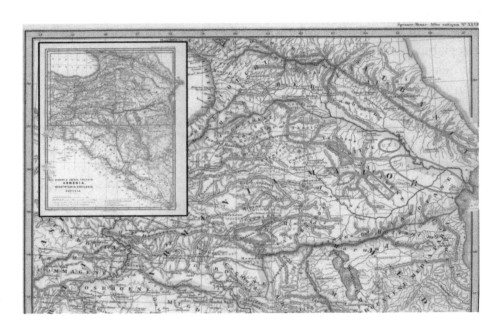

INSET FROM THE MAP OF THE ANCIENT LANDS BY THE GERMAN CARTOGRAPHER AND GEOGRAPHER KARL VON SPRUNER MERTZ (1803-1892) - PUBLISHED IN 1865, SHOWING BOTH ARMENIA MINOR AND ARMENIA MAIOR WHICH COVERED MOST OF TODAY'S AZERBAIJAN INCLUDING ITS CAPITAL BAKU THAT FELL WITHIN THE 15TH ARMENIAN PROVINCE OF PAITAKARAN (PHAITAKARAN IN MAP, CIRCLED), THE KURA RIVER (CYRUS CORUS IN MAP) AS THE ARMENIAN KINGDOM'S BORDER WITH CAUCASIAN ALBANIA, THE 12TH ARMENIAN PROVINCE OF UTIK (UTI IN MAP, CIRCLED) AND THE 10TH PROVINCE OF ARTSAKH (IN RECTANGLE ON MAP). ONE OF SEVERAL MAPS THAT MENTION ARTSAKH (LATER CALLED KARBAKH BY THE PERSIANS). NOWEHERE ON THE MAP IS THE COUNTRY OF AZERBAIJAN LISTED, BECAUSE AZERBAIJAN DID NOT COME INTO EXISTENCE UNTIL 1918 PUBLIC DOMAIN, FROM WWW.DAVIDRUMSEY.COM

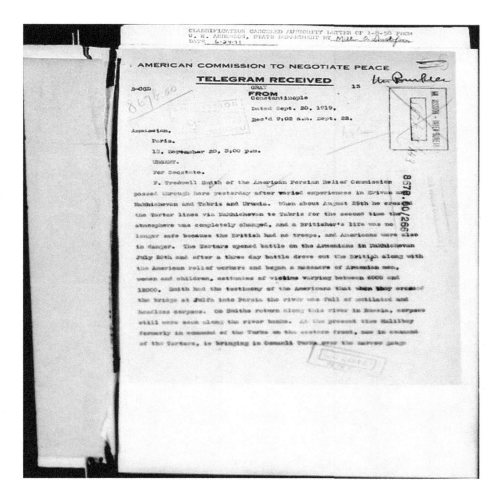

A telegram dated September 20, 1919, from American Commission to Negotiate Peace, describing the massacre of Armenians in Nakhichevan: "The Tartars opened battle on the Armenians in Nakhichevan... drove out the British along with the American relief workers and began a massacre of Armenian men, women and children, estimates of victims varying between 6000 and 12,000. Smith had the testimony of Americans that when they crossed the bridge at Julfa into Persia the river was full of mutilated and headless corpses" Wikimedia commons. Series: General Records, 1918-1931. Record Group 256. File: M820 Roll542

1987: Another Armenian Tree!

THREE YEARS HAD PASSED SINCE I had left Lebanon, and here I was, a freshman biology student at the local Cal State University, still working on my accent. I was accepted at UCLA, but I had turned it down. My counselor at Grant High School had told me that, one day, when I realized UCLA's standing, I would regret that decision. I was not sure why I had zero desire to attend UCLA. I told the counselor that my decision was based on the fact that I did not have a car yet to drive all the way to Westwood. I thought that sounded like a good valid reason.

Life was great in 1987. I was a full-time student and held a job at the pharmacy of the Student Union building on campus. I felt I was positioning myself on a good path until an earthquake of magnitude 5 introduced me to the other facet of living in California!

I was sitting in the cafeteria on the roof of Sierra Hall when everything started shaking. A group of Armenian students who had graduated from Holy Martyrs Ferrahian, the first private Armenian school established in Southern California, tended to always occupy the same set of benches in the middle. I guess this was a different kind of "tree" to congregate around. Except this tree was shaking now and sending these students into a frenzy. As suddenly as it came on, the jolting halted, and so did the rattling of the glass panels. Soon, the Armenian students were settling back onto their benches. Although I had tried to befriend them, their bond seemed to be somewhat exclusive. Armenian students from other schools tended to orbit around this group, like satellites around a mother planet.

Something about these Ferrahian students, their expressions, their involvement in the Armenian Student Association on campus, and their demeanor, in general, reminded me of my childhood school of Nshan Palandjian Djemaran. The longing that called for me all those years ago rekindled as I observed the interaction between them. I stayed, however, in my own orbit, which ran with those of other "outsiders" such as Serj Tankian (he would later become the lead singer of the band System of a Down) and many others who were non-Ferrahian graduates. Thankfully my orbit was not a lonely one. Several of my friends from Grant High School were also there, and we kept in touch as often as our class schedules permitted. Among them was Mariana, a Turkish Armenian, or a *Bolsahay* as Armenians hailing from Istanbul were referred to. Mariana and I would carry on our own conversations on a side table away from the "tree." We seemed to have many things in common. However, when her childhood friend Siranush would join us, I would feel like a third wheel. Theirs was a deeper friendship. After all, they came from the same country, had similar experiences, and their families had known each other for many years.

So it was that during one of those encounters, where Mariana and Siranush had yet again immersed in their heated gossips, slipping in Turkish words that I did not comprehend, that I blurted out something half-mindedly that ended up changing my life forever...

Malatya?

It was spring 1988.

ON THAT MORNING, AND AS it had become all too common, conversations about current world events, in particular the shocking Sumgait pogrom of Armenians in Azerbaijan, campus activities, and gossip about other Armenian students gave way to yet another "Mariana and Siranush tangent." They went on in their fluent Armenian, mixing in the occasional Turkish words in a most familiar way. Unbeknownst to them, I cringed inside with every Turkish word they uttered. I kept this disdain private because I knew that it belonged to me alone. I recognized that mixing Turkish words came as naturally to Turkish Armenians as mixing Arabic words did with Lebanese Armenians. I reminded myself that my mother's grandparents spoke mostly in Turkish. And yet... I looked over to the "tree" from the side of my eyes, the mostly Lebanese Armenian Ferrahian students. My mind drifted to something that had been calling on me from afar. I could not describe what it was. A whisper. A gnawing feeling. A call of some sort. I returned my attention to our table, not giving up on my budding friendship with Mariana and Siranush. "You know, I am Turkish Armenian, too," I said, surprising even myself! The attention grabber worked. They both stopped halfway in their conversation and turned to me. "You are?" Siranush asked, her big green eyes brimming with disbelief and humor. "Yes, my dad is from Malatya," I added. The word flowed with ease out of my mouth, but hearing it stopped me in my tracks! "Malatya?" I had no idea where this word came from! For a second, I doubted myself and wondered if it was the correct name of the region my father referred to while talking about the origins of his family. My father's stories had become white noise to my ears. "I am in trouble now!" I told myself. "What if this is not the right region?" "What if there is no place called Malatya?" I risked making a fool of myself if I had, in fact, just invented this word. "What?" said Mariana, almost choking. "Really?" exclaimed Siranush, her shiny eyes fully focused on me. "I mean, my father's parents were from Malatya," I corrected quickly. "Wait. *I* am from Malatya!" said Siranush. My surprise at this revelation was overshadowed by my great relief that Malatya was indeed the name of an actual city! "You are? No way!" I reacted, thrilled that my efforts at forging a closer bond with these girls were perhaps paying off. "Oh my God! I can't believe it," continued Siranush; "I have to tell my dad!"

That night, I told my father, too. He was very happy to hear that I had found a fellow Malatyatzi. Of course, this news opened the gates to the flow of the white noise again, but I now had a newfound interest in listening to my father's stories from the old country. The next day, and to my delight, this revelation was the main topic of our hangout at the school cafeteria. Siranush informed me that the Armenian community of Malatya was a small tight-knit bunch and that her father knew all the families. She added that her father was asking if my father knew the names of his relatives. She went on to suggest that my father write down names of relatives that he could recall so that she could show them to her father. This was now becoming very intriguing! I could not wait to get home. Did my father even know the names of his relatives? Lo and behold, the white noise that I had shut out throughout my childhood was full of all sorts of colors and details. When I told my father about what Siranush had suggested. "Of course, I know the names of my relatives!" he replied. He wrote down the names of his maternal uncle and cousins on a piece of paper. "These are my nene Maryam's relatives? How do you remember their names?" I asked him. "I visited Malatya with my mother when I was about 11, 12," he said. "And my cousin Bedros visited us once in Lebanon many years ago," he added. "But after that, we lost all contact," he finished. I was speechless! I took the piece of paper on which my father had neatly inscribed the names of his Malatya relatives to school and handed it to Siranush. I had no expectations of anything coming out of this exercise, except the following day, Siranush informed me with great excitement, that her father knew all the individuals on that list! He knew them and their families "very well," and some of them were even "here in California!!"

They say life is full of coincidences. But for me, this was more than a chance discovery! Deep inside, I felt as if the shadows that had been following me all my life were finally closing in on me. We came all the way from Lebanon to California. We could have fled to another country or even another part of the United States. I then attended Grant High School out of all the high schools, made a friend named Mariana, declined to go to UCLA, wanted to go to the local Cal State University, met another girl called Siranush, opened my big mouth to utter the word *Malatya* when I could have very well mentioned *Adana,* where my mother's side of the family is from, and ended up finding long-lost relatives completely unknown to me! It was unreal! I looked at the names on the paper: Maynuel, Bedros, and Krikor (will leave out the last name). Hmmm... Who were these people?

(I will be spelling my father's maternal uncle's name as Maynuel to differentiate it from his paternal uncle's name of Manuel; essentially, they were both named Manuel)

Turkish Armenian Relatives?

NEEDLESS TO SAY, THIS TURN of events took my friendship with Siranush to a different level. The amazing discovery we stumbled upon overtook our conversations, as we enthusiastically proceeded to organize a meeting between my family and my newfound relatives. These were my grandmother Maryam's relatives. It suddenly occurred to me that as a child, I had never realized that Nene had no family of her own in Lebanon. This revelation was quite intriguing. Siranush explained that a certain Vartug, daughter of my father's cousin Krikor from the list of names we turned in, had recently moved with her husband Yeghia from Central California to where we lived in Los Angeles! Siranush's family had reached out to her with the news about my father, and she was apparently as eager to meet us as we were to meet her. The day of the get-together was upon us, and my father was very excited as we climbed up the stairs to Siranush's home. Her parents had invited both families over, and everyone was looking forward to meeting each other. Siranush opened the door, eyes gleaming and a big smile on her face. She introduced us to her parents, who greeted us in Armenian. Then, her father took over in Turkish and introduced us to Vartug, her husband Yeghia, and her sister Ilda. Here stood an elegant tall lady in advanced pregnancy, with hazel blue eyes she often cast down in shyness and gleaming marble-like skin that reminded me of my grandmother Maryam's. Her smile never left her face as she acknowledged my father as "George Dayday" (Uncle George in Turkish) and went on to tell him that she had informed her father Krikor, in Istanbul, about this meeting and that he was elated that we had found them! While her husband spoke perfectly fluent and impeccable Armenian, she only spoke Turkish. Yeghia, a round-faced, super-friendly, and articulate man, said a few heartfelt words about the amazing happenstance that had brought us together and proceeded to inform us that Ilda had just moved to California after completing her graduate studies in Turkey. Unlike Vartug, Ilda had darker features and brown eyes. A very skinny girl, she was a little more reserved and again did not speak a word of Armenian.

For the next couple of hours, Betty and I sat quietly as our parents attempted to communicate in Turkish with Vartug and Ilda. As they spoke, their Turkish became better and better, it seemed, because both Vartug and Ilda started nodding their heads affirmatively in recognition of certain key events that had taken place in their family. Betty and I were mesmerized by what was unfolding in front of our eyes. Vartug and Ilda were finishing the sentences of my father. Strangers who previously did not know of each other's existence were recounting the same events and completing each other's accounts of the same torn story. The gaps that my father was unsure of they filled in with invaluable information that made his eyes twinkle with the moisture of tears as he nodded his head with a grateful smile. Ilda explained that, in the early 1930s, there was a Turkification movement, during which the "Surname Law" was passed that required Armenians living in the eastern provinces of Turkey (where Malatya is) to change their last names. They had the option of either dropping the traditional Armenian "ian" suffix from their family names or taking on as last name the Turkish word describing their profession. She went on to say that the Arpadjians had changed their last name at that time to a name descriptive of their line of work. "Ilda (will leave out last name)" instead of "Ilda Arpadjian," I told myself quietly. How cruel for a government to force survivors who had lost family in the Genocide to let go of even their sacred bond to them, their last names! I had no idea about

Turkey's forceful Turkification of the remaining Armenians within the old Armenian provinces.

As the night advanced, the story of our families was woven together and the holes sewed in. The resulting tale blew me away to pieces. It also became evident to me that, while aware of their family's story, Vartoug and Ilda were not well-informed about the larger details of the calamity that befell the Armenians living in Turkey during the latter years of the Ottoman Empire. Yeghia told us that, in Turkey, it was forbidden to mention the Armenian Genocide, and accusing someone of being Armenian was treated as blasphemy. Speaking Armenian was also frowned upon, especially in the middle and eastern parts of the country. The entire period of the First World War was skimmed over in history class, and alternate stories were taught at schools. Fearful of persecution and concerned for the safety of their families, survivors spared their descendants from hardship by intentionally not sharing their Genocide experiences with them. Most of these stories were taken to the grave, lost forever. Absence of history and memory compromised the makeup of the ethnography of the Turkish Armenians. Yeghia was a formidable storyteller! He said that he owed his Armenian to his iron-willed grandmother, who forced him to speak his mother tongue behind closed doors in the safety of their home in Istanbul. He went on to say that Ilda was just now finding out about the truth of what had happened to the almost two million Armenians living in Turkey between 1915 and 1923! He added that there were only five Armenian families still living in Malatya. I started struggling with keeping my focus on the topic, which was now turning to the current politics of the region. There was a lump in my throat. I kept on going back to the family story that had unfolded earlier. I felt truly sorry for my grandmother. As a matter of fact, I started understanding her better. I was too young when she passed away. Had I known all this back then, I would have implored her to tell me her story as a firsthand account.

Although, at first, the idea of having Turkish-speaking relatives was hard for me to digest, as my newly discovered relatives described the ordeals that the remaining Armenians in Turkey had continued to endure, I realized how little we the Armenians on the outside knew about what life was like for the ones who had stayed behind. The Turkish Armenians, at times described by Diaspora Armenians as sellouts who had "become Turks," had a lot to educate the rest of us about. I wanted to know all about the aftermath when the lands were emptied of Armenian families, neighbors, farmers, storekeepers, artisans, where delicately cultivated mulberry and apricot trees in courtyard gardens hunched over and shriveled, the caring touch of their owners forever gone, where rows upon rows of once vibrant houses and shops lay empty and silent, the souls of their owners still lingering around unfinished daily chores. How did it feel for the remaining Armenians to witness the confiscation of Armenian properties by the government, the appropriation of ancient Armenian historic monuments, the enrichment of politicians with Armenian assets, and the settlement of Muslims into Armenian homes and businesses? It must have taken great courage and strength for them to stay on.

They Are Dead, Dead...

Practically every Armenian family has a Genocide story because practically every Armenian is the descendant of a Genocide survivor. The story of my paternal grandparents that unraveled that evening took further shape over the next several years with the collaboration of my father, my newfound relatives, and family members in different countries who were more than happy to contribute any details passed down to them. My father's amazing treasures of old family photos and collected memorabilia were indispensable. Research on my part also helped me put the events into historical context. It goes like this.

MALATYA IS KNOWN FOR ITS apricots (one of the symbols of Armenia) and also for its Koefte (meat and wheat shell stuffed with ground meat). Situated at the southwestern edge of the Armenian Highlands, it is a city with more than six thousand years of history, during which it was invaded and ruled by many ancient people such as the Hittites, Cimmerians, Scythians, and Urartians. The Urartians, who had created the Iron Age Kingdom of Van in the mid-9th century BC, around the lake with the same name (Lake Van), are identified as the immediate ancestors of the Armenians, the people of Ararat (highest mountain in the region). Shortly after being conquered by the Iranian Medes in the 6th century BC, Urartu re-emerged as Armenia. The Kingdom of Armenia, also referred to as the Armenian Empire (from 321 BC to 428 AD), evolved under the rule of three successive royal dynasties: the Orontid, the Artaxiad, and the Arsacid. It was later divided between two empires. Eastern Armenia came under the suzerainty of the Persian Sasanian Empire, while Western Armenia became part of the Roman Empire. Malatya was a major center of crossroads in the province of Armenia Minor in Western Armenia. In 330AD, the eastern provinces of the Roman Empire, including Western Armenia, became known as the Byzantine Empire. In 392 AD Emperor Theodosius I divided Armenia Minor into two provinces: First Armenia with its capital of Sebastia (now Sivas) and Second Armenia with its capital of Malatya (also known by its Greek name of Melitene).

MAP SHOWING ARMENIA DIVIDED BETWEEN THE BYZANTINE (WESTERN ARMENIA) AND PERSIAN (EASTERN ARMENIA) EMPIRES. MINOR ARMENIA UNDER BYZANTINE RULE WAS DIVIDED INTO ARMENIA I WITH ITS CAPITAL OF SEBASTIA AND ARMENIA II WITH ITS CAPITAL OF MELITENE, THE GREEK NAME FOR MALATYA. REPRINTED WITH PERMISSION FROM COPYRIGHT HOLDER ARMENICA.ORG - WWW.ARMENICA. ORG, CC BY-SA 3.0, BYZANTINE ARMENIA, 387-536. NO CHANGES WERE MADE.

THE CATHEDRAL OF ANI, COMMISSIONED BY ARMENIAN KING SMBAT BAGRATUNI IN 989, SITTING IN RUINS IN EASTERN TURKEY (WESTERN ARMENIA) ACROSS THE BORDER FROM CURRENT DAY ARMENIA. ANI, THE CITY OF 1001 CHURCHES AND CAPITAL OF THE BAGRATUNI ARMENIAN DYNASTY, WAS CAPTURED IN 1064 BY THE INVADING SELJUK TURKS, AND ITS POPULATION WAS MASSACRED AND DISPLACED. PHOTO © MATTHEW KARANIAN, REPRINTED WITH PERMISSION FROM *THE ARMENIAN HIGHLAND*.

Hundreds of years later, in the early 11th century, a long stretch of cold weather and famine in the steppes of Central Asia forced nomadic Seljuk Turks from the Altai Mountains of Mongolia to venture south and eastbound in search of green pasture for their herds. Adopting the religion of Islam for political expediency, they infiltrated the Persian Empire and later the Muslim Caliphate, first as slaves in Persian armies, then as hired mercenaries, and later as tribal allies. In 1064, the Seljuks attacked the ancient Armenian city of Ani at the eastern edge of the Byzantine Empire, ransacked it, and slaughtered its inhabitants. As the Byzantine Empire weakened, the Seljuks continued raiding and acquiring more and more of its lands. The local Armenians, Byzantines, and even Muslims did not know how to defend themselves against these mobile brutal forces that had nothing to lose and everything to gain by raiding the towns of sedentary settlements. The Seljuk reign was short-lived, however, as they were ousted by multitudes of Mongols who had followed behind them. In the early 1230s, the Mongols ruled over Western Armenia and divided it into Emirates or "Beyliks." One of these Emirates was run by Osman I, a descendant of Oghuz Turks from the Kayi tribe in Central Asia. The name Ottoman (*Osmanian* in Armenian) was derived from his name. Eventually, the Ottoman dynasty grew in power and took over the rest of the Emirates. In 1453, the city of Constantinople, the center of the Byzantine Empire, succumbed to the Ottomans, ending the 1,100 year Byzantine reign. What eventually became known as the Ottoman Empire expanded to include Western Armenia, Bulgaria, Romania, Greece, Hungary, Macedonia, Egypt, Jordan, Lebanon, Syria, Palestine, parts of Arabia, and the north coast of Africa. Many Christian cultural monuments and places of worship were confiscated and converted to Islamic structures, barns, or storage facilities. The Haghia Sophia (Great Wisdom in Latin) Greek Orthodox Christian church built in the early 530s by Byzantine Emperor Justinian I was converted to a mosque under Mehmed the Conqueror. The bells, altar, and religious relics were destroyed, mosaics depicting Jesus and the Virgin Mary were mostly plastered over, and the mihrab, minbar, and four minarets were added (converted to a museum in 1935 by the secular Turkish Republic, it was converted back into a mosque in July of 2020 by Erdogan, the current Turkish president). It is the most prominent landmark of Istanbul, the name given to Constantinople by the Turks since 1930.

Malatya was captured by the Ottoman army in 1516 and came under the official rule of the Ottoman Empire along with the rest of Western Armenia starting in 1623. The lands of Eastern Armenia, on the other hand, were conquered from Persia by the Russian Empire in 1828, with the Treaty of Turkmenchay (as previously mentioned in the chapter about Karabakh). After thousands of years of Greek, Roman and European coexistence and common history, the Armenians were now being subjected to Mongolian Turkic rule. The Turkic ways were the same everywhere: they came, they killed, and expelled the local leaders, took over, renamed cities and infrastructure, Turkified the people, and made the land and everything in it theirs. Under the rule of the Ottomans, indigenous Armenians, along with Jews and other minority Christians such as the Greeks and Assyrians, were treated as second-class citizens and called "Giavours" (Infidels). For a while, Armenians and Jews had to wear blue or purple shoes to indicate their status as minorities. Later, the decree was for the Armenians to wear red shoes to be further distinguished. Minorities were not accorded equal rights and could not sue Muslims, which left them defenseless and prone to all sorts of abuses. The Ottomans gave the Armenian Patriarchate in Constantinople spiritual and limited civic leadership over the six Armenian vilayets (Provinces) in Anatolia that made up the Armenian homeland: Van, Erzurum (or Karin), Harput (or Kharpert, also known as Mamuretulaziz), Bitlis, Dyarbekir (or Tigranakert), and Sivas. Through the years, the geographic and demographic continuity of Western Armenia began to break with the settlement of Turks and other Muslims as well as increasing sociopolitical unrest under Ottoman rule. Nevertheless, Armenians remained a large sector of the population, with some villages that were completely Armenian. Malatya was part of the Harput Vilayet, where Armenians are said to have been innovators and leaders in commerce, agriculture, and the silk business.

It is in this Malatya that my grandfather Sarkis Tavitian and my grandmother Maryam Arpadjian were born. Originally from Erzurum,[29] the Tavitians were successful textile merchants,

---

29 Erzurum, a city in Turkey in the north eastern part of Anatolia, that was once known by its Armenian name of Karin

specialized in fabric dyeing, and seemingly quite influential. My great-grandfather, Garabed Tavitian, and his two brothers, Manuel and Nishan, were highly esteemed for their trade. They lived in the city in adjacent homes in a cul-de-sac and owned established businesses in the marketplace. Their workplace was a family hub, where great grandmother Varter, Garabed's wife, was known to drop by in the early afternoons to help ring the dyes out of the fabrics. My grandfather Sarkis shared the curiosity and progressive thinking of his generation of Malatyatzis in that he constantly inquired about new innovations and technologies being forged in the European textile industry. He once told my father about how he and his brothers had one year put in an expensive order for German fabric dyes without telling their father, Garabed. Although open-minded, Garabed belonged to the old school of thought that was suspicious of transactions made with remote companies in foreign countries and swore by the philosophy of needing to inspect a product with "your own eyes" prior to purchasing. Months had gone by without a sign of the order, prompting Sarkis and his brothers to disclose their secret business dealing to the fury of their father. Then one day, during a cold winter storm, when the bone-chilling air and political unrest had quieted the cobbled streets, a delivery wagon emerged through the fog and fluttering snowflakes. The driver took his time inspecting the lineup of shops, passing by the apothecary, the dried fruit stalls, and displays of colorful kilim rugs until he halted his horse in front of the Tavitian workshops. "Are you the Tavitian fabric dyers?" he asked my grandfather and the small crowd of relatives that had emerged out of the shops, curious about the delivery wagon that had appeared out of nowhere. In response to their affirmative answer, the driver announced, "I have an order for you from Germany." It would be thanks to those German-manufactured fabric dyes that the Tavitians would amass their fortune in the years ahead.

The Muslim Turks saw the Christian minorities they ruled over as their war spoils. They considered them second-class subjects to whom they had left trades deemed inferior, while they exclusively held positions in the government and military. In time, this arrangement inadvertently led to the Christian sector accumulating great wealth because most professions, trade industries, and agriculture were left to them to cultivate. They were also more educated, and many sent their children to complete their education in France's Sorbonne and Venice's Mkhitarist School. In the late 19th century, while the Armenian vilayets in Eastern Anatolia were struggling with mounting harassment and additional taxation by local Kurdish and Turkic tribal warlords who were taking advantage of the weakening reach of the Ottoman government, an elite section of Armenians in the western urban areas had gained the confidence of the Sultans. This class of wealthy Armenians held prominent positions in all economic sectors, including the silk industry, architecture, construction, customs, and currency. Some had even attained positions in government. "16 of the 18 most important bankers of the Ottoman Empire were Armenian,"[30] and a multitude of renowned mansions, palaces, and mosques were designed and built by the Armenian Balyan family of court-sponsored architects (Among them Dolmabahce Palace, Ortakoy Mosque, and Topkapi Palace).

The Muslim Turks, who considered themselves superior to their minority subjects, grew envious and resentful of this wealth, knowledge, and prosperity. To keep them in check, disproportionately high taxes were maliciously imposed on Christians who were punished by beatings and fines when unable to pay them. At the beginning of the 20th century, life for the Armenian peasants in the countryside was becoming particularly treacherous as they were left at the mercy of local tribesmen who, in the absence of central authority, abused their self-proclaimed powers by extorting the locals of their

---

30 Astrig Tchamkerten, *Calouste Sarkis Gulbenkian: The Man and His Work* (Lisbon: Gulbenkian Foundation Press, 2010).

earnings, livestock, and properties.[31] They even took away a son or a daughter in reprisal for unpaid "taxes." The Western region of the Armenian Highlands, as Eastern Anatolia was known for millennia prior to the Turks' arrival, was being ravaged by thousands of incoming Muslim nomads, Circassians, Chechens, Kurds, and Turkmen fleeing the Russian armies, political instability in northern Iran, and the Balkan wars. These newcomers, many of whom were chased out of the revolting European territories of the Ottoman Empire, preyed on the vulnerable Armenian families, stole their property, and raped and abducted Armenian women with impunity. Any kind of resistance was met with assault and death. Cases that made it to the courts were handled like charades where false witnesses were called and falsehoods concocted, leading complicit judges to dismiss the cases or, worse yet, punish the victims instead for disseminating "lies" and insulting their Muslim overseers. Complaints about this state of affairs and pleadings for government oversight fell on deaf ears, which prompted the better-off Armenians in urban areas to use whatever influence they had to appeal to foreigners on behalf of their brethren in the east and some eastern Anatolian Armenians to acquire guns from Russia and form militias to protect their villages. The Ottoman government was simply not interested in protecting its Christian citizens. On the contrary, fresh out of its devastating losses in Europe, it was letting the newly arrived "muhajirs" (refugees) take their revenge on them. The plan was to rid the land of its Christian communities by making life miserable for them, and many did leave.[32]

The persecution of Armenians seemed to come in response to their recurring demands for safety and equality. It also attracted the scrutiny of foreigners monitoring the decline of the Ottoman Empire. The Turks resented this international outcry with passion.

---

31 Benny Morris and Dror Ze'evi, *The Thirty-Year Genocide: Turkey's Destruction of Its Christian Minorities, 1894–1924* (Cambridge, MA: Harvard University Press, 2019), Rural Decline.
32 Morris and Ze'evi, *Thirty-Year Genocide*, A Rural Community Under Siege.

Pressured by the Europeans and Russians to ease the oppression of its Christian minorities, the government would hint at impending reforms to appease the foreigners and then orchestrate a disturbance or provocation designed to taunt Armenians into defending themselves. This self-defense would then be exaggerated, taken out of context, and propagated as "treacherous rebellion" in order to incite the Muslim population against the Armenians and provide an excuse for their wholesale persecution. Mobs formed in response to impassioned calls for Jihad would descend upon the Armenian population and slaughter thousands with impunity. A case in point is the 1894-1896 Hamidian massacres, named after the Red Sultan Abdul Hamid II, during which upwards of 300,000 Armenians were put to the sword by state-sponsored pogroms. Foreign arbitrators and Armenian representatives were appealing to the government to draft a new Constitution offering minorities certain rights. This interference by foreigners angered the Sultan, who vowed to teach the "impudent" Armenians a lesson and "solve the Armenian Question once and for all." The Armenian Question referred to the autonomy of the Armenian territories. Muslim Turks saw the further breakdown of their empire as the ultimate motive behind these proposed reforms. They were incensed by the thought of Armenians gaining rights, vying for autonomy, and possibly an eventual independent state following in the footsteps of Greece, which had broken away from the empire and gained its independence in 1821. The possibility of losing the Anatolian Armenian lands conquered by their valiant ancestors was seen as a line in the sand, and fighting against it with all their might was a sacred act. The Sultan's solution to the "Armenian Question" was the wholesale murder of Armenian men, the destruction of their homes, and the forceful conversion to Islam of thousands of Armenian women and children. The intent was to chip away at the prospect of an independent Armenia. While the city of Malatya was mostly spared, Armenian villages in its rural countryside were completely eradicated. It is said that 7,500 Armenians from Malatya perished during those massacres.[33]

An established businessman who had regular dealings with merchants in neighboring areas as well as deep ties and friendships in both the Armenian and Turkish communities, my great-grandfather Garabed was a wise and shrewd man who did his best to be a step ahead of brewing developments in order to safeguard his family. When the decree came in the summer of 1915 for all Armenian grown men to report to the town center, he did not like it and decided not to comply. As the authorities started searching houses and arresting men, he hid in previously dug-up ditches in his garden along with his sons Napoleon, Sarkis, and Krikor (an inspiring and quite eloquent young man who often held community meetings at home, Napoleon died around 1918-1920 at the age of 29 from complications of kidney failure. Years prior, he had developed a kidney disease while rendering his military service under harsh and unsanitary conditions).

Garabed, always vigilant and proactive, had dug up trenches in discreet areas of his fruit tree garden. "If one day the need arises," he had thought, "they will provide a quick temporary hiding place." That need seemed to be inching ever closer in early 1915, when news came from neighboring areas that over 200 renowned Armenian community leaders, politicians, writers, journalists, poets, physicians, and clergy were arrested on the eve of April 24. Among them were poets Siamanto and Daniel Varoujan, prominent figures in what seemed to be an era of flourishing Armenian cultural and intellectual renaissance expressing itself with newfound nationalistic zeal. With distant territories of the empire poised to break free from Ottoman rule, the Armenian community was allowing itself hope for its own future independence. Garabed, a regular presence at the local Armenian church where for many years he had been serving as a *Taghagan* (delegate), was putting together bits and pieces of

33 Raymond Kévorkian, *The Armenian Genocide: A Complete History* (London: I. B. Tauris, 2011), 382

news concerning the fate of those arrested. He had concluded that things "did not look good," and the air smelled of another purging about to be unleashed upon the Armenians.

A year prior, on February 8, 1914, Russia, France, Britain, and Italy had succeeded in convincing the Ottoman regime to sign the Armenian Reform Package that was set to make one province out of the six Armenian vilayets to be governed by a Christian Ottoman or a European Governor General. This ill-fated Reform Package was quickly annulled by the Turks in December of 1914, a few weeks after the Ottoman Empire entered World War I on the side of Germany and the Central powers against the Allied Powers of France, Britain, and Russia (the United States, Italy, and Japan would join later). CUP Leader Cemal Pasha has later said about the empire's decision to join the war, *"Our sole goal was to be freed by means of this world war from all the foreign treaties that existed, each of which was a blow to our internal independence. The ripping up of the agreement concerning the reforms of Eastern Anatolia (Armenian provinces) was also desired."*[34] Dubbed "the sick man of Europe," the Ottoman Empire was spiraling downward, losing more and more of its Balkan and Eastern European territories to Christian nations. In an attempt to expand eastbound with a Pan Turanic dream of joined Turkic nations, War Minister Enver Pasha had marched his troupes towards the Russian Empire with the goal of reaching Baku. The Russians were quick to convince Armenian reservists living in Eastern Armenia within the Russian Empire, along with Armenians who had fled from Anatolia, to join the Russian forces and help push back the Turkish army. In return, they had promised to help the Armenians liberate the Anatolian Armenian lands, which had fallen into a vulnerable predicament in the wake of the nullified Armenian Reform Package. What resulted was a catastrophic defeat for the Turks in Sarikamish, with the decimation of their troops, who were ill-equipped for the harsh

---

34 Taner Akçam, *The Young Turks' Crime Against Humanity:, The Armenian Genocide and Ethnic Cleansing in the Ottoman Empire* (Princeton, NJ: Princeton University Press, 2012), 129.

winter conditions and had been forced to march for hours in the snow. Enver, humiliated by his miscalculations, was quick to blame the Armenians for this failure, and thousands of Armenians living in the eastern front lines were massacred in revenge for the ostensible suspicion of collaborating with the enemy. Anger simmered among the Turks, who were being fed poisonous rhetoric by the government about the Armenians preparing to attack the Turkish army from the rear as a fifth column. This was a fabricated lie with no collaborated evidence meant to fan the flames of hatred against the Armenians. All the Armenians were doing was defending their people, which was the only option they were left with since all peaceful discourses to secure basic human rights had failed against an ever brutal regime. The Russians and Europeans, on the other hand, were enlisting Armenians in their armies to take advantage of their zeal to protect and liberate their people.

The Turkish pattern of false propaganda aimed at inciting the Muslim Turks was eerily predictable to Garabed. He feared that the workings of an impending massacre could have already been set in motion in response to the 1914 signing of the Armenian Reform Package, similar to the 1890s Hamidian massacres that were triggered by then Constitutional reform proposals. Deep inside, he was convinced that the Turks would never give up an inch of anything and that they rather see all Armenians gone. Ironically, the Young Turks had also exploited the Armenian aspiration for liberty by enlisting them and other minorities in their coup of Sultan Abdul Hamid's government with reassurances that their vision of government was more westernized and democratic with equality and justice for all citizens. They had promised concrete social reforms in exchange for help during the countercoup and the final toppling of the Sultan.

It was at this juncture that Armenians, as well as other Christian minorities, were allowed to serve in the armed forces. But after seizing power, it was the leading branch of these same Young Turks, the Committee of Union and Progress (CUP) with its Triumvirate

Pashas, Talaat Minister of Interior, Enver Minister of War, and Djemal Minister of the Navy, that seemed to be taking advantage of the chaos of WWI to push forth a most sinister plan of ethnic cleansing. Determined to hold onto the territories in the mainland of the disintegrating empire, it seemed that the CUP would stop at nothing. So when the town crier had announced that all Armenian grown men needed to report to the town center, my great-grandfather and his sons had not complied. The eerie quiet in the streets was interrupted by hoof sounds as mounted soldiers approached. Observing the scene from behind their second-story shutters, the Tavitians were quick to determine that the authorities intended on searching the homes for the men. My great-grandfather, my grandfather, and his two brothers had run to their secret hiding place under the trees of their expansive garden. Muffled sounds of gates opening and family members being questioned in Turkish drifted to their ears as they waited under rocks and bushes.

When "the storm finally passed," Garabed, accompanied by his sons, resurfaces ever so cautiously only to be told by distraught family members that his brothers Manuel and Nishan were seized from their homes and taken to the "Karakol," police station. (A family story says that one of the brothers was discovered hiding in a tree). A day or two later, Garabed, blinded by the instinct to save his brothers, heads to the police station with a bag of English gold coins. There, ignoring the obvious perils and relying on the respect he had earned in the community, he walks up to *gendarmes* (police officers) and quietly tries to bribe them into releasing his brothers. The officers eye the bag of coins and look around. One of them finally responds: "You are too late! They have already been taken away." By now, Garabed had most surely heard through the grapevine about the bodies of killed men travelers were coming upon in valleys and remote fields throughout the country. He freezes for a moment, stupefied. Only a few days prior, he was together with his brothers Manuel and Nishan in the marketplace, fretting over everyday transactions, customer complaints, and shipments of merchandise detained in war-torn ports. The stomach-churning realization hits him like a ton of bricks. "They are going all out! They are finishing what Abdul Hamid started!" There seemed to be a brazen well-organized systematic program whose synchronized and uniform execution throughout the land belied advanced well-studied planning.

First, the enlisted Armenian soldiers at all army fronts were disarmed, sent to labor camps, and disposed of. This eliminated the remote possibility of the Armenian community calling upon its conscribed soldiers to put up an effective self-defense. Armenians were then ordered to turn in all their weapons. Community leaders and clergy were beaten and tortured in order to disclose where "the guns were hidden." The whereabouts of some self-defense ammunition hidden in churches and public centers were thus revealed under duress. Many families resorted to purchasing new weapons and turning them in to free their loved ones from captivity and cruelty. Photographs of those "captured weapons" were then published in newspapers as proof of activities of unrest and rebellion. Public hangings and the display of the cut-off heads of supposed traitors were designed to strike fear among the masses. Next, the top political leaders, physicians, journalists, and writers were arrested and murdered. The community had consequently lost its voice and was, in a sense, decapitated. There was no one to guide it or communicate its plight to the outside world. All adult males were now being arrested and killed, leaving behind the helpless elderly, women, and children who were being relocated because of the government's mistrust of "the treacherous Armenians who were siding with the Russians." This was, of course, the adopted guise of the decades-old objective of securing land by eliminating its rightful owners. The few Armenian militia *fedayee* bands formed to put up some semblance of self-defense were not organized at a military level and in no way a match to the Turkish army.

Livid and in shock, Garabed heads back home to inform his brothers' wives and children of the terrible news. I can only imagine how he felt, leaving the Karakol, having failed to save his brothers, knowing that he himself was living on borrowed time. No amount of money could bring them back. Soon afterward, the authorities deport his brother Nishan's widow and four children: Khosrof, Meguerdich, Markrit, and Satenig. Entire families were being told that they were to be relocated for "their safety" until the war ended. This was another absurd lie, meant to coax the Armenians to co-operate and leave. Malatya was miles and miles away from the war frontlines on the Bosporus and in the Caucasus. The order said to pack immediate needs and leave everything behind and meet at the town center. Their homes were going to be kept untouched until their return, and they were forbidden to sell anything they owned. Indispensable tradesmen who offered necessary services to the armed forces as well as to the infrastructure of the country could apply for a special permit to stay on. Garabed, determined to postpone his family's deportation as long as he could, presents himself to the town authorities to apply for this exemption. His pride put aside, he waits patiently for his turn; then proceeds to fill out exemption forms for his family and as many relatives as he can. Halfway into this process, the office runs out of copies of the form, and the officer behind the desk asks him to turn in the forms that he had already completed. My great-grandfather hesitates. He needs an additional copy of the form in order to turn in the names of a few more relatives. He walks away from the desk towards chairs in a waiting area as another officer announces that they have no additional forms left and orders the remaining Armenians in line to go home and prepare to be deported.

Overwhelmed by the heavy task at hand, Garabed sits on one of the chairs, holding on to the cushion to calm his nerves as the names of his relatives keep on looping in a torturous refrain in his mind. Anguished complaints rising from the line of Armenians add to his misery. In his desperation, he does the only thing that was left to do. He shuts out everything happening around him and starts reciting the Lord's Prayer: "Ya Sourp Adsvadz, Oh Dear Almighty… Hayr

Mer vor Yerginkn es… Our Father in heaven…" As he aims his eyes at the sky, the edges of his fingers encounter what feels like a piece of paper. He pulls the piece of paper from under the cushion and looks at it. It was a copy of the form he was looking for! Without a minute to spare, Garabed fills out the names of his remaining family members. He then makes the case for the indispensability of his family's expertise in fabric dyeing. He explains that the Tavitians are currently the only expert fabric dyers in the area, and the military, as well as the aristocracy, have come to depend on the excellent quality of their fabrics. "Their deportation would be detrimental for the area's garment industry." The officer looks impressed and tells my great-grandfather that, from that day on, his family will be under the protection of the government and will be allowed to stay with approved identification cards on the one condition that they immediately hire local Muslim Turks and teach them all the ins and outs of their craft. To this day, the Tavitians profess having been "saved by a piece of paper."

Luck, however, had not smiled upon my grandmother's family in another neighborhood of Malatya. Maryam Arpadjian, her parents and younger brother, her older sister Nartuhi with her two children Lucine and Kegham, and her sister Elizabeth were all waiting in the middle of the ensuing chaos for the caravan of deportees to take shape. Her 16-year-old brother Maynuel, as well as her sister Nartuhi's husband, were already taken away by the authorities with the rest of the able-bodied young men. Her parents had packed valuables, money, and food for their journey. They had stepped out of their home, leaving behind the safety, warmth, and precious memories it beckoned onto them. All around them were acquaintances and families stricken with uncertainty and fear, clutching carefully prepared bundles of travel clothes, dried fruits, breads, and cheeses to sustain them in the journey ahead. Muslim spectators, gendarmes with bayonets, and Turks with red fezzes perched on horses were circling them, all waiting for the moment the caravan would start its journey on foot. On the night we met them, our newfound relatives completed my father's sentences, and he theirs, as they told about what ensued next.

As the line of deportees swelled and the hour drew near, more and more Turkish and Kurd spectators appeared, adding to the panic of the deportees. They had heard that groups of Muslims often followed caravans of deportees in order to attack, rape, and loot them in remote areas. Cries of helplessness at first muffled were now becoming more audible in the crowd. As my grandmother's family tries to stay together in the mayhem, they suddenly discern their Turkish next-door neighbors negotiating with a gendarme and pointing towards their direction. As the dreaded order comes for the lines to start marching, their neighbors, man and wife, hurry towards them and notify them that they had arranged for the adoption of the Arpadjian kids. The lady pushes the children behind her and stands her ground. Maryam and her siblings are motioned by their parents to do as their neighbors say. A gendarme was now bellowing at my grandmother's parents to get moving. After a last glance, her parents advance towards the deportees. Maryam and her siblings start crying for their parents but obey them in staying put with their Turkish neighbors. At the last moment, as the caravan was turning the corner of the street, my grandmother's younger brother cries, "I want to go with mommy!" He breaks his siblings' hold and runs after his parents.

No sooner than the dust from the line of deportees settles that a horseman who had witnessed the scene from the sidelines approaches the Arpadjian children with his assistant, points at Elizabeth, and proclaims, "Send that one to my home." Both my father and Vartug disclose that they had heard from their parents that Elizabeth was exceptionally beautiful. The horseman was a wealthy and well-reputed *Agha*.[35] Elizabeth is sent to his home as the rest of the children head to their neighbors' house. It is then that Nartuhi realizes that her son Kegham is missing and nowhere to be found. She had lost

---

35 Agha was an honorary title given to a civilian or military officer. Some court functionaries were also given this title

sight of the boy in the chaos and mayhem. Once in the shelter of their neighbors' house, she unleashes a desperate cry for her son. Fearful of revealing their true identities, cognizant of the necessity to lay low, the siblings feel helpless as Nartuhi's desperation and cries about her son worsen day by day. In the meantime, Elizabeth agrees to marry the agha, who already had two other wives, on the condition that he retrieves her brother Maynuel from the authorities. With the help of the last family photo they had taken, the agha identifies Maynuel at a labor camp and secures his release. Maynuel joins his sisters at their Turkish neighbors' home. Nartuhi's lamentations about her son Kegham do not cease until they eventually drive Maynuel to his feet. At 17, he takes off, vowing not to return until he finds his nephew Kegham. He spends the next several months traveling from one village to the next, disguised as a Turk, looking for his nephew. Almost a year into his search, he arrives at a village where he goes through his routine of inquiring about the child, at this point barely going through the motions, dreading the looming fact that he will soon need to give up and head back home, when he hears a voice calling, "Dayday, dayday," "Uncle, uncle." Kegham, now almost a year older, had recognized him among the pedestrians. He had survived in the streets with other abandoned Armenian orphans, feeding on scraps of food tossed their way.

For a while, they all live with their Turkish foster parents, helping and assisting with chores. The agha ends up marrying Elizabeth, a circumstance that inspires shame in her siblings, who distance themselves from her. Marriage between a Christian Armenian and a Muslim Turk was a disgraceful taboo at the time. When the massacres ease off, Maynuel goes to work. He works day and night and saves all his earnings. He finally presents himself at the door of his parents' house. When the Turks who had broken into it open the door, he offers them his hard-earned savings and purchases his family's home from them.

In the meantime, Nishan Tavitian's (my great grandfather Garabed's killed younger brother) deported sons, Khosrof and

Meguerdich, make their way back home minus their mother and sisters Markrit and Satenig. The caravan of deportees they had joined was forced to march on foot for months on end, exposed to the elements and without food or water. It seemed that they were being herded in circles so that they died from hunger and exhaustion. In an interview I conducted in 2019 with Mrs. Marie Tavitian Bedoyan, Nishan's granddaughter, she informed me that her father Khosrof would tell her that wherever the gendarmes let them camp, his mother would sleep in the middle with two kids on each side because she wanted them at an arm's length from her. One day, exhausted from walking endless miles while keeping her four young kids in tow, she places her youngest infant daughter Satenig under a tree and carries on with the other three. When the caravan is ordered to camp for a break, she secures her three children with other deportees and goes back to the tree only to find that her Satenig is no longer there. Weeks later, her daughter Markrit, exhausted and feeble from hunger and dehydration, is lying on the ground, unable to continue with the caravan. When her mother prods her to stand, an inpatient gendarme comes over and kicks the child so hard that he sends her to the other world. Khosrof and Meguerdich continue on with their mother until the morning they wake up to find her dead, lying in the position she was sleeping in between the two of them. We do not know under what circumstances the two brothers return to Malatya. It is possible that my great-grandfather was able to locate them when international organizations assisted with the resettlement of orphans. All we know from family accounts is that the two orphaned brothers were, from that point on, under the care of their uncle Garabed.

The few remaining Armenians in Malatya do their best to fend for their families. From a community of 20,000 prior to the Hamidian massacres, only about 200 remain, mostly artisans.[36] They witness the government's precipitous settlement of Muslim refugees into the

---

36 Akçam, *Young Turks' Crime*, 248.

homes of their Armenian relatives, friends, and neighbors who were deported with assurances that their houses and properties would be safeguarded by the government and returned to them after the war. As survival dictates, community members set up clandestine meetings between prospective single Armenians with the particular intent to settle orphans into homes. The Tavitian household was ready to welcome some joy after older son Napoleon's death from kidney failure. So it was that Sarkis, son of Garabed Tavitian, was set up to meet Maryam Arpadjian on the way to the hammam (the great baths). My grandparents were married very possibly at night-time in a quiet ceremony not to attract attention. Maryam settles in with the Tavitians. Theirs was apparently quite an elaborate compound with adjacent houses in a cul-de-sac. According to one of the descendants we later located in New York, Bible verses were etched in a semicircle at the entrance of each house. On the right side of my grandparents' wooden gate, a piece of stone etched with a prayer from a destroyed Armenian church was incorporated into the wall of the fence.

As I came to learn, this is how my family coped.

The Tavitians feel terrible for the tragic plight of young Khosrof and Meguerdich, who had come back from the deportation routes terribly emaciated. Great grandmother Varter makes nourishing the two boys a household priority, even asks my pregnant grandmother to give her portions to poor Khosrof and Meguerdich. Maryam and Sarkis are soon blessed with the birth of their first child, a daughter. They live as best as they can under the cloud of war and the ongoing persecution of their compatriots until one fateful night, which our research and discussions place around 1923. The war had ended in 1918. The Ottoman Empire was defeated, and its Middle Eastern territories were divided among the Allied Powers. Kemal Ataturk, a hero of the Gallipoli battle (a singular but important battle won by Ottoman Turkey during WWI), had risen to power as the first president of the newly formed Republic of Turkey. By spearheading the Turkish National Movement and declaring Turkey a Republic,

Ataturk had halted the partition of the mainland of Turkey by the Allies and was advancing a nationalist movement of Turkification.

My grandparents' new baby was colicky and, on that particular night, was crying inconsolably.

Great grandmother Varter decides to fetch some fresh water for the baby from the well in the courtyard. As she lowers the bucket, she notices in the water the reflection of ropes being lowered from the fence wall. Looking up, she discerns the shadows of men about to jump over. Panic-stricken, she starts screaming at the top of her lungs. At this, Garabed opens the door. One of the assailants hits him on the forehead with the butt of a baton. Garabed loses consciousness momentarily and collapses onto the floor. Hearing the commotion from their bedroom, my grandfather Sarkis reaches for his handgun[37] just as their door is flung open. The man at the door has a turban covering his head and mouth. Their eyes meet. "*Ahmet senimisen*? Ahmet is that you?" asks my grandfather, recognizing his so-called friend from the marketplace. Ahmet's eyes, previously filled with evil determination, lose their focus, and he abruptly recoils to head back out. My grandfather, shocked by the assault and not knowing what else is ensuing in the rest of his household, aims and shoots after the attackers, hitting one of them in the leg. As he reaches the courtyard, he comes onto a scene of utter chaos. His cousins next door were jumping over their fences to come to their rescue, and his mother was wailing over his father in the doorway as several disguised men, alarmed by the sound of gunshots and fearing being outnumbered, were running toward the fence. They help their injured friend over and disappear beyond the walls.

According to my mother, my grandmother Maryam called that day the day of *Atash Oglu Ylderem Ordusu* (The Turkish word-by-word translation is "Fire Sons Lightening Army"). Apparently, my grandmother opened up on occasion to my mother while they cooked in the kitchen and told her about that evening. Years later, other

---

37 According to relatives, the government protection they gained through the exemption they received allowed my grandparents to keep a gun.

relatives introduced to us by Ilda and Vartug confirmed this terminology. They repeated the same name, "Atash Oglu Ylderem," given to the mobs that included criminals released from jails to attack, loot, and "finish off" the remaining Armenians in Malatya and elsewhere *ad libitum*. For many years, according to Ilda, people would apparently point out a limping man and tell each other that he was the one Sarkis Tavitian had shot!

The entire Tavitian clan sat together that evening, trying to recover from the assault they had endured and to come up with a much-needed exit plan. It was Garabed, his head still aching from the blow he had received, who decided their next step. They all had to leave immediately. He would stay behind to see what he could salvage from his business and would follow them later. Somehow, word was sent out to my grandmother's family and her sister Elizabeth about what they planned on doing. Even before the first light of dawn, a caravan of several donkeys, carrying the wives and children of my great-grandfather's deceased brothers, Manuel's widow, her eldest son Hagop with his wife Nvart and toddler Manuel (named after his killed father), her younger son Avedis, daughters Hripsimeh and Noyemzar (at this point in my research I could not find out about what had happened to the third daughter, Terfanda. I only knew that she had not made it to Lebanon), Nishan's orphans Khosrof and Meguerditch, my grandfather Sarkis and his brother Krikor, my grandmother Maryam and her newborn and great grandmother Varter, all disguised as Kurds, made its way towards the mountains leading down to Syria. They took with them food, water, and many small rugs to lay down on in the forests and fields ahead. They wore special fabric belts in which were sewn most of their 24-carat gold jewelry as well as cash. Also in their cargo were special large oil cans prepared years prior, with secret compartments at the bottom where they had hidden their English gold coins. Anyone who looked down into them would only see the oil. Ilda added that, for years after the Armenians left, Turks would open holes in the walls of abandoned homes and dig in the ground of courtyards and gardens to find "hidden gold and treasures" the owners thought they would come back for. As they climbed hills and mountains, they witnessed from afar an atrocious carnage. They stayed away from prying eyes as long as they could. *Chetehs*, criminals whom the government had released from prison and enlisted to massacre Armenians, came upon them several times. My father says that is how they came to lose most of the jewelry and money they had in their belts. They bribed some Chetehs into staying away from them by offering jewels and money, while other Chetehs downright robbed them. They finally made it into disease-infested Aleppo, Syria (part of the Ottoman Empire then).

Aleppo was where the caravans of thousands of deportees from all corners of the country were led and, from there, forced into death marches into the Syrian Desert. They were denied food and water. They were robbed, raped, mutilated, shot at, massacred, and burned alive by waves of Kurds, Chetehs, and Turkish gendarmes as they dragged their emaciated bodies through the desert of Deir El Zor. This was the end of the road for thousands of Armenians who were deported or relocated away from the supposed "war zones" in order not to assist the Russians! Gendarmes bet on the sex of fetuses as they cut open pregnant women's bellies. Children were stolen away from their parents' arms, thrown in harems, or sold as slaves. Young boys were taken away, circumcised with kitchen knives or swords, and forcefully converted to Islam, forever losing their Armenian identity. Malaria, typhoid, and dysentery ran rampant because of rotting cadavers. Rivers on the deportation routes such as the Euphrates are said to have run red with the blood of freshly massacred men, women, and children and were later infested with decaying body parts. The final destination, the desert of Deir El Zor, is the mass grave of thousands who were rounded and killed there. To this day, all you have to do is scrape the top layer of dirt on mounds of soil to find bones.

The Tavitians arrive in Aleppo, having lost most of the money they had on hand, but with all the gold coins at the bottom of the oil cans intact. A few months after settling in, my grandparents' first-born falls ill with one of the diseases plaguing the area (most likely Typhoid). Unfortunately, she is unable to recover and dies. Hearing that conditions for refugees were better in Beirut, the Tavitians move to Lebanon, which was at that point under a French mandate. Great-grandfather Garabed joins them there, safe and sound, but forever a broken man. He never discusses the trials and tribulations he went through during his solitary journey out of Turkey. He only mentions that the authorities would inquire about his sons during regular visits to his shop. He would tell them that they were running business-related errands in Aleppo and would soon be back. His experiences must have affected him deeply as he unfortunately never recovers from his internal turmoil and passes away about eight months after arriving in Beirut in 1926. His sons Sarkis and Krikor open a fabric and custom tailoring store in downtown Beirut, and they name it the *Tavitian Frères*.

The store becomes quite a landmark where famous politicians, high-ranking military, and the Lebanese bourgeois come to have their suits made. Years later, it is mentioned in several publications, including Henri Edde's *Le Liban d'ou je viens*.[38] They also rent apartments on two floors in a new building in Gemmayze. Sarkis and Maryam are blessed with three more children: Ankine, Garbis, and my father Kevork. My grandfather's brother Krikor marries Haigouhie Kassakian, and they have two sons, Vahak Napoleon (named after his deceased uncle) and Edward. My father fondly remembers his grandmother Varter asking all the grandchildren to sit in a circle on the floor and telling them, "*Dghak mer yerkereh bidi yerkenk*, children we are going to sing our songs." He recalls her conducting an Armenian song from Malatya with her meaty hands, a song that started with the word *lucine* (moon). Years later, my sister and I were raised in the same apartment as my father. Upon Sarkis

---

38 Henri Edde was a famous Lebanese architect and later politician. He served as Lebanon's Minister of Public Works and Transport in 1970, and Education Minister in 1972

and Krikor's deaths, the Tavitian Brothers store passed on to their children. It burned down in 1975 during the Lebanese Civil War, 50 years after its opening. In the safe, the deed of the house in Malatya, ever so carefully and preciously saved for decades by my grandfather Sarkis, sat in layers of baked ash.

Arabo's Song (written in the 1890s by Fahrat, the Armenian *ashough* (bard) from Moush, in memory of freedom fighter Arabo)[39]

Khuzhan askyar zork e zhoghovel	Mobs of soldiers have gathered
Yekel msho dashtn e patel	Surrounded the plain of Moush
Sultan kuze jnjel mezi	The Sultan wants to wipe us off
Zartir lao mernim kezi	Awake my son, I die for you
Kheghj mshetsin merav lalov	Poor Moushetsi died drowned in tears
Otar yerkêrner man galov	Walking through foreign lands
Merav turkin partkê talov	Died paying taxes to the Turk
Zartir lao mernim kezi	Awake my son, I die for you
Inch anitsem turk askyarin	Should I curse the Turkish nation
Vor êspanets joj apoyin	Who have killed our chief Arabo
Mer huys toghets ororotsin	They left our hopes in the cradle
Zartir lao mernim kezi	Awake my son, I die for you

---

39 https://musicofarmenia.com/song-number-seventy-nine-zartir-lao

THIS IS A MORE THAN 100-YEAR-OLD PHOTOGRAPH FROM MY FATHER'S COLLECTION OF THE BURIAL OF HIS UNCLE NAPOLEON TAVITIAN, GARABED TAVITIAN'S ELDEST SON. IN THE FRONT ROW FROM LEFT TO RIGHT, STANDING NEXT TO THE PRIEST IS MY GREAT-GRANDFATHER GARABED. NEXT TO HIM IS MY GRANDFATHER SARKIS WITH HIS HEAD LEANING DOWN, AND NEXT TO HIM IS HIS COUSIN HAGOP (GARABED'S BROTHER MANUEL'S SON). HAGOP HAS PLACED HIS RIGHT HAND OVER HIS BROTHER AVEDIS'S SHOULDER. NEXT TO HAGOP IS MY GRANDFATHER SARKIS' YOUNGER BROTHER KRIKOR LOOKING DOWN TOWARDS HIS DECEASED BROTHER NAPOLEON (YEARS LATER, HE GAVE HIS OWN SON VAHAK, NAPOLEON'S NAME AS MIDDLE NAME). NEXT TO KRIKOR IS AN OLD MAN (POSSIBLY A RELATIVE OR MATERNAL GRANDFATHER) HOLDING ON TO KHOSROF AND MEKERDICH (MY GREAT-GRANDFATHER GARABED'S YOUNGER BROTHER NISHAN'S SONS). NOTEWORTHY IS THE ABSENCE OF MANUEL AND NISHAN, WHICH MAKES US THINK THIS PICTURE WAS TAKEN AROUND 1918-1920 WHEN THEY WERE ALREADY KILLED.

MY GRANDMOTHER MARYAM AND GRANDFATHER SARKIS
(PHOTOS FROM FAMILY COLLECTION)

A PICTURE OF THE TAVITIAN BROTHERS FABRIC STORE IN DOWNTOWN BEIRUT. MY FATHER IS STANDING IN THE MIDDLE, MY GRANDFATHER SARKIS IS ON HIS RIGHT, AND HIS UNCLE KRIKOR IS ON HIS LEFT. THE STORE BURNED DOWN IN 1975 AT THE START OF THE LEBANESE CIVIL WAR. PHOTO FROM MY FATHER'S COLLECTION.

MY GRANDPARENTS MARYAM AND SARKIS (TOP ROW), MY AUNT ANKINE, GREAT GRANDMOTHER VARTER AND MY UNCLE GARBIS (BOTTOM ROW). MY FATHER IS NOT IN THIS PHOTO BECAUSE HE WAS NOT BORN YET. FROM OUR FAMILY'S COLLECTION.

ONE OF THE LAST STANDING HISTORIC ARMENIAN HOUSES IN
MALATYA (REPORTED TO HAVE BEEN DEMOLISHED IN 2019)

PHOTO © 2022 MATTHEW KARANIAN, REPRINTED WITH
PERMISSION FROM *THE ARMENIAN HIGHLAND.*

Questions and More Questions

IT IS ONE THING TO hear a chronicled story. It is another to mentally process it. Questions swarmed my mind when I first heard my paternal grandparents' story. I wanted to know what happened to the siblings my grandmother had left behind in Turkey. I wanted to know more about her brother Maynuel. He was left in charge of his sisters, spent a year looking for his nephew, and worked hard to gather enough money to buy his parents' home back from the Turks who had broken into it! What determination and what courage! Vartug and Ilda shook their heads positively: "Yes, he was a very strong man!" He later married an Armenian girl named Vartuhi and had five children of his own: Bedros, Elmas, Krikor, Manoushag, and Yepraksi. Vartug and Ilda were Krikor's children. I was stunned with the realization that I was looking at the grandchildren of my grandmother's brother Maynuel! They also spoke of their other sister Elizabeth whom they hoped we would meet soon. "Elizabeth?" I inquired. "Yes, father named her after his aunt," smiled Ilda and added that their grandfather Maynuel had not approved of that name and acted a bit reserved around their sister. "So, what happened to Elizabeth, my grandmother's sister?" I inquired. They shared that she passed away quite young, apparently from uncontrolled high blood pressure. She had, of course, most likely converted to Islam, at least outwardly, and had children with the agha. Ilda remembered the names of a couple of them: Saadet and Makbule. "Did you guys used to see them?" I pressed further. "No, not really" was the answer. I wondered if Elizabeth's own grandchildren knew that their grandmother was Christian Armenian.

I was quite astonished when I first found out that my father had visited Malatya with his mother in 1951. My grandfather Sarkis had apparently refused to join them. When I inquired why that was the case, my father said that as an energetic child, he kept on prodding his father to come along on their trip, but his father, who was a quiet man, would not respond. One day, however, he motioned to my father to come near him and whispered softly, "Son, one day during the Genocide, I was disguised as a Turk when the authorities started hurtling Armenian refugees close to the bank of the river. I ran up the hill and hid behind a rock. They had brought butchers and started slaughtering the Armenians and throwing them in the river, which turned red in no time. Son, I do not wish to go back because I still hear their cries!" My father says that his father's confession affected him so that it still rings in his ear. I read in several books that many deportation routes passed through Malatya. We do not know in what context my grandfather was near a river when he witnessed those killings. Was it during another raid in Malatya before the family's exemption from deportation, or were these deportees passing through when they were attacked? Most Genocide survivors did not want to talk about what they had endured and witnessed. They were very likely suffering from post-traumatic stress[40] and opted not to face their hurtful past.

My father told us about his trip to Turkey with his mother. He remembers crossing over a valley via train. He was speaking in Armenian to his mother, and two Turkish men sitting across from them recognized the language. As they were passing over the deepest point of the valley, one of the Turks pointed to my grandmother and father and told his companion in Turkish, "We slaughtered so many of these Giavours in this valley!" My grandmother became distraught and started shaking. She advised my father to stay quiet

---

40 Rubina Peroomian, *Literary Responses to Genocide, The Second Generation Responds* (Yerevan: Armenian Genocide Museum-Institute, 2015), pg. 26

when they were in public. I found the unabashedly racist and vile remark of that Turkish passenger to be quite a bold admission of the deeds his countrymen had committed.

My father remembers that his uncle Maynuel kept him busy with chores such as watering the trees in the garden. He also recalls his mother taking him to a Turkish household, where children ran towards them, calling his mom by an endearing Turkish word. He says he never made much of it back then. I could tell from his distant look that he was trying in vain to recall further details of that visit. My grandmother never told him who those people were and why she wanted to visit them. We can now guess that they were her sister Elizabeth's children and that, like the rest of her siblings, my grandmother kept that inconvenient family secret under wraps. I found Elizabeth's fate particularly tragic. She most likely felt powerless in facing her circumstances. After all, her parents were not around, there were no authorities protecting her community, and she, like hundreds of other Armenian women, was at the mercy of Turkish men preying on their vulnerability. How could she have fought the agha? Resisting could have cost her and her siblings' lives. How traumatizing and disturbing it must have been to be forced to marry into a Turkish household while her parents were driven to their death by Turks. And how wrenchingly hard it must have been to be forced to convert to Islam, forever letting go of her people's age-old traditions and the Christian faith into which she was born. How can anyone survive the loss of their identity? It is perhaps not surprising that she suffered from hypertension! And yet, she must have been such a strong woman to be able to summon her courage to convince the agha to help get her brother Maynuel released and assist her family in weathering the many challenges they would face.

My grandmother wished to see her Malatya home one last time. My father describes walking through a gate and a courtyard. The two-story main house on the left "looked like a mansion," and there were stables and workers' quarters facing them. When they knocked on the door, a Turkish lady opened and looked at them attentively.

My grandmother asked if she could possibly take a look inside the house because she used to live there. The lady understood and bid them inside. As she neared her old bedroom, my grandmother started shaking uncontrollably again. She observed that everything "was left in the same way" as she remembered it as a newlywed. My father remembers that the room had diamond-shaped wood wall paneling. The lady was kind and hurried to fetch a glass of water for my grandmother. Before leaving Turkey, they took several family portraits with my grandmother's relatives as was the custom in those days, for the sake of memory, *hishadag*. My father was also able to fulfill the one favor his father had asked of him: to find their "*teinturier*" fabric dyeing stores and dip his fingers in one of the dye barrels. My father describes dipping his fingers in a large container full of a dark colored dye and returning to Beirut with the proof of the fulfillment of his promise. He had taken his father's wish very seriously and had made sure to have someone take him to the marketplace where his family's stores were by then being run by Turks.

FRONT ROW, SEATED, FROM LEFT, KEGHAM, HIS WIFE AND CHILDREN, MY
GRANDMOTHER MARYAM, MY FATHER, MY GRANDMOTHER'S BROTHER MAYNUEL'S
ELDEST DAUGHTER ELMAS. TOP ROW, FROM LEFT, THE REST OF HIS CHILDREN: BEDROS,
YEPRAKSI, MANOUSHAG, AND KRIKOR (VARTUG & ILDA'S FATHER). MAYNUEL HAD
OPTED NOT TO BE IN THE PICTURE. PHOTO FROM MY FATHER'S COLLECTION.

It seems that my grandmother felt comfortable opening up to
my mother about her past. Maybe she wanted to spare her own
children from the details of her ordeal and found in my mother a
discreet confidante to whom she could unburden things weighing
on her heart. In the privacy of our kitchen, she would tell her about
the night they escaped from Turkey, the night of *Atash Ylderem,* as
she called it. She would also confide to my mother that she often
thought about her younger brother, whom they failed to hold back.
She would wonder about his fate. Her parents and brother had
walked away with the other deportees on that fateful day, never to be
heard of again. There were, however, stories about young Armenian
children who were snatched away from their parents and abducted
by Turks, Kurds, or Bedouin Arabs, Islamized and assimilated into

Turkish society. "What if he survived?" she would wonder. "What if Kurds raised him?" "She always wondered," shared my mother.

Our first meeting with our long-lost relatives was a shock to my system. I had grown with the story of the Armenian Genocide, but discovering the unique story of my father's family brought it home on a different level. Most of the characters involved were strangers to me except for my grandmother Maryam whom I had come to know in my early childhood. My beautiful, patriotic grandmother apparently had to stand behind and watch as her parents were marched to their death. Did her parents put on a brave face and feign normalcy not to alarm their children just like my parents did during the Lebanese war? Did they assure them that they would be safe with their Turkish neighbors? Did they advise them to stay strong and that they would surely reunite when the war ended? And how did they comfort and distract their youngest boy on the deportation route? Did they tell him stories, jokes? Sang to him? How long did his young legs endure the miles and miles of travel on foot? How did they meet their fate? Who died first? Where are their remains resting? We will never know.

That evening, I felt the curtain surrounding my life start folding aside to finally reveal what had been following me throughout my life. All the strange feelings embedded in my DNA, the inexplicably familiar foreign smells and sentiments that would invade my heart and my senses out of nowhere, all were explained and laid to rest. As the conversation woven out of Armenian and Turkish words continued between my parents and my newfound relatives, I mentally stepped away to a place where things were peacefully clear. Suddenly, my feet grew cold, and the night breeze was causing goosebumps on my skin. My parents were out. It was nighttime on our balcony in Dhour Choueir. The moon was bathing us with its light. I was shivering. "Dessar! Do you see? They are gone... gone...! They are dead, dead!" Echoed my grandmother's anguished voice...

"I see, Nene. I see now..."

Hit the Books

It was fall of 1988. I was working as an intern pharmacist at a chain drug store. One day, a tall, large-built man in his sixties approached the counter to pick up his prescriptions. When I asked for his last name, he pronounced it so fast that I requested that he spell it out. I had been in the country for all of four short years and was still honing my English. My slight accent was not lost on this gentleman, who became visibly irritated and spelled out his name so quickly that I could not grab the sequence of the letters in his long Scottish or Irish-sounding name. I was forced to ask him to spell his name out one more time: "slowly please.*" At this, he snapped in a derisive tone, "Where the hell...What part of the world are you from? Why don't you go back to where you came from?" I was astounded, but I kept my composure as I found a match to the spelling in the computer, verified his date of birth, and located his prescription orders. "Can you spell my last name?" I muttered under my nose as I took his medication vials out of the bag to consult him on their usage. He squinted, tilting his head sideways as if asking, "Did you say something?" I feigned nonchalance and carried on with my work.*

Yes... where was I from, and why was I here?

WHILE ONCE I IGNORED MY father's ancestral stories, I had now become consumed with them! I wanted to know everything, every last detail. I started reading ferociously about the Armenian Genocide. I wanted to comprehend how this atrocious calamity had befallen my people. It seemed that my schooling in Lebanon had focused mainly on the era where Armenia had taken up Christianity, the different Armenian kingdoms and dynasties, and from there had transitioned to the literary work of authors and poets from the time of the Genocide and its aftermath. There were big gaps in my knowledge about the times preceding and between those eras, and I was eager to uncover all the missing information. I wanted to go even further back and find out about the origins of the Armenians. I wanted to learn about Urartu, ancient Armenia, established in 860 BC. That's 860 years before Christ! I hoped to delve more into the stories of the Armenian kingdoms and medieval princehoods and the different powers that came to rule over them. What was life like under the Byzantine, Persian, and later the Ottoman and Russian Empires? How did the Genocide take shape, and how did we end up with the small Soviet Republic of Armenia?

I learned that in 782 BC, the Urartian King Argishti founded the city of Erebuni, the ancient name of today's Yerevan, capital of Armenia, and that Armenians were so eager to take up Christianity in the year 301 that they had effectively destroyed all traces of their pagan past and built new churches and monuments atop the foundation of pagan temples. I read that the famous Silk Road passed through our ancient city of Ani (capital of the Armenian Bagratid Dynasty) and that the Armenian Kingdom of Cilicia on the southern Mediterranean coast was founded in 1198 by the refugees of the principalities of Ani after its destruction by the Seljuk Turks. I also discovered that the crusaders had a dominant presence in the Kingdom of Cilicia, where they acquired architectural techniques of castle building, particularly the construction of arches and circular towers! The European castles they were accustomed to up to that point were built in the shape of a square.

I returned my attention to the Genocide. In the 1980s, rumors circulated within the Los Angeles Armenian community that the Turkish lobby had stopped not one but several productions of the movie adaptation of Jewish author Franz Werfel's novel *Forty Days of Musa Dagh*. I was oblivious to what the story was about, so I picked up a copy and began reading. When I was done with the book, I understood why Turkey would object so vehemently to the movie version coming out. After all, the novel was based on the true story of 5,000 Armenians who had refused to obey the order of deportation, knowing full well that it was tantamount to a death sentence. They had instead retreated to Moses Mountain, *Musa Dagh*, in today's Hatay province of Turkey and put up a resistance for 53 days. As a Turkish army unit started a full-blown offensive on the refugee camp, these desperate, hungry, diseased, and injury-ridden Armenians resorted to climbing down the opposite side of the mountain and were finally rescued by French naval ships that detected the huge Red Cross flag they had sewn and placed on the side of the mountain. While thousands of Armenians had been killed without anyone knowing how they had met their deaths, those on Musa Dagh had lived to tell the world how Turkey was hell-bent on killing men, women, and children for the mere reason that they were Armenian.

To my astonishment, I learned that most of the Musa Dagh Armenians were later resettled in the town of Anjar in Lebanon's Bekaa Valley, the same valley where my family went to visit my mother's cousin Hagop and where many Lebanese Armenians fled to during the civil war! I could not believe how close to the actual locales that had witnessed the fateful events of that period I had lived! (The story of Musa Dagh was finally told in a short clip in the 2016 movie *The Promise,* starring Christian Bale and Oscar Isaac).

My next readings were the personal accounts of the American ambassador to Turkey from 1913 to 1916, Henry Morgenthau Sr., in *Ambassador Morgenthau's Story,* a memoir covering his candid talks with CUP leaders and his real-time efforts to relate to Washington the atrocities he was witnessing. Interior Minister Talaat Pasha, the main mastermind of the Armenian Genocide, could not have been any more explicit to the American ambassador about the political expediency of getting rid of the indigenous Armenian minority. He even went as far as to ask him to help submit the names of Armenians who held policies with American life insurance companies, saying, *"they are all practically dead now and have left no heirs to collect the money. It, of course, all escheats to the State. The Government is the beneficiary now."*[41] In a time when communication channels were so rudimentary, how would Talaat have known that all Armenians had "died with no surviving children" had he not ordered their killings himself? Why would he assume that they were all dead if, in fact, the government only intended to "deport" them? He even asked Morgenthau, *"You are a Jew; these people are Christians. The [Muslims] and the Jews always get on harmoniously. We are treating the Jews here all right. What have you to complain of? Why can't you let us do with these Christians as we please?"*[42] And in the clearest terms, he went on to explain the reason behind CUP's decision to exterminate the Armenians: *"The great trouble with the Armenians is that they are separatists. They are determined to have a kingdom of their own, and they have allowed themselves to be fooled by the Russians"*[43] This was a stunningly frank rationalization of the need to wipe out the indigenous Armenians in order to keep their lands. Morgenthau went on to say, *"When the Turkish authorities gave orders for these deportations, they were merely giving the death warrant to a whole race: they understood this well, and in their conversation with me, they made no particular attempt to conceal the fact."*[44]

At a 1988 Armenian Student's Association Genocide commemoration gathering at the university, we were shown clips of testimonials gathered by Professor Richard Hovannisian, chair of Modern

---

41 Henry Morgenthau, *Ambassador Morgenthau's Story* (1918; repr., London: Forgotten Books, 2015), 339.

42 Morgenthau, *Ambassador Morgenthau's Story*, 333, 334.

43 Morgenthau, *Ambassador Morgenthau's Story*, 347.

44 Morgenthau, *Ambassador Morgenthau's Story*, 309.

Armenian History at UCLA. I remember the room going completely quiet. Here we were, Armenian American students hailing from Lebanon, Iran, Russia, Iraq, Armenia, and other countries sitting shoulder to shoulder miles away from our roots in a lecture hall in California! The heart-wrenching details recounted by survivors videotaped by loved ones did not leave a dry eye in the hall. This was our story, the story of all our grandparents, unraveling in most horrific firsthand accounts! As the years went by, Professor Richard Hovannisian's compilation of oral history culminated in over 1,000 survivor testimonials, which can be accessed today at the University of Southern California Shoa Foundation's Visual History Archive. The many books he has written about the history of Armenia and the Armenian Genocide, in addition to the books published by the equally distinguished Armenian historian Vahakn Dadrian, such as the *German Responsibility in the Armenian Genocide,* explained the sequence of events and the different players and factors involved. I was surprised to learn that the Germans, allies of the Turks in WWI, helped them with the planning of their genocidal activities and assisted them in offensive attacks on Armenian villages and civilians when all the while many German nurses, missionaries, and dignitaries were sounding the alarm about the atrocities being committed against Christian Armenians. This made the German Parliament's recognition of the Armenian Genocide in 2016 all the more devastating to the denialist Turkish stance.

Many non-Armenian writers have also taken up the subject matter, such as English journalist and author Robert Fisk who researched the story of the orphanage of Antoura, Lebanon, where under the directive of Ottoman Minister of Navy Jemal pasha, Armenian orphans who had just lost their parents were forcibly Turkified, starved, and beaten for speaking Armenian. Published in 2014, *An Inconvenient Genocide,* by human rights barrister Geoffrey Robertson QC shed light on the complicity Western powers were embroiled in to cover up the Armenian Genocide and obstruct the legal process of justice and reparations for this crime in return for strategic geopolitical favors from Turkey. It explains in clear terms how the recognition of the Armenian Genocide has in many ways become a political bargaining chip with Turkey in the hands of powerful nations and the United States in particular. It is summoned whenever Turkey strays out of line as a NATO ally, triggering Turkish paranoia about the prospect of land and monetary restitutions, and is then returned to the pocket of the American political system to the dismay of Armenians who have been waiting for over decades for justice.

I next read *Vahan Cardashian: Advocate Extraordinaire for the Armenian Cause* by Vartkes Yeghiayan, a compilation of the eloquent letters and observations addressed to the United States government by Vahan Cardashian, a Turkish Armenian lawyer who graduated from Yale in 1908 and was practicing law in New York while the Genocide was taking place in his homeland. The book exposes the inner workings of the U.S. Congress, the politics surrounding the different treaties, and how the Ottoman Empire's Western Armenian lands that President Woodrow Wilson had awarded to the Armenians by arbitration in the Treaty of Sevres were bartered away in the creation of many new partnerships with Turkey, including a percentage of Mosul oil negotiated by the U.S. Standard Oil Company. Cardashian became the initiator of Armenian American activism.

It was, however, the books written by contemporary Turkish historian Taner Akçam that enlightened me the most. Here was a Turkish scholar, one of few, who researched and lectured openly about the Armenian Genocide. I found his books *From Empire to Republic Turkish Nationalism & the Armenian Genocide* and *A Shameful Act: The Armenian Genocide and The Question of Turkish Responsibility*, based on official documents from Turkish government archives most revealing and eye-opening. Akçam's books helped me form a satisfactory understanding of the Triumvirate's state of mind and the economic and demographic factors that came into play in their decision to exterminate the Armenians and confiscate their assets.

His latest book published in 2016, *Killing Orders: Talat Pasha's telegrams and the Armenian Genocide,* earned him the nickname of the "Sherlock Holmes of the Armenian Genocide." By studying the encryption codes in hand-duplicated copies of telegrams sent by Talaat that were acquired during the Genocide from a Turkish officer, Akçam proves the authenticity of the telegram messages and uncovers the highly coveted "smoking gun" of the official order to kill Armenians. His research of Turkish government archives of the same time period has produced the same encryption codes, proving they were not random or concocted numbers.

The fact remains that today's Eastern Turkey comprises the lands of Western Armenia. It is laden with the remnants of Armenian fortresses from the 9th to 7th century BC, such as Urartu kingdom's Van fortress, Armenian cities dating from the 5th century such as Ani, monasteries, and castles from the medieval ages, as well as churches from the Ottoman Empire era. These cultural and religious sites were converted to mosques or barns and given Turkish names, but mostly they are allowed to be vandalized and destroyed in a multitude of ways in order to eliminate all traces of the civilization that produced them. Some of these ruins are displayed to tourists without a single mention of the word "Armenian" on them. The intentional omission of the origins of these monuments, the deliberate destruction of Armenian symbols, letters and artifacts, churches, medieval ruins, and ancient cemeteries, the deceptive revision of history and the appropriation of monuments as Turkish, and the active efforts of denial by the perpetrator nation make the Armenian Genocide an ongoing crime.

In their attempt to secure the land for the Turkish people, the CUP Triumvirate had seen the destruction of the indigenous minorities as the only solution to the definitive eradication of their prospects for autonomy. Not only was the Ottoman Empire in financial ruin and losing distant territories, but it was also facing the prospect of ending up with a fraction of land in the event the Greeks, Armenians, Assyrians, Kurds, and other indigenous peoples on its mainland declared their own national independences. The reason the Ottomans were so passionately opposed to offering their subjects equality and autonomy was that equality and autonomy were in direct contradiction to the system of governance they had created. Equality and autonomy would lead to the separation of the nations they had assembled together in order to create their empire. Calls for freedom emanating from their subjects were seen as acts of treason against their way of living. The connotation of "rebellion" was applied to minorities who were previously cooperating under duress. The ruled indigenous nations were expected to be willing participants in their own homelands' occupation. The Ottomans used their legal system as well as excessive taxation to keep these communities in check. They were forced to accept their subjugation as second-class citizens and not question the ruling class. Any other reaction was deemed unacceptable, disloyal, and "treacherous."

As the remote Ottoman territories where Turks were a minority started shrinking, letting go of the imperial model and creating a nation for Turks in the example of other nations within the mainland of the empire was announced as an urgent holy war by the Turkish leadership, and all crimes to that end were justified to the Muslim population. Purging of the Christian indigenous minorities was also necessary to create a homogenous nation made up mostly of Muslim Turks in order to establish "Turkishness" as an ethnicity. Everything that belonged to the unwanted Christians was up for grabs, even their genetic makeup. This was in line with the Turkic cultural tradition that glorified conquest and considered the capture of spoils as the befitting right of brave conquerors. The six Armenian vilayets were seen as particularly problematic and, in the eyes of the Turkish leadership, the Armenians, in general, had become rivals in wanting to create their own sovereign nation from the empire's mainland. "Turkey for the Turks!" became the mission of the Ottomans as the prospect of losing all their occupied lands became a looming existential threat, and World War I gave the perfect cover to execute it. Jihad authorized the Muslim population to take part in the most heinous crimes against humanity: deportees were attacked and ransacked, men were tortured, dismembered, beheaded, hanged, skinned alive, had their eyes gouged out, nails pulled out, horseshoes nailed in the soles of their feet. Priests were crucified, pregnant women had their bellies cut open and fetuses pulled out, women were raped, sold as slaves, and thrown into harems. Thousands of children were abducted, entire groups of deportees were burned alive in churches and caves, slaughtered with all sorts of axes and hatchets, starved to death, shot at, and drowned in seas.

It took another 28 years for the coinage of a new word, "Genocide," in 1943 by Yale professor Dr. Rafael Lemkin to describe the crime of extermination of an ethnic group. In his own words in a 1949 CBS interview, Lemkin said he saw the need to create a name for such a crime *"because it happened to the Armenians..."* and international laws needed to be enacted to punish and prevent such a crime.

The creation of a Turkish nation also involved the transfer of capital wealth and real estate ownership from the Christians to the Muslims. This not only provided the capital the financially troubled Ottoman government was looking for, but it also helped with the settlement of Muslim refugees from the Balkans and elsewhere into Christian homes and the creation of a Muslim middle class to take over Christian-run businesses and industries. It is with this in mind that they were inclined to hold back Christian professional tradespeople long enough for them to train Muslims in their crafts. My grandfather's family, for example, was exempted from deportation and given protection by the authorities on the condition that they train local Muslims in fabric dyeing. From the destruction of ancient monuments and cultural treasures to the forceful conversion to Islam, the confiscation of movable and unmovable properties and wealth, the transfer of knowledge of the trades, to the wholesale murder of men, women, and children, the CUP had devised a premeditated, elaborate, multi-layered system of annihilation. It wanted Western Armenia without the Armenians, and it can be said that it was successful in achieving just that.

The Armenian Genocide was a Turkish policy that had started with Sultan Abdul Hamid II, kicked into high gear by the Triumvirate Pashas (who, during the same period, also orchestrated massacres of Armenians in what was to become the country of Azerbaijan), and finished by Mustafa Kemal Ataturk, the founding father of the Republic of Turkey. It is not only one of the most documented and studied genocides, but it is also one of the most devastating based on percentage of population killed. After all that was said and done, of the estimated 2.4 million Armenians who lived on the Ottoman mainland prior to the Hamidian massacres, almost 75% to 80% were killed between 1894 and 1923 (this precludes the number of Armenians who were massacred by the Azeris within the same time span). Christian minorities, who combined formed a substantial 20% of the Empire's population in 1914, are today at a meager 0.2% of the Turkish population. While Armenians attributed the famous Ottoman comparison of Armenians to "cancer" to xenophobia and bigotry, it is now becoming more evident that the Turkish leadership had employed scientific and mathematical precision of demographic reengineering in eradicating the "cancerous" community and rendering it powerless. From deporting to resettling in largely Muslim areas, separating members of communities by a distance of a given number of kilometers, prohibiting the founding of Armenian schools in Anatolia, keeping the Armenian population below 10% and even 5% to keep it from having government representation, to forceful conversion to Islam and outright massacres for expediency's sake, the goal was to clear the land of a viable Armenian presence and solve the Armenian Question once and for all. The immediate activation of corrupt laws to oversee the confiscation and distribution of the movable and unmovable assets of the deported Armenians and the resettlement of Muslims in their homes also attest to the fact that Turks saw the ousting of Armenians as final. My grandmother's childhood house and the house she shared with my grandfather were both immediately settled by Muslims. At no time were there any attempts by the government to return these to their owners/heirs, nor to make monetary restitution for them.

As sinister, inhumane, and methodical as it was, the Armenian Genocide was also a testament to human resilience, goodwill, and survival against all odds. It would be a terrible omission not to mention all the American missionaries, European and Canadian nurses, Arabs, and even Turks and Kurds who saved Armenians. Particularly noteworthy is the crucial role that American Ambassador Henry Morgenthau Sr. played in the 1915 founding of the Near East Relief Foundation. It was the United States' first modern-day large-scale humanitarian project of the 20th century, which set the standard for future overseas humanitarian assistance by using for the first time celebrity spokespeople, captivating visuals, and real-life stories. Americans living in that era remember the "Save the Starving Armenians" campaign, which raised millions in aid and saved as many as 132,000 orphans. Many in today's Armenian Diaspora are descendants of the orphans saved by the Near East Relief, in addition to orphans and survivors who were taken up by other countries. Discovering the fact that the American newspapers of the day had covered the Armenian massacres in real-time and the Near East Fund had literally prevented the extinction of my people both astonished and humbled me as an Armenian American. While I was currently living in an America that had no recollection of those events, I felt extremely grateful for the generosity and humanity that my adopted country had shown to the immediate survivors of the Armenian Genocide.

Many Armenians had also saved themselves by converting to Islam, forever turning their backs on their ancestry. Others who were converted to Islam by force kept their Armenian identity secret. They clung to their Armenian names and the names of their deceased parents and siblings as long as their memory allowed them. Many survived massacre scenes by sheer luck, covered by a pile of dead bodies or fleeing their capturers in the ensuing chaos or in the dead of night.

While the CUP went to extreme lengths to censure the events, including forbidding photography and limiting the carnage to the Anatolian villages and remote deserts miles away from the capital and the prying eyes of foreigners and journalists' lenses, a German soldier and medic, Armin Wegner, managed to capture many of the iconic photographs of the Armenian plight. Armin Wegner's secret routes of sending his letters and photographs to Germany and the United States were later discovered, and he was arrested by the Germans at the request of the Turkish authorities. He continued fighting for the Armenians, however, and wrote a letter to American President Woodrow Wilson asking him to create a free and independent Armenia. He later became one of the earliest voices to condemn Hitler in his treatment of the Jews. Finally, the stubborn will for perseverance and survival kept deportees walking at all cost, their bodies nothing more than skeletons, their miraculous survival surprising even the Turks. They stopped to bury the fallen or take on the onslaught of renewed attacks. Some ate the meat of dead animals, and some ate the flesh of dead friends and relatives in order to survive the intentional starvation they were being subjected to. They suffered from symptoms of dysentery, malaria, typhoid fever, and dehydration but kept on moving, leaving behind the slaughtered remains and scattered skeletons of their children, relatives, and neighbors in the open fields of their forbidden homeland and the deserts of Syria. The few who survived took upon themselves the duty of perpetuating precious new generations.

Playing a distinct role in the fight for survival were the outnumbered and outgunned Ottoman Armenian citizens who volunteered to form irregular units of *fedayeen* (freedom or resistance fighters) and took up arms to defend their villages and families. Their activities were mostly overseen by the leaders of the Hnchak, Tashnak, and Armenagan Armenian political parties, whose efforts of national defense and liberation were portrayed as treasonous by the Ottomans. While all weapons were confiscated from Armenian civilians, being under the protection of the government while he taught his craft to local Muslims had allowed my grandfather to keep a gun. By wielding it on the eve of Atash Ylderem, he was able to protect his family and chase the attackers away. The cooperating unarmed masses, on the other hand, were led to their deaths like cattle. While the heroic tales of many of the Armenian *fedayeen* ended up buried under the rubble of their obliterated villages or were stifled at the gallows, it was the valiant efforts of many others, such as the citizens of Van and Musa Dagh that saved lives. These citizens refused to give up their guns and be slaughtered like sheep. They held on to dear life, buying precious time, hoping that the Christian Allies would come to their rescue or their brethren in the Russian army would reach them on time.

The Russian army, with its Armenian volunteer units on the front-lines, did, in fact, reach deep into Anatolia, as far in as Erzurum. However, once at the sought-out posts, instead of assisting with the liberation of the Anatolian (Western) Armenians as promised, the Russians disbanded their Armenian battalions and started retreating by order of the Bolshevik Revolution's leadership, leaving the Armenians to their fate. The Tsarist regime had fallen with the ousting of the Imperial Romanov family. In March of 1918, The Russians and the Ottomans put an official end to their war by signing the Peace Treaty of Brest-Litovsk. Taking advantage of the Russians' withdrawal, the Ottomans proceeded to attack Erzurum. Out of ammunition and outnumbered, the Armenian units sustained major losses and abandoned their positions. The Ottomans continued advancing, taking back even the territories that had previously come under Russian control in 1855 and 1878, such as Kars. The fleeing Armenian population was subjected to rape, plunder, and all sorts of atrocities by the incoming Turkish army, which was now entering Eastern Armenia.

Faced with true annihilation, the Russian Armenian volunteers, together with Tashnak party leaders and remnants of Anatolian irregular units, formed an impromptu army and made a last stand in Yerevan. It is with heroic victories in battles at Sardarapat, Karakilisa, and Abaran that the Armenian armed forces, together with the public at large, dealt major blows to the Turkish army and succeeded in pushing it back. Church bells rang incessantly, calling to arms men, women, children, and even the clergy to fight for their lives and their nation's survival. These crucial victories halted the Ottoman goal of wiping out Armenian existence and creating a Pan Turkic bloc, a desire that still burns in Turkish and Azeri propaganda and remains a security threat for the current Republics of Armenia and Artsakh.

On May 28, 1918, in the political vacuum caused by the fall of the Russian Empire and on the heels of the victories it registered, the Armenian leadership took a leap of faith and declared the independence of the first Republic of Armenia, comprised mostly of the Eastern Armenian lands previously under Russian rule. The defeat of the Ottoman Empire and the end of World War I in November of 1918 prompted the Armenians to defend some of their remaining positions in Western Armenia while waiting for the Allies to materialize their vow to reward them and punish the Ottoman Turks for the atrocities they committed. The new Armenian Republic was not only poorly armed but also burdened by 300,000 desolate refugees who had fled from Anatolia (Close to 180,000 of these refugees would die by 1919). The Treaty of Sevres was signed in August of 1920, awarding Armenia most of the Western Armenian provinces in Turkey, in addition to access to the Black Sea at Trabizon. However, in total disregard for the League of Nations' official recognition of sovereign Armenia, and the terms of the Treaty of Sevres that called for Turkey to also recognize the sovereignty of Armenia as well as withdraw its armed forces from the territories awarded to the Armenians, Mustafa Kemal, who was now forging an alliance with previous foe Russia, in violation of the Armistice ceasefire, attacked Armenia in 1920 in what he called the Eastern Operation of the Turkish War for Independence from the "occupying" Western

Allies. The name "Turkish Armenian War" that is also given to this operation is misleading and intends to distract from the Turkish side's blatant contempt of the Treaty of Sevres by presenting the invading aggressor with superior military advantage, and the victim, barely coming out of a genocide, as equals. At the same time, the Bolshevik Russians advanced to reoccupy Eastern Armenia (while the future Azeris, the Tatar Turks, were attacking the Armenians in Nakhichevan, Zangezur and Karabakh). Attacked on both sides, the newly established fledgling Armenian Republic surrendered to the Russian Red Army, as the alternative was genocide by Turkey, and reluctantly agreed to annex itself to the newly forming Soviet Union in order to safeguard its people. The first independent Armenian Republic that had lasted only two years thus became the symbol of an unattained dream of sovereignty that Armenians continued yearning for.

ARMENIAN ORPHANS OF THE ORPHANAGE IN ALEXANDROPOL (GYUMRI IN TODAY'S ARMENIA) FORMING A MESSAGE OF THANKS TO AMERICA AND THE NEAR EAST FUND. SOURCE: NEAREASTMUSEUM.COM HTTPS://NEAREASTMUSEUM.COM/2019/10/30/ HOUSE-RESOLUTION-296-RECOGNITION-AND-REMEMBRANCE-OF-THE-ARMENIAN-GENO

The Treaty of Sevres and Justice for Armenians

How can a country deport three-quarters of an indigenous minority population, murdering the majority of them, confiscating their properties, assets, and lands, annexing their ancestral homeland... and get away with impunity? I wanted to know...

SINCE THE 1970s, ARMENIAN COMMUNITIES around the world, made up of direct descendants of survivors, have taken it upon themselves to revive the Armenian cause and work towards recognition and justice for the Armenian Genocide. Their grassroots efforts are constantly curtailed by a powerful Turkish lobby and an official campaign of denial that has gagged the mouths and covered the eyes of powerful nations terrified to upset a strategic geopolitical partner with acute sensitivities. And yet, from what I found out, back in 1920, it was these very same countries that had championed the Armenian cause and come monumentally close to leveling harsh retributions at Turkey. They pushed to convict those who had perpetrated massacres and had awarded three of the Armenian vilayets of Anatolia to a sovereign Armenia several times the size of current-day Armenia. Most notably, Ottoman Turkey conceded to their terms! The same Turkey that today emphatically denies having committed the Armenian Genocide and adheres to a self-imposed national dementia.

The Allies first held the Paris Peace Conference to set the terms of peace with the defeated Central Powers. Some of their chief accomplishments were the creation of the League of Nations (predecessor of the United Nations), the idea of awarding territories previously held by Germany and the Ottoman Empire as "mandates," mainly to Britain and France, and the drawing of national boundaries by referendum to more closely reflect ethnic boundaries. They invited many diplomats and countries to participate and contribute to their proceedings, including an All-Armenian Delegation (headed by Boghos Nubar Pasha and Avedis Aharonian), which presented a proposed map for a unified Armenian state that included Western Armenia with all six Armenian Turkish Vilayets, the province of Trabizon, and four districts of Cilician Armenia, in addition to Eastern Armenia including Javakhk, Nakhichevan, Karabakh and Zangezur (also known as Syunik). To protect the integrity of the new state, the delegates also asked for Armenia to be put under the protectorate of an Allied power. Five treaties were signed at the Paris Peace conference. The fifth one was the Treaty of Sevres.

The Treaty of Sevres, drawn fifteen months after the November 1918 Armistice of Mudros that put an end to WWI, was the closest the Allied nations came to holding Ottoman Turkey accountable for the crimes against humanity it had committed. The newly established independent Republic of Armenia was suffering from a terrible humanitarian crisis. Thousands of livestock were slaughtered and consumed by the invading Turkish army in 1918, and thousands more were taken away on their way out by early 1919. The granaries were bare, and there was a serious shortage of food. Skeletal refugees who had poured into Yerevan escaping from the Genocide were dying by the thousands due to hunger and the breakout of Typhus.[45] Surrounded by Turkish and Bolshevik forces, the Armenians were waiting anxiously for the Allied nations to act on

---

45 Richard G. Hovannisian, preface to Bedross Der Matossian, *The First Republic of Armenia (1918–1920): On Its Centenary: Politics, Gender, and Diplomacy* (Fresno, CA: Press at California State University, 2020).

their wartime promises of rewarding them with their ancestral lands in Western Armenia and righting all the wrongs they had suffered at the hands of the Ottomans. While the Russian Empire had been more sympathetic towards the Armenians, the revolting Bolsheviks seemed to have a completely opposite view. The resulting Russian change of heart in regards to the liberation of the Armenians of Western Armenia had been quite detrimental. This betrayal belied the Bolshevik ambitions of reoccupying the newly independent Transcaucasian countries, and reinstating Russian imperialism with a modified version of their fallen empire. The Russians did not like the fact that the Allies had acquired the Ottoman territories, and were planning on awarding lands, including those that until recently were under their control, to the Armenians. Previous foes, the Russians and Turks now had a common objective: to push the Europeans and Americans out of their region. The Russians, in fact, wanted the fallen Ottoman mainland, with its maritime borders and access to the critical Dardanelles, for themselves. In 1917, they had abandoned the Armenian troops to the mercy of the Turks, whom they now considered more desirable allies. However, with the support of the British, who arrived in Kars after the withdrawal of the Turkish troops as dictated by the Armistice, the Armenians regained their positions there as well as several other surrounding cities in Western Armenia. They even installed an administration in Nakhichevan in preparation for the Treaty of Sevres, which was set to award them even more of their ancestral land.

The treaty was signed on August 10, 1920, in Sevres, France, by the victorious Allies represented by Britain, France, Italy, and the United States, and the defeated members of the Central Powers, the Ottoman Empire, Germany, Austria-Hungary, and Bulgaria. Russia was not a party to this treaty since it had already exited the war by signing the Peace Treaty of Brest-Litovsk with the Central Powers earlier in March of 1918. The treaty of Sevres divided the Ottoman mainland into British, French, Italian, and Greek zones of influence and placed British mandates over Iraq and Palestine and

French mandates over Lebanon and Syria. The British also called on the Americans to vote on a mandate over Sovereign Armenia, whose borders were to be drawn by U.S. President Woodrow Wilson's state department.

I studied in amazement the sections in the Treaty of Sevres dedicated to extracting justice for Armenia. The following were some of those terms:

ARMENIA.

ARTICLE 88.

Turkey, in accordance with the action already taken by the Allied Powers, hereby recognises Armenia as a free and independent State.

ARTICLE 89.

Turkey and Armenia as well as the other High Contracting Parties agree to submit to the arbitration of the President of the United States of America the question of the frontier to be fixed between Turkey and Armenia in the vilayets of Erzerum, Trebizond, Van and Bitlis, and to accept his decision thereupon, as well as any stipulations he may prescribe as to access for Armenia to the sea, and as to the demilitarisation of any portion of Turkish territory adjacent to the said frontier.

ARTICLE 90.

In the event of the determination of the frontier under Article 89 involving the transfer of the whole or any part of the territory of the said Vilayets to Armenia, Turkey hereby renounces as from the date of such decision all rights and title over the territory so transferred. The provisions of the present Treaty applicable to territory detached from Turkey shall thereupon become applicable to the said territory.

ARTICLE 144.

The Turkish Government recognises the injustice of the law of 1915 relating to Abandoned Properties (Emval-i-Metroukeh), and of the supplementary provisions thereof, and declares them to be null and void, in the past as in the future.

The Turkish Government solemnly undertakes to facilitate to the greatest possible extent the return to their homes and re-establishment in their businesses of the Turkish subjects of non-Turkish race who have been forcibly driven from their homes by fear of massacre or any other form of pressure since January 1, 1914. It recognises that any immovable or movable property of the said Turkish subjects or of the communities to which they belong, which can be recovered, must be restored to them as soon as possible, in whatever hands it may be found...

ARTICLE 230.

The Turkish Government undertakes to hand over to the Allied Powers the persons whose surrender may be required by the latter as being responsible for the massacres committed during the continuance of the state of war on territory which formed part of the Turkish Empire on August 1, 1914. The Allied Powers reserve to themselves the right to designate the tribunal which shall try the persons so accused, and the Turkish Government undertakes to recognise such tribunal. In the event of the League of Nations having created in sufficient time a tribunal competent to deal with the said massacres, the Allied Powers reserve to themselves the right to bring the accused persons mentioned above before such tribunal, and the Turkish Government undertakes equally to recognise such tribunal.[46]

With their signatures, the representatives of the Ottoman Empire at the Sevres recognized the sovereignty of Armenia, whose borders were drawn by the U.S. State Department. It included three instead of all six Armenian Vilayets that the Armenian delegates had asked for at the Paris Conference as well as access to the Black Sea at Trabizon. It did not include any of the Cilician lands that the Armenians had asked for. Cilicia was instead placed in France's zone of influence. The Allies also included language acknowledging the historic Armenian lands in the Caucasus (Karabakh), directing in the treaty's Article 92 that the state's eastern border demarcation be finalized in direct negotiations with neighboring Azerbaijan and Georgia and that the League of Nations would decide those borders itself in the event an agreement was not reached (as also discussed in chapter about Karabakh).

Article 92

The frontiers between Armenia and Azerbaijan and Georgia respectively will be determined by direct agreement between the States concerned.

If in either case the States concerned have failed to determine the frontier by agreement at the date of the decision referred to in Article 89, the frontier line in question will be determined

---

46 Treaty of Peace Between the Allied and Associated Powers and Turkey Signed at Sèvres, August 10, 1920, accessed April 10, 2021, https://wwi.lib.byu.edu/index.php/ Section_I,_Articles_1_-_260.

by the Pricipal Allied Powers, who will also provide for its being traced on the spot.[47]

The Ottoman government's representatives also agreed to turn in the perpetrators of massacres and allow an international court to try them, as well as return all confiscated property and businesses to their owners or to the communities they belonged to. The American government was set to vote on a mandate over Armenia during negotiations. Coming at the heel of the end of WWI, the treaty's terms reflected all the wartime righteous promises the outraged Allies had made in response to the heinous WWI Ottoman crimes that were still fresh in everyone's consciousness, promises that lamentably would turn out to be too good to be true.

The Treaty of Sevres was doomed for failure for several reasons. First, the terms of the treaty were conditional on their ratification by the Ottoman government and the principal Allied Powers, who, opting not to put additional troops on the ground, relied on Turkish repentance and cooperation. For the nationalist conservative Turks, this offered the opportunity to buy time, reassemble and rise up against the moderate Turks, who had agreed to the terms of the treaty, as well as the Allied powers which were now occupying Constantinople. The treaty was set to diminish the size of the Turkish mainland dramatically, a scenario that Turks had been agonizing over ever since their territories in the Balkans and Eastern Europe had started breaking away. In order to retain the mainland where most Turks lived, the CUP had preemptively massacred indigenous minorities, including three-quarters of the Armenian population, to stop the formation of an independent Armenia.

Pressured by the British, who were overseeing Constantinople, the Sublime port (the government of the last Sultan of the Ottoman Empire) established the Turkish courts-martial (1919-1920) and

---

47 DiPublico.org, Derecho International, *The Treaty of Sèvres, 1920 (The Treaty Of Peace Between The Allied And Associated Powers And Turkey Signed At Sèvres August 10, 1920)* Oct 22, 2010.

blamed its rival, the CUP, for all the atrocities and war crimes perpetrated during WWI. Notably, these trials took place after the CUP Triumvirate Pashas responsible for the Genocide had safely fled the country following the Armistice. Damning evidence in military records was produced from different provinces. A first list of CUP officials was tried and convicted for subversion of the Constitution, wartime profiteering, and massacres of the Armenians and Greeks, and the CUP Triumvirate, Talaat, Djemal, and Enver were sentenced to death in absentia (Operation Nemesis of the Tashnak Armenian Revolutionary Federation would later hunt these fugitives from the law and assassinate them). The Turkish courts found that it was the intent of the CUP to exterminate the Armenians via its Special Organization and ordered the disbanding of the party. Soon, however, the implementation of the terms of the treaty of Sevres came to a halt with the launch of the Turkish National Movement led by Mustafa Kemal (later known as Ataturk), a celebrated officer who took charge of the Ottoman army.

This movement eventually gave rise to the Turkish War of Independence waged against the Allied nations and the moderate Turks who had capitulated to them. As the nationalists gained ground, a provisional government replaced the sultanate and announced that considering the political divisions and lack of national unity, it could not ratify the Treaty of Sevres. Under mounting pressure from the Kemalists, the Turkish tribunals stalled their proceedings and did not return additional convictions for the remaining CUP operatives. This frustrated the British, who took the trials away from the Turkish courts and transferred them to an international court in the British colony of Malta. There, the detainees were held for three years while the British, French, and Americans studied laws that could permit the conviction of war criminals outside the jurisdiction of their areas of residence. Their work was sabotaged by the lack of transparency of the Turkish courts-martial and their refusal to submit documents of evidence in their possession.

The European international courts finally contended that there was no legal framework available that allowed moving the trials forward. In the early 20th century, there were no international laws in place to prosecute war criminals. The word "Genocide" was not even invented yet. Subsequently, the international courts stopped their proceedings and released their detainees in exchange for 22 British POWs whose lives Kemal kept on threatening in retaliation to the trials. Kemal proceeded to apprehend the Turkish representatives who had signed the Treaty of Sevres by stripping them of their Turkish citizenship, and executed several of their supporters. He halted the proceedings of the courts-martial altogether and pardoned those who were serving sentences! All incriminating evidence was destroyed or lost. Even prior to the proceedings of the courts-martial, testimonials exist by Turkish and German officials regarding the Triumvirate having purged archives leading up to the Armistice and Talaat pasha burning a suitcase full of documents in the basement of a friend before fleeing the country.

Having regained control of most of the Ottoman mainland, the Kemalists took up the CUP mantra of *Turkey for the Turks* in earnest by massacring more Greeks, Armenians, and now Kurds who were working on a referendum for the borders of a sovereign Kurdistan also based on the terms of the Treaty of Sevres (The Kurds failed to produce a referendum outlining the borders of a Kurdish homeland. An indecisiveness that would prove to be quite costly). Violent uprisings against Allied forces, particularly in the French zone of influence in Cilicia (south center of today's Turkey) that prompted the Franco-Turkish wars (1918-1921), further eroded the resolve of the Allies. The French, who had deployed a French Armenian Legion (unit in the French army made up of French Armenians and foreign Armenian volunteers), wanted to control the coal mines of their zone of influence and return the refugees of the Armenian Genocide back to their homes. Guerrilla warfare and brutal terrorism by the Turks in the entire region of Cilician Armenia, especially in Marash, prompted the withdrawal of the

French units who, ashamed of abandoning the Armenians to their fate, chose to cover the hoofs of their horses with sacks and retreat in the dead of night, leaving the Turks to massacre the Armenian refugees (5,000-12,000 killed) who had just resettled in the area. Hundreds of Armenian churches, schools, and monuments in the area were then destroyed.

Catolicos Sahak II of the Great House of Cilicia[48] managed to escape from Sis (last capital of the Armenian Kingdom of Cilicia) with some members of his parish. After a journey through Syria, he established the Holly see of Cilicia in Antelias Lebanon in 1930. Growing up, I came to love the main church in Antelias. I attended many wedding and holy day masses there and had aspirations of spending a whole lifetime enjoying its services!

The second reason the treaty fell apart was Kemal's cunning enlistment of Russian aid in his war against the Greeks, and his promises of siding with the Bolsheviks against the "Allied Western Imperialists who wanted to take over the region." He excelled in propaganda warfare assigning to the West that which the West had vilified about the Ottomans: Imperialism. Since the Turkish institutions were bankrupt, the Russians offered Kemal serious amounts of gold and weaponry to battle the Allies. Russia's backing proved to be critical in Kemal's fight for an independent Turkish republic. The Greco Turkish war culminated in 1922 with the Turks setting the coastal city of Smyrna (the area of influence the Treaty of Sevres had offered to the Greeks) on fire, killing another 100,000 to 180,000 Greeks and Armenians in the blaze. Kemal also started negotiating with the Allied nations separately and pinning them against each other. It did not help that the latter were distracted,

---

48 The Armenian Catholicosate had moved southbound to Sivas in 1058 after the fall of Ani, the Bagratid capital, eventually settling in Sis, the capital of the Armenian Kingdom of Cilicia. In 1441 a new Catholicos of All Armenians was elected in Holy Etchmiadzin, while the retiring Catholicos in Sis remained as the Catholicos of the House of Cilicia. Since 1441, the Armenian Apostolic Church has had two catholicosates: the Catholicos of All Armenians in the Mother See of Holy Etchmiadzin and the Catholicos of the House of Cilicia (in Antelias, Lebanon since 1930).

clamoring for their part of the spoils of victory. In particular, Britain, France, and the United States were embroiled in a major quarrel regarding the acquisition of oil fields in Mosul, Iraq. Ironically, while these countries put aside their noble plans of achieving justice for the Armenians, it was Armenian oil expert Calouste Gulbenkian[49] who ended up resolving their quarrel. Britain, with its mandate on Iraq, was to receive half the share of the oil that was still to be recovered from reserves, and France and the United States were to get a quarter share each.

Thirdly, a most devastating blow to the Armenians came shortly prior to the signing of the Treaty of Sevres from the one country that had been essential in preventing their extinction: America. My heart sank as I read about the vote that took place in the American Senate on May 29, 1920, regarding a mandate over greater Armenia to help it transition to full independence. While U.S. President Woodrow Wilson was given the authority to draw the border between Armenia and Turkey in an arbitral award, the U.S. Senate rejected the proposed American mandate over Armenia 52 to 23, based on military and governing concerns in a hostile region. The Bolsheviks had assembled their forces and were poised to invade Armenia in order to reoccupy it and prevent an American mandate. In return for their cooperation, they were willing to return to the Turks the Armenian lands in Anatolia. The Wilsonian Armenia proposed in the Treaty of Sevres was the embodiment of the Armenian nation's 600-year yearning for an independent, free and united homeland. Oh, to be able to roam free along the shores of Van, the foggy plains of Mush, the mountains of Sassun... The U.S. Senate vote screamed the tragedy of Armenia, the dream of unification of the fatherland that slipped from a precipice while coming so close to be realized.

---

49 Calouste Gulbenkian, born in Constantinople, had studied petroleum engineering at King's College, London, and had been the driving force behind the formation of the Turkish Petroleum company. Known as Mr. 5 Percent for his personal share of Middle Eastern oil, when Gulbenkian died in 1955, he was the richest man in the world.

The Treaty of Sevres proceeded without a mandate over Armenia, which proved to be the downfall of the Armenians who needed a strong guarantor of the security and integrity of the lands being awarded to them in a most hostile environment. For a nation that had earnestly adopted Western ideals and values, this was a major letdown. The American missionaries in the Ottoman mainland had played a big role in educating thousands of Armenian pupils and instilling in their minds the concepts of national identity and freedom. They were on the frontlines of protecting the Armenians and informing Washington about the atrocities they were being subjected to at the hands of the Ottomans. Thousands of articles were written by major American newspapers informing the world about the plight of the Ottoman Armenians and garnering the support of Americans. Between 1894 and 1922, The New York Times had published hundreds of articles about the Armenian massacres; 124 articles in 1915 alone.[50] The constant flow of news from the missionaries, along with the reports of the American Ambassador Henry Morgenthau Sr. perpetuated the founding of the American Near East Fund in 1915 in response to the Armenian and Assyrian Genocides. If it were not for the Near East Fund setting up refugee camps and caring for thousands of orphans, the Armenian people would have probably not recovered. American assistance, however, would stop at humanitarian aid. Without the support of a major Western power, Armenia became easy prey to Russia and Turkey.

Confident that the Allies would not come to the assistance of the Armenians, and in complete defiance of the Treaty of Sevres, Kemal reoccupied Western Armenia and proceeded to invade the fledgling new Armenian Republic (Eastern Armenia). This time, however, he was coordinating his military advances with his allies, the Russian Bolsheviks, who attacked Armenia from the east. Exploiting the burgeoning rivalry between the Allies and the Russians, Kemal had

---

50 Margaret C. Tellalian Kyrkostas, "U.S. Media Coverage," University of Minnesota: Center for Holocaust & Genocide Studies, https://cla.umn.edu/chgs/collections-exhibitions.

succeeded in enlisting the full support of the Russians who, just a couple years prior, had used the Armenians in their advancement into the Ottoman Empire. The Bolshevik-Turkish rapprochement was not lost on the Allies, who were now wary of a Russian Turkish partnership, and were reevaluating their support of the Armenians. The Armenian leadership pleaded to the Allies for their intervention but received no response, a predicament that would sadly repeat. Kemal promoted this operation as the Eastern Front of the Turkish War of Independence from "Western Imperialism". Attacked from all sides, the Republic of Armenia, with its refugee crisis, military disadvantage, and fear of annihilation by the Turks, surrendered to the Bolshevik Red Army in December of 1920, and agreed to join the Soviet Union as the lesser of two evils (the concensus is that were it not for the Soviet takeover of Eastern Armenia, over time, it would have been annihilated by Turkey). The Russians annexed Eastern Armenia and hoped to persuade Kemal to also join the Soviet Union. Using the leverage at hand, Kemal bargained for additional lands from the defeated Armenian Republic for both Turkey and the new SSR of Azerbaijan, and the Russians obliged with the treaties of Moscow and Kars (transferring several provinces to Turkey, and Nakhichevan and eventually Karabakh to Azerbaijan, as mentioned in the chapter on Karabakh). Armenia's borders with SSR Azerbaijan were decided by Stalin instead of the League of Nations as specified in the Treaty of Sevres. Kemal wanted to maximize Armenia's loss of land to diminish its future capability of territorial claims from Turkey and to leave the door open to the culmination of a Turan linking Turkey to Azerbaijan. In their pact to divide the Armenian lands with Turkey, the Bolsheviks even promised to stifle any nationalist movement and sabotage any efforts by the Armenians to regain their Western lands or get reparations for the genocide. Having won the War of Independence and thrown the Allies out of Turkey, Kemal played his hand and pushed for the replacement of the Treaty of Sevres with the Treaty of Lausanne. The Armenians whose units had served in the Russian, British and French armies were excluded from this treaty and further decisions concerning the fate of their homeland. Signed on July 24, 1923, the Treaty of Lausanne ended all conflict between Turkey and the Allies, who were now vying for a Turkish alliance to counter the Bolshevik expansionist plans. Turkey gave up all claims to the previous remote Ottoman territories, and the Allies accepted its new borders.

In October of 1923, the new Republic of Turkey was established, with Kemal, now known as Ataturk, as its first president. Ataturk went on to westernize Turkey, at least outwardly, and kept Turkey's independence by playing the West against the East. Europeans were hopeful and eager to welcome Turkey to the ranks of civilized nations. The book on Western Armenia and the matter of justice for the Armenians were effectively closed. What remained of Eastern Armenia was dismissed as being part of the Soviet bloc. Soon the Allies joined in Turkey's game of forgetfulness and distortion of facts in order to keep their strategic geopolitical ally against the Soviets happy. The same America that possessed the most damning archives on the Armenian Genocide feigned ignorance and started using words more favorable to the Turkish lobby, such as "the alleged" massacres, "civil war," "losses on both sides," etc. Iraq, Palestine, Lebanon, and Syria, who at times resented the British and French and saw them as colonialists, eventually gained their independence from the mandates. While Armenia, as a Soviet republic, ended up with a fraction of its historic lands, the Kurds and Assyrians failed in attaining independent statehoods altogether. In recent years, the Kurds have apologized to the Armenians for their role in the Armenian Genocide. Many have Armenian great-grandparents abducted as children during the massacres of their parents, Islamized and made Kurdish. They see themselves as victims of the Turks who, having used them during the Armenian Genocide, had proceeded to force them to Turkify. The Kurdish language, folklore, ethnic attire, names, as well as the words "Kurd" and "Kurdistan" became officially banned in Turkey. Whoever used the Kurdish language or practiced anything pertaining to the Kurdish culture was arrested and imprisoned. When the Kurdistan Workers' Party rose up against the oppression of Kurds with the intention of founding an independent Kurdish state, the Turkish leadership, along with the United States, the European Union, Australia, and Japan, designated it as a terrorist organization.

Justice for the Armenians has thus been obstructed for the last 106 years, a shameful stain upon civilization. If the leading nations of the world had taken a united stand in making Turkey come to terms with its past crimes and make reparations for them, they would have set a strong precedent, upheld justice, and stood on the right side of history. Instead, enabling Turkey to cover up its crimes for the sake of political expediency has created a culture of treachery, deceitfulness, human rights violations, corruption, and territorial conflicts. The Jewish Holocaust, as well as many genocides that followed, took place in many ways because of the terrible missed opportunity at the conclusion of WWI for a decisive punishment and unequivocal show of intolerance to man's inhumanity to man. In his own words, Hitler pitched his genocidal plans to his generals a week prior to Germany's invasion of Poland, using the world's neglect of the Armenian cause as a reassuring blueprint, saying, "who, after all, speaks today of the annihilation of the Armenians?" Had America invested in a mandate over Armenia, would the region have been in a different place now? No one, of course, knows how things would have turned out. Had justice been served, however, the Armenian and Turkish people could have had the chance to move on from their painful past in the example of the Germans and the Jews. Instead, the wounds and animosities continue to fester.

Although the Treaty of Sevres was never ratified, it remains the single official contemporaneous document where territories of Western Armenia in current-day Turkey are identified and acknowledged by the League of Nations to be part of Armenia, where massacres based on ethnicity are admonished and attempted to be punished, and a legal framework for the return of confiscated properties and assets is outlined in the clearest of terms. The Treaty of Sevres wakes feelings of animosity among conservative Turks as they see it as the treaty that came veritably close to making them lose all the land that their ancestors had conquered. They often pride themselves on having nullified it and replaced it with the Treaty of Lausanne.

However, the Treaty of Sevres was never officially annulled, as that would have cancelled all the other parts of the treaty, in particular those pertaining to the Middle Eastern countries and the map of the Middle East as we know it today. Secondly, the Treaty of Lausanne cannot qualify as a replacement of the Treaty of Sevres because it does not include all the participating signatories of the Treaty of Sevres and does not address all its parts, in particular those pertaining to the Armenians. The Treaty of Lausanne was more of a victory lap for Turkey, as it basically forced the exhausted Europeans and Americans to sign on the dotted line of its one-sided wish list of terms pertaining to Anatolia. And since it was to its liking, Turkey hurried to ratify it. The Europeans and Americans, having secured their interests in the Middle East and Eastern Europe, were also satisfied and ratified the treaty, while justice for the Armenians was sacrificed at the altar of power exclusive to big nations. Armenia simply did not have much to offer, while Turkey controlled the maritime strategic straits of the Bosphorus and Dardanelles. Russia saved Turkey from the brink by preventing its partitioning by the West and assisting it in escaping justice. The West was not interested in the Caucasus. It was, however, invested in pulling Turkey away from the USSR and making it part of NATO. The borders between Turkey, Armenia, and Azerbaijan were left in their arbitrary state, not backed by any viable treaty signed by an independent Armenia, a fact that continues to drive Turkey and Azerbaijan to find a multitude of ways to force Armenia to officially recognize their current (Soviet-era) borders.

MAP COURTESY OF CITIZENSHIP OF WESTERN ARMENIA. IN THIS MAP, THE DOTTED
BORDERS REPRESENT THE MAP PRESENTED ON FEBRUARY 12, 1919, TO THE PARIS PEACE
CONFERENCE BY THE UNITED ARMENIAN NATIONAL DELEGATION BY INVITATION OF
THE ALLIED NATIONS NEGOTIATING HOW TO DIVIDE THE FALLEN OTTOMAN EMPIRE.
THE MAP INCLUDED ALL SIX PROVINCES OF OTTOMAN TURKISH ARMENIA—VAN, BITLIS,
DIYARBEKIR, KHARPERT, SIVAZ, AND ERZURUM, IN ADDITION TO THE PROVINCE OF
TRABIZON, FOUR DISTRICTS OF CILICIAN ARMENIA, AS WELL AS THE FIRST REPUBLIC OF
ARMENIA (EASTERN ARMENIA) INCLUDING JAVAKH, KARS, NAKHICHEVAN, ARTSAKH
AND THE PLAINS SURROUNDING IT. THE ALLIES AGREED TO GIVE THE ARMENIAN
STATE ONLY THREE OF THE SIX OTTOMAN ARMENIAN PROVINCES (VAN, ERZURUM,
AND BITLIS) AND AN OUTLET TO THE BLACK SEA AT TRABIZON (AREA WITH DIAGONAL
LINES). THEY ALSO ACKNOWLEDGED THE FIRST REPUBLIC OF ARMENIA AND THE
ARMENIAN LANDS IN THE CAUCASUS, RESERVING THE RIGHT TO DECIDE ARMENIA'S
BORDERS WITH GEORGIA AND AZERBAIJAN, IN CASE AN AGREEMENT WAS NOT REACHED
BETWEEN THE THREE COUNTRIES. WITH ITS NEW WESTERN BORDER, THE COUNTRY
WAS REFERRED TO AS WILSONIAN ARMENIA SINCE AMERICAN PRESIDENT WOODROW
WILSON DREW ITS BORDERS WITH TURKEY. BOTH MALATYA FROM MY FATHER'S SIDE
AND ADANA (AND ALL OF CILICIAN ARMENIA) FROM MY MOTHER'S SIDE WERE LEFT TO
TURKEY BASED ON THE TERMS OF THE TREATY OF SEVRES (AS SHOWN IN THIS MAP). THE
LANDLOCKED COUNTRY WITH SOLID BLACK BORDERS IS TODAY'S REPUBLIC OF ARMENIA,
THE LITTLE THAT REMAINS OF THE ARMENIAN STATE IN ADDITION TO THE REPUBLIC
OF ARTSAKH (THE MAP REFLECTS ARTSAKH'S BORDERS PRIOR TO THE 2020 WAR)

Map showing the boundaries of Armenia as awarded by PRESIDENT WILSON.

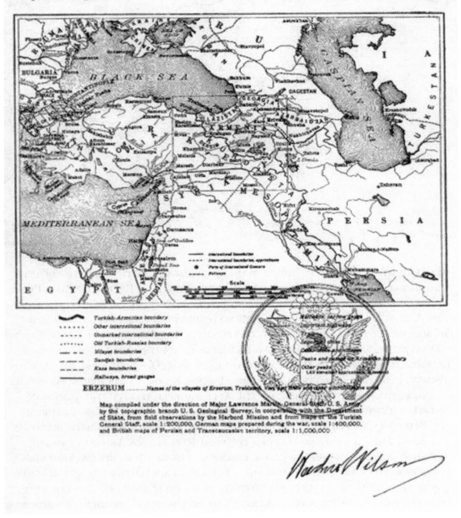

1920 MAP OF WILSONIAN ARMENIA AS AWARDED BY PRESIDENT
WOODROW WILSON'S ARBITRAL AWARD (BEARING THE GREAT SEAL OF
THE UNITED STATES). DOCUMENT PUBLISHED BY THE UNITED STATES
GOVERNMENT. PUBLIC DOMAIN. SOURCE: ARMENIAPEDIA.ORG

WIKIMEDIA FILE: BOUNDARY BETWEEN TURKEY AND ARMENIA AS DETERMINED
BY WOODROW WILSON 1920, PRESIDENT OF THE UNITED STATES OF AMERICA
/ FROM THE PRESIDENT WOODROW WILSON PAPERS (THE PRESIDENT'S
SIGNATURE APPEARS ON THE LOWER PART OF THE MAP). SOURCE: LIBRARY
OF CONGRESS. AUTHOR: WOODROW WILSON. PUBLIC DOMAIN.

Those Who Stayed Behind

WHEN I FIRST MET MY grandmother's relatives and realized that they did not speak Armenian, were not versed in Armenian history or the details of the Genocide, and even their last name was changed, I was overwhelmed with the enormity of the crime committed against my nation. It was not just deportations and massacres. It was the systemic and intentional dissemination of all the layers that made up a society. Everything from culture, language, religious relics, history, community, archeological treasures to individual family trees and heirlooms were desecrated and torn apart with the dual intentions of annihilating a people by genocide and rendering it unrecognizable by ethnocide. Growing up in the era of poet Daniel Varoujan and composer Father Gomidas, my grandmother spoke impeccable Armenian; and yet these second-generation descendants of her family had already lost their mother tongue. They were born in a community where only a handful of Armenians were left, where once thousands had thrived. As a student majoring in biology, I likened this to an unnatural and sudden mutation in the gene pool of a people that manifested its dramatic changes within the span of only one or two generations. A national identity was modified into another, a lineage torn up and altered to look like a different race! This was the impression on the surface, and yet underneath, there were a plethora of unspoken experiences begging to be uncovered after years of silence and hiding. Indeed, there was so much more that we, the Armenians in the Diaspora, were unaware of concerning our brethren left behind. While we were rebuilding our lives and communities in foreign lands, the Armenians in Turkey were enduring ongoing and ever-evolving phases of the Genocide. Many truths and facts started emerging in the late 1990s, in the age of computers and social media, where encouraged by the seeming democratization of Turkey, individuals started putting their guard down and opening up about their experiences. While the Armenian community in Istanbul, where foreigners were abuzz, was accorded a seemingly more tolerant treatment, it was becoming evident that there was a hushed secret layer within the Turkish population of the eastern provinces, that of the hidden Armenians.

Ataturk built upon the groundwork lain by the CUP Triumvirate for a homogenous Turkey with only one ethnic majority and one religion. He turned the entire destiny of the defeated Ottoman Empire around by inventing a new image for the "Turk" and the Turkish nation. He adopted Western ideals, secularized the new Republic, at least outwardly, insisted that Turks dispose of their fezzes (red felt hats with tassels) and old garbs in exchange for European clothing, and changed the alphabet from Perso-Arabic to Latin, effectively promulgating a disconnect with the Ottoman past. This gave way to a national amnesia of events and facts whose archived records in the Arabic alphabet were no longer comprehensible, such as the verdicts from the 1919-1920 Turkish court tribunals that had charged Ottoman leaders of crimes against humanity. Court documents bearing the evidence based upon which the CUP leaders were convicted disappeared, and the Turkish leadership embarked on institutionalizing an alternate history devoid of unpleasant facts surrounding WWI events.

While this metamorphosis was being showcased outwardly, the persecution of minorities and of Armenians continued, manifesting itself in Ataturk's Turkification reforms starting with the Surname Law of 1934[51] (See chapter: *Turkish Armenian Relatives?*). The use of

---

51 Rubina Peroomian, *And Those Who Continued Living in Turkey after 1915, The Metamorphosis of the Post-Genocide Armenian Identity as Reflected in Artistic Literature* (Yerevan: Armenian Genocide Museum-Institute, 2008, 2012)- p. 192

Armenian endings such as –ian or –yan or Greek endings such as –is, -dis, -pulos and –aki, among others, were forbidden. Everyone had to take on a Turkish surname.[52] It is inconceivable to imagine an American President ordering the abolishment of all ethnic-sounding last names and mandating the taking of English ones! So it is that in 1934, my grandmother's surviving brother Maynuel had to obey this law and drop the most important and personal link he had with his murdered parents: their last name, Arpadjian. In exchange, and as the law had suggested, he had taken on as surname the Turkish word that described his profession. The name Arpadjian would only be whispered as a family secret by the grownups. Additionally, a series of laws were enacted to facilitate the transfer of Armenian wealth to the state, giving a legal semblance to policies of outright plunder, such as the law of *Emval-I Metruke* "Temporary Law of Expropriation and Confiscation" (Law of Abandoned Properties) which legalized the confiscation of Armenian properties if the "owners did not return," authorized the settlement of Muslim refugees from the Balkans into seized Armenian homes, and allowed the state to fill its coffers with Armenian wealth. These properties were not "abandoned" of course. Their owners were forcibly kicked out, deported, and murdered! According to my newfound cousins, my grandmother's brother, Maynuel, had to buy back his own parents' home from Turks who had broken in and were living in it! Any and all pretexts were used to extort the wealth of Armenians. A special Commission for the Administration of Abandoned Property was put in place for the storage, distribution, and sale of Armenian properties and the al-location of the resulting funds to specific government departments within the newly forming Turkish state. Some of these funds were even used to cover the expense of deporting! In the thick of the Genocide, laws were adopted by the CUP that forbade Armenians from selling their properties, receiving promissory notes for them,

---

52 "Soyadi Kanunu," accessed April 10, 2021, https://web.archive.org/web/20170107165807/http://www.nvi.gov.tr/Files/File/Mevzuat/Nufus_Mevzuati/Kanun/pdf/soyadi_kanunu.pdf

or claiming them back from authorities that were supposed to supervise them! Armenians were lured into the deportation routes by fake assurances that their homes would be safeguarded by the authorities, while in effect, the settlement of Muslims in their homes sometimes took place within hours of their departure. Armenian real estate properties, personal and business bank accounts, and valuables were unscrupulously stolen by the State and used to balance the sheets of the new Republic of Turkey. Opportunistic corrupt dignitaries lined their pockets with Armenian wealth, and Turkish shops sold all sorts of stolen Armenian jewelry, priceless artifacts, furniture, rugs, and antiques.

While churches and schools were repurposed as military headquarters, hospitals, warehouses, or barns, sprawling real estate properties were turned into hotels, government buildings, military bases, and palaces. Two such properties that stand out are Injirlik, the American airbase in Turkey, and Cankaya Kosku mansion which was used by Ataturk as his presidential mansion and is currently the residence of the Turkish Vice President. Injirlik's runways, warehouses, and commercial buildings sit on land that previously held several houses, farmland, and businesses that belonged to Armenians whose descendants still have the deeds of their stolen ancestral properties. The Cankaya mansion was previously the Kasabian estate owned by Ohannes Kasabian, a jeweler and merchant whose property was confiscated by Turks when he had fled the Genocide. Turkey has repeatedly threatened to shut down Injirlik if America recognizes the Armenian Genocide. I was shocked to find out that confiscation of Armenian property was not exclusive to the Genocide years. Looting of Armenian homes and businesses was allowed by the Turkish government again in 1935, as well as during the 1955 and 1974 riots.

Next came the Turkification and appropriation of all historical sites that belonged to other cultures. Thus, the famous Armenian island of Akhtamar was renamed Akdamar, and Mount Ararat became Mount Agri. In the far eastern suburbs, Armenian villages that were emptied of their inhabitants sat in their ghostly emptiness for years because Turkish villagers were scared of taking over the properties of murdered folk. But, slowly, through the passing years, the Armenian names of these villages were changed to Turkish ones, and the bulldozers leveled the ghostly homes to make way for new roads, shopping centers, and residential buildings. Armenian churches were actively scavenged for treasure, bombed by the army, or used as stables and their stones recycled as building materials in Turkish or Kurdish homes. To this day, many homes in villages have odd stones with crosses and Armenian engravings on them.

During the Kemalist years and in the years that followed, special government commissions were created to change the "ethnic" names of streets, villages, rivers, and mountains, often according them phonetically similar-sounding names. The Special Commission for Name Change (Ad Degistirme intisas Komisyonu) was created by the Ministry of Interior in 1952 to take on the task of changing the names. Approximately 28,000 topographic names were changed, including over 12,211 villages and towns and 4,000 mountain, river, and other topographic names.[53][54][55] This policy continued well into the 1980s until no "foreign" and "confusing" sounding topographic, street, monument, and town center names remained. Non-Turkish names of places were designated as "divisive" and "inappropriate" by the state, which warranted their alterations. If the story did not suit their narrative, the Turks simply came up with creative alternate facts to force the story to fit their narrative. Not only were imported maps mentioning historical regions such as

53 Ali Çaksu, ed. *Balkanlarda slam Medeniyeti II. Milletlerarası Sempozyumu Tebli leri: Tiran, Arnavutluk, 4-7 Aralık 2003* [Proceedings of the Second International Symposium on Islamic Civilization in the Balkans, Tirana, Albania, 4–7 December 2003] (Istanbul: Research Center for Islamic History, Art and Culture, 2006).

54 Harun Tunçel, "Türkiye'de smi De i tirilen Köyler" [Renamed Villages in Turkey], *Fırat Üniversitesi Sosyal Bilimler Dergisi* 10, no. 2 (2000): 23–34.

55 Kerem Öktem, "The Nation's Imprint: Demographic Engineering and the Change of Toponymes in Republican Turkey." *European Journal of Turkish Studies, 7.* (2008). doi:10.4000/ejts.2243. Retrieved 18 January 2013.

Armenia and Kurdistan prohibited but it is said that the state went as far as paying foreign map makers not to mention "Armenia" on their maps. Pictures of Armenian villages and churches taken before and after the Genocide are very critical to the preservation of the Armenians' collective identity and memory. They are naturally very sad to look at. Old black and white prints depicting villages with narrow streets and residential structures with protruding second stories and church complexes with the typical Armenian apostolic architecture, and current pictures where the same villages have disappeared from the landscape or have been replaced by modern cities, strewn here and there with the partial silhouette of the remains of ancient Armenian structures. The name of every Armenian village altered to Turkish, every Armenian church blown to oblivion, and every ancient Armenian cemetery desecrated add to the psychological agony of being the victims of this ongoing, ever-morphing unpunished crime. The Armenian people hang on passionately to these precious disintegrating fragments of their story. And yet there is a myriad of other information beneath the surface waiting to be uncovered, besides the fact that Kharpert is now Harput, Zeitun village is now called Suleymanli, Arax River is Araz, Kayl Ket River is Kelkit, and Norashen is Norsin.

In the early 1940s, the transfer of Christian wealth that was legalized by several temporary Ottoman statutes during the Genocide continued, this time in the form of a national taxation called Varlik Vergisi (Wealth Tax or Capital Tax) imposed by the government of the Republic of Turkey. This 1942 tax, applied to fixed assets, was created under the pretext of raising funds for military defense in case Turkey needed to enter WWII. In the tradition of taking advantage of the cover of world events, the main intention of this temporary tax was to financially ruin the remaining non-Muslim minorities, obliterate them economically, and transfer their wealth into the hands of the state. This extremely disproportionate taxation that targeted non-Muslims effectively destroyed the remaining Armenian, Greek, and Jewish merchant class. Christian Armenians had to pay 232%, Jews 179%, and Christian Greeks 156% compared to the 4.94% tax rate of Muslims![56] This tax could not be challenged in court and had to be paid in cash within 15 days from notice. The panic and chaos that ensued were unimaginable. Folks auctioned off their belongings, businesses, and homes at dirt-cheap prices, even borrowing cash from relatives to pay the taxes, and many committed suicide. This tax accomplished the same goals of the Genocide without the dirty business of massacring, and whoever did not comply was arrested by the authorities on legal grounds of evading taxation! Those arrested were sent to labor camps in Eastern Anatolia, from which many never returned. This tax was severely condemned by Britain and the United States. By the time it was repealed, however, those who survived it were left in ruins and ended up leaving the country, accomplishing the actual intent of the law.

This criminal taxation was news to me! I was shocked when I heard about it from my newfound cousins. Can you imagine paying 232% tax on fixed assets! If 100% is the value of everything you own, where would you get the remaining 132% from? I had to ask how my grandmother's relatives had survived this ingenious way of ethnic cleansing. The answer I received was even more surprising. The agha who had married my grandmother's sister Elizabeth had used his influence to spare his wife's family from this taxation! Wow! There was even more... Laws were put in place that prohibited Armenian schools in Turkey from expanding. As a matter of fact, it was extremely difficult, if not impossible, to get a permit to refurbish or renovate an Armenian school. The maintenance and upkeep of Armenian churches, schools, summer camps, and community centers continue to be sabotaged by the legal system so that they fall in disrepair, close their doors, and disappear. The entire episode of the Armenian Genocide during WWI is skipped from academia, and hateful lies about Armenians are fed to students.

---

56   Corry Guttstadt, *Turkey, the Jews, and the Holocaust* (Cambridge, UK: Cambridge University Press, 2013), 75; Andrew G. Bostom, *The Legacy of Islamic Antisemitism: From Sacred Texts to Solemn History* (Amherst, NY: Prometheus Books, 2008), 124.

The Armenian Genocide remains taboo, and the leadership continues to manipulate the legal system to come up with creative laws to silence dissent. "Article 301" of the Turkish Penal Code that took effect in 2005 makes it illegal to insult Turkey, the Turkish nation, Turkish government institutions, and Turkish heroes. It is a law that can be applied at the government's discretion to any critical expression regarding the state and its governing bodies. In the 1990s, the Armenian Genocide was at the peak of its denial and cover-up phase, where the Turkish government lavished upon American and other politicians free trips to Istanbul and generous payments for contracts with its lobbying firms. Turkey spent millions to cover up the Armenian Genocide, and its lobbies in America were among the most powerful. They stopped the truth from surfacing for years by halting the production of Genocide movies, convincing American Presidents such as George W. Bush and Barack Obama to stop Armenian Genocide Resolutions from passing, and even paying historians to rewrite history with made up lies.

The subject of the so-called "hidden Armenians," or Islamized Armenians, is now attracting great interest. As the Turkish genetic makeup has shown, there is much more Armenianness in Turkey than the Turks allow themselves to accept. Material, physical and cultural destruction could not eradicate the deep-rooted Armenian existence on the cellular, genetic level.

I would have loved to be able to locate my grandmother Maryam's sister, Elizabeth's descendants, and ask them if they knew that she was Armenian. What was her life like? Why did she have an untimely death? Was her name changed to a Turkish one, like it was done to women who were married into Turkish households? How did the agha's other wives feel about her?

Counting how many Islamized or hidden Armenians currently live in Turkey, on the other hand, remains a challenging task, considering the country's sensitivities to the subject and this sector's fears of being discovered. Recent estimates place that number around four to five million.[57] Like the torn pieces of a once beautiful Armenian carpet, with its hues of blues, purples, and reds, patches of the Armenian people live strewn, spread, and lost in the masses but always striving to be found and reunited.

KHTZKONK MONASTERY (PHOTO ON THE LEFT FROM EARLY 1900S) BUILT BETWEEN THE 7TH AND 13TH CENTURIES DURING THE ARMENIAN BAGRATID KINGDOM, IN DEGOR, NEAR THE CITY OF ANI IN THE DISTRICT OF KARS, WESTERN ARMENIA. ACCORDING TO LOCALS, THE CHURCH COMPLEX WAS BLOWN UP WITH EXPLOSIVES BY THE TURKISH ARMY IN THE LATE 1950S. ONLY THE CHURCH OF SAINT SARGIS SURVIVES. THIS IS THE FATE OF THOUSANDS OF ANCIENT ARMENIAN CHURCHES ACROSS TODAY'S TURKEY. CURRENT PHOTO ON THE RIGHT (2014) COURTESY OF ANI HOVANNISIAN'S DOCUMENTARY FILM *THE HIDDEN MAP*.

---

57 "More Than Half of 4–5 Million Islamized Armenians Confess That Their Ancestors Have Been Armenian," ArmRadio.info, November 5, 2013, http://www.armradio.info/?part=1&id=179965.

Sovietization

In 1920, ONCE EASTERN ARMENIA became a Soviet Socialist Republic, the Bolsheviks embarked on neutralizing all nationalist activity by exiling Armenian leaders, mostly those belonging to the Tashnak party, to labor camps in Siberia and executing military leaders, including the heroic generals of Armenia's celebrated victory of Sardarapat. Their message was, "You either submit to us or we will leave you to be massacred by the Turks." In subsequent years, Lenin and Stalin would also arrest, submit to torture, and kill thousands of Armenians, including prominent intellectuals and writers such as Yeghishe Charents and Zabel Yessayan (a survivor of the Armenian Genocide), physicians, and even Khoren I, Catolicos of the Armenian Church. Once again, the prospects of freedom and independence were curtailed. The land was desired minus the rights of its owners. Books about Turkish atrocities and stories of survival during the Genocide were banned by the Soviets. Cultural institutions were stripped of nationalist and patriotic nuance, and churches were sabotaged or closed, and their message ridiculed. In fact, several Christian churches and even mosques were destroyed by the Soviets throughout the USSR. While Kemal Ataturk was Turkifying the remaining Armenians in Turkey, the Soviets were Sovietizing the ones in SSR Armenia. Their campaign to stifle all nationalistic layers in the Armenian society was so terrorizing that it trained Armenians to mistrust each other, avoid nationalism, turn in their own compatriots, and conform to the institutionalized Soviet mold, at least outwardly.

A mere 25 years after the genocide, when the Armenian nation was trying to recover from its catastrophic loss of population, the Soviets sent to the frontlines of WWII's Great Patriotic War against Nazi fascism, somewhere between 300,000 to 500,000 Armenians from all over the Soviet Union (a proportionately substantial number from the smallest Soviet republic), almost half of whom were killed or went missing in action. In return for this sacrifice, the Soviets eased the suppression of national identity in Armenia, allowed some patriotic books and movies, and reduced the restrictions on the Armenian Church. They even considered undoing the Treaty of Kars and returning to Armenia the lands given to Turkey. In light of the start of the Cold War, however, Turkey strengthened its ties with the West. The Western nations, in their effort to join Turkey to NATO, stood against the reversal of the Treaty of Kars, so that Turkey keeps the ancestral Armenian lands instead of the Soviet Union!

In an unexpected hazard, while researching, I came across the familiar names of professors I had heard floating at my old Armenian school in Beirut, Nshan Palandjian Djemaran. Names I had hoped I would revisit in higher grade levels had I stayed at the school. Upon further research, I discovered that poet and playwright Levon Shant, born in Constantinople in 1869, and Armenian Literature professor Nigol Aghpalian, born in Tbilisi in 1875, were both members of the Tashnak party and had held high ranking positions in the government of the first Armenian Republic of 1918! Levon Shant was one of the vice presidents of the Armenian Parliament and in 1920 had headed the Armenian delegation in negotiations with Moscow that led to Armenia being annexed to the Soviet Union. Nigol Aghpalian was appointed minister of education of the first Republic of Armenia in 1919. Both were imprisoned by the Bolsheviks when Armenia surrendered to the Russians. They were freed from jail when the Armenian Revolutionary Federation (ARF/Tashnak party) took control of Yerevan in its last attempted anti-Bolshevik revolt that started on February 13, 1921. The bodies of 21 Karahisar and Sardarabad war heroes that the Bolsheviks had killed with axes in the jails were also retrieved. On April 2, 1921, the outnumbered ARF forces retreated to Zangezur and joined Garegin Njdeh in the short-lived Mountainous Republic of Armenia (southern Armenia),[58] which was itself taken over by the Bolshevik army in July of 1921. As a result of the Armenian resistance, however, Zangezur, today's Syunik, remained part of Armenia. The Bolsheviks proceeded to clean the country dry of the little food it had, and burned all cultural and historic literature they could find, to deplete it of its ethnic identity. Levon Shant and Nigol Aghpalian fled the country and eventually settled in Beirut, Lebanon, where they established Nshan Palandjian School in 1929. Levon Shant was the school's first principal as well as one of the founders of Hamazkayin Armenian Educational and Cultural Society. Both had continued serving the cultural, social, and political needs of the Lebanese Armenian community until their deaths. Upon Levon Shant's death in 1950, Simon Vratsian, born in 1882 in Nor Nakhichevan and last Prime Minister of the first Republic of Armenia, had taken over as the principal of Djemaran! He had accepted the position of Prime Minister of the first Republic of Armenia in 1920 and was the one left with the difficult task of handing Armenia over to the Bolsheviks. During the February 1921 ARF uprising, he had founded the Salvation Committee of the Fatherland, which was meant to govern the country until a new government was elected. With the failure of the uprising however, he had fled through Armenia's southern border into Iran and from there to Europe. In 1945, he presented a petition to the UN General Assembly at San Francisco, California, appealing for the restoration of Wilsonian Armenia. He had eventually settled in Lebanon. Years later, a young Richard Hovannisian[59] showed up in Beirut from Fresno, California. With the guidance of Simon Vratsian, he

---

58 Area including today's Vayots Dzor and Syunik areas in Armenia with some parts of present day Azerbaijan in the West in Nakhichevan and in the East in Artsakh.
59 Professor Emeritus and Historian, UCLA, Armenian Educational Foundation of Modern Armenian History.

prepared the foundation of his self-directed Ph.D. dissertation on Armenian history, which paved the way for an entire body of work in the English language where he pieced back together the multitude of layers of the Armenian story. Finally, Nshan Palandjian's beloved professor, writer, and poet Moushegh Ishkhan, was born in Sivrihisar near Ankara in 1913. He was orphaned at the age of two during the Armenian Genocide. He had escaped to Syria where he lived for a few years. In 1930, he settled in Lebanon, where he attended Nshan Palandjian as a student and later became a teacher there. He ended up publishing novels, poems, plays, and a series of textbooks on Armenian Literature that generations of Armenians in the Diaspora used in their studies.

I was finally uncovering the hidden truths that were tugging at my subconscious while attending my beloved childhood school! I discovered the stories behind the names of these individuals, who had carried on as unassuming everyday professors away from the homeland they had fought for. They were heroes of a generation of Armenians who rescued our nation from extinction with their bold sacrifices and patriotism and who had simply chosen the best out of the worst options they were dealt. All that the Armenians wanted was freedom; freedom they bled for, fought for, and had continuously been exploited for. It must have been so difficult to be in exile, yearning for the elusive and unattained dream of an independent state!

Occupied by the Soviets and dismissed by the Europeans and Americans for being part of the Soviet bloc, the little Soviet Republic of Armenia somehow managed to safeguard its culture, music, and history within the secret confines of communism. In time, it even started making strides in the Soviet education and industrial systems. It remained a closed, tucked-away nation until 1991, when, in the wake of the fall of the Soviet Union, it declared its second independence.

Wedding in the Mountains

In May of 1991, in what became known as Operation Ring, Soviet Internal Special forces and SSR Azeri Omon forces, committing systematic human rights abuses and viciously killing hundreds, expelled the villagers from the fully Armenian inhabited Shahumyan district in Azerbaijan (part of historic Artsakh), as well as the Armenians of Shushi, Martakert and Hadrut within the Nagorno-Karabakh Oblast.[60] The operation was considered as the official beginning of the armed phase of the Karabakh war, and is also viewed as ethnic cleansing. While the collapse of the Soviet Union dominated world news, the Karabakh war had become a central issue in the lives of Armenians all over the world.

On September 2nd, 1991, the Armenians of Karabakh, who had always considered Stalin's decision to award their land to Azerbaijan unjust, announced their independence from the Soviet Union, and formed the Republic of Nagorno-Karabakh. Armenia followed suit in announcing its independence on September 21st. We all rejoiced as Lenin statues were toppled in our homeland, and our ancestral Tricolor flag was raised. On October 18, 1991, Azerbaijan, in its turn, declared its independence from the Soviet Union. A month later, on November 26, 1991, the Azeri parliament abolished the autonomous status of Nagorno-Karabakh and declared an all-out war against the oblast, essentially to cleanse the area of Armenians and absorb it into its lands once and for all. The Azeri government was not

---

60　Human Rights Watch/Helsinki (1994). *Azerbaijan: Seven years of conflict in Nagorno-Karabakh.* New York: Human Rights Watch, p. 9.

entitled to remove the autonomous status of Nagorno-Karabakh by any legal measure or stand against the Karabakh people's right to self-determination. Moreover, it no longer had any jurisdiction over Nagorno-Karabakh, because the autonomous enclave had already seceded from the Soviet Union. On December 10, 1991, the people of Karabakh announced, by referendum, the independence of the Republic of Nagorno-Karabakh (82% of all voters participated, and 99% of them voted for independence). The unrest escalated as senior officers in Turkey took early retirement and arrived to help the Azeri forces. Karabakh was completely blockaded and was being subjected to massive tank, Grad missile, and air bombardments. Essential supplies of food, fuel, water, and medicine reached critical lows, and gas and electricity were cut off by the Azeri government.

Conditions were abysmal. Those thrown out of Azerbaijan in a tempest were reeling with the shock of the barbaric assault they had endured and facing new challenges as refugees. They had to choose between settling into a blockaded Karabakh being shelled daily or an Armenia going through tough socioeconomic times. It was during this time that famous Armenian American singer Cher visited Armenia on a humanitarian trip. She described how citizens were cutting trees in parks to provide firewood for their homes during the cold winter, as the country had no fuel and only sporadic electricity. In February 1992, about two hundred Azeri civilians were killed, caught in the crossfire between Armenian forces and Azeri armed fighters who were interspersed among civilians, using them as human shields, as they were retreating from Khojaly (the killings in question took place miles away in Agdam). During the 1980s, Khojaly, a town near the only airport within the Nagorno-Karabakh Oblast, was the focus of a robust settlement program, where the Azeri government was actively settling Azeris and Meshketian Turks from Central Asia. During the war, they used it as a base from where they continuously shelled Stepanakert, the

capital of Karabakh, causing many civilian deaths.[61] The Armenian
side had previously warned the town of their imminent offensive,
and had announced through loud speakers that a humanitarian
corridor was secured for the evacuation of the residents, however,
the Azeri authorities had ordered the people not to surrender the
town (per witness testimony).[62] During the offensive, the civilians
started fleeing along with armed Azeri militia in two different directions. When they arrived at Agdam, which was at the time still
under Azeri control, a shooting allegedly erupted between the two
sides, and Armenian fighters along with the 366th CIS Guard Motor
Rifle Regiment are said to have opened fire indiscriminately upon
the crowd (mostly civilians with armed troops mixed in) that appeared from the direction other than the one of the humanitarian
corridor. Claims linger about Armenian irregular militia, in the
heat of the gunfight, having taken revenge for the Sumgait pogroms
endured by their families, as well as the incident being orchestrated
by the Azeri opposition leadership itself in order to oust their then
President Ayaz Mutallibov. The official number of victims released
by Azerbaijan immediately after the incident was much lower than
the number later disseminated. (At the time, the Helsinki Watch
and the Human Watch Report held both sides accountable for the
tragedy and found no proof that the Armenian fighters acted on
orders of their commanders). However, Azerbaijan maximizes the
incident's anti-Armenian propaganda value, going as far as calling
it a genocide to sow hatred and undermine the Armenian side's
legitimate accusations of genocide. Unabashedly, two months later
in April of 1992, the Azeris massacred over 100 Armenians in the
village of Maraga. Baroness Cox of the British House of Lords, who
has done extensive humanitarian work in war-ravaged Karabakh,

61 "Human Rights Watch World Report 1993 – The Former Soviet Union". Hrw.
org. Archived from the original on 18 February 2015. Retrieved 28 April 2014.
62 De Waal, Thomas (2004). *Black garden: Armenia and Azerbaijan through peace and
war*. ABC-CLIO. p. 172. ISBN 0-8147-1945-7. Archived from the original on 3 June
2016.

witnessed the decapitated and mutilated bodies of the Armenian civilians in the aftermath of the Maraga massacre and has written and spoken about it on many occasions since. Also in 1992, with the agreement of both Armenia and Azerbaijan, the Minsk group, chaired by France, Russia, and the United States, was formed by the Organization for Security and Co-operation in Europe (OSCE) to mediate and find a peaceful solution to the conflict.

Since Karabakh was just an oblast with no structured military force, the Azeris must have anticipated that it would be easy to occupy. They perceived the vulnerable transitional period from the Soviet Union as their most opportune moment to annex the area. What they miscalculated was the sheer will of the hardened Karabakh people and the support that arrived against incredible odds from Armenia and the Armenian Diaspora. Although outnumbered and facing a superior military offensive, the Armenian forces led a more organized and smarter warfare, fighting for their homeland and their very existence. By 1993, they even carved out a buffer zone that reattached the lowlands of Karabakh that were absorbed into Azerbaijan in 1923. These areas, which became known as the "seven territories surrounding the oblast," also provided a security belt between the Armenians and the Azeri forces. Almost the entirety of historic Artsakh was now back in Armenian hands. The Karabakh fighters' heroic achievements became legendary, lifting the dignity and national pride of Armenians all over the world. Things started shifting when the Armenian side captured the Lachin corridor, finally linking Karabakh to Armenia. I will always recall the rejoicing when Shushi was liberated next on May 8, 1992 through a daredevil operation called "Wedding in the Mountains" that entailed climbing up the jutting steep cliffs of the impregnable mountain plateau over which the city sits and surprising the enemy from unexpected angles. Many of the fighters knew they would be sacrificing their lives, but it was critical for them to liberate Shushi from where the Azeris were bombing Stepanakert day and night. The success of the operation was a turning point in the war, as it finally allowed the Stepanakert residents, who had been living in basements for months on end, to see the sun and with it feel tangible hope for a normal life. One exhausted but jovial fighter, whose ancestors were from Shushi, found their graves, doused them with wine in celebration, and hunkered down beside them all night! The ghosts of the 20,000 Shushi Armenians slain in 1920 seemed to celebrate with us in that imaginary "wedding" of victory!

In 1994, with pleas from the Azeri side, a Russian brokered ceasefire took effect. The Republic of Karabakh was also a signatory of the agreement, which legitimized it as a political entity with a say in the security of its people. Thousands lost their lives on both sides in an unnecessary war against an indigenous people's wish to live in freedom and peace in its historic homeland. A purported estimate of 724,000 Azeris migrated or were displaced from Armenia, Karabakh, and the surrounding seven territories as a result of the war (According to a 1994 Human Rights Watch report, the number of Azeris who left Armenia was roughly 167,000). From the estimated 350,000-500,000 Armenian refugees who left Azerbaijan, many eventually came to America. In a show of solidarity with its Azeri brethren, Turkey proceeded to close its border with Armenia, blockading it from both sides. This left only two outlets for Armenia: one through Georgia in its north and another into Iran to its south. To our bitter disappointment, having announced that it is the guarantor of the security of the Armenians of Karabakh, Armenia opted not to rejoin the province, fearing retaliation by the Turks. Instead, it chose to abide by Russia's roadmap of attaining an independent status for the region, a decision that left the fate of Karabakh in limbo. It also projected the erroneous impression that Karabakh was a separatist region of Azerbaijan, when in fact, it had never legally belonged to it. It was simply a region that Azerbaijan, a brand new country, contested. "Contesting a land" does not make the land in question automatically the property of the party contesting it!

As the years passed, Azerbaijan, using Western words and terminology as a ruse, weaved an alternate tale where Armenia was constantly depicted as an occupier, gradually winning the information/public opinion war, while perpetually advocating for its "right to defend itself." Armenia, on the other hand, relied exclusively on the OSCE mandated peace process, instead of simultaneously screaming its truth to the world!

Photo of Shushi following the March 1920 massacre and destruction of the Armenian quarters. Ghazantchetsots Cathedral in the background (with its crosses and dome still intact) Public Domain

THE ARMENIAN QUARTERS OF SHUSHI NEGLECTED AND DESTROYED FURTHER
IN THE YEARS FOLLOWING THE MARCH 1920 MASSACRE AND THE EXPULSION
OF REMAINING ARMENIANS. GHAZANTCHETSOTS CATHEDRAL MINUS ITS DOME
CAN BE SEEN IN THE BACKGROUND. WIKIMEDIA COMMONS. PUBLIC DOMAIN

May 9th, 1992, Picture taken in front of Ghazanchetsots Cathedral. Armenian forces liberate Shushi with the daring operation of "Wedding in the Mountains". Source mentioned as Westernarmeniatv. com in article by Armedia.am, Liberation of Shushi: *The Turning Point of the "Wedding in the Mountains," May 8, 2019.*

The Reawakening of the Monster

"Hrant Dink is visiting Los Angeles. Do you want to attend his talk?" Ilda asked me. "I am not able to. Maybe next time," I answered.

IN THE EARLY 2000S, A Turkish Armenian journalist by the name of Hrant Dink emerged. It so happens that he was born in none other than my grandparents' Malatya. At the time, Turkey was at the height of its westernization and promoted itself as a democratic modern country with ambitions of joining the European Union. It is in this environment that Dink's daring lone voice reverberated and started the unthinkable: a conversation about facing the Turkish past. This was such a bold move by an Armenian columnist in Turkey that it propelled many to think or hope that Turkey was indeed changing. With his bilingual Turkish Armenian weekly newspaper Agos, Dink entered unchartered territory, opening a dialogue about how Turks felt about what their ancestors had done, analyzing their feelings of denial, shame, and hurt. He raised awareness about Armenian issues in the Turkish community with the hopes that understanding each other's challenges would pave the way for peace and reconciliation. One of Agos' goals was to promote a social path to democracy, including freedom of speech and debate.

Dink's most valuable reportage was about "hidden" Armenians in Turkey. As a child of separated parents, he lived in Tuzla Armenian

Children's camp during many summers in his childhood. It is there that he met his future wife, Rakel. In meeting Rakel, he became acquainted with the Varto clan to which she belonged. Apparently, in 1915, the Varto clan that originated from Van was ordered to relocate like the other Armenians in the region. However, during their journey, the clan was attacked, and five of the families escaped to nearby Mount Cudi, where they settled in caves and remained cut off from the rest of the world for 25 years. They came to believe that they were the only surviving Armenians! They eventually emerged and assimilated into the nearby Kurdish population, speaking Kurdish exclusively but aware of their Armenian ethnicity and Christian religion.

Through his work as a columnist and because of ads placed in Agos newspaper by Genocide survivors looking for relatives, Dink uncovered the existence of an even larger population of hidden Armenians: those who had been forced to convert to Islam or had converted in order to survive. He spoke about an entire generation of Turks who are now discovering that one of their grandparents, the grandmothers, in particular, were Armenian. A case in point was Turkish lawyer and human rights activist Fathiye Cetin, who had grown up thinking that her entire family was Turkish Muslim, until one day her maternal grandmother disclosed to her that she was a Christian Armenian by birth. As a child, she was torn from her mother's arms and adopted by a Turk during a death march. This story hit close to home and made me think of my grandmother's sister, Elizabeth's grandchildren. Fathiye went on to publish her famous memoir *My Grandmother: An Armenian Turkish Memoir.* She later became Hrant Dink's lawyer.

At every point in his life, Hrant Dink experienced all the discrimination and persecution that came with being an Armenian living in Turkey. When he took over the Tuzla Armenian Children's camp and started running it with his wife, he was accused by the state of raising Armenian militants! Later, as his columns began informing about Armenian history and culture and advocating for transparency, he became the target of lawsuits and endless court cases claiming he was undermining national security and was insulting Turkishness. The onslaught of criminal charges picked up major steam following an article he wrote in Agos, claiming that Sabiha Gokcen, the adopted daughter of Kemal Ataturk and the first Turkish female air force combat pilot, was in fact an Armenian orphan Ataturk had discovered at an orphanage in Bursa. The article spoke about Hripsime Sebilciyan, an Armenian originally from Gaziantep in Southeast Turkey, who was claiming to be Gokcen's niece. This caused such a vitriolic public outrage that it was a challenge escorting Dink and his lawyers in and out of courtrooms with angry mobs spitting and hurling all sorts of insults and objects at them. On January 19, 2007, Hrant was shot three times in the head in front of the Agos newspaper offices by an ultranationalist teenager named Ogun Samast. By this time, the country had veered far from secularism and democracy with the rise of the Justice and Development Party (AKP), which entered the political arena as a "moderate" but gradually became more and more conservative and hardline Islamist.

At the time of his death, Dink was on trial for violating Article 301 of the Turkish penal code, which was enacted two years prior in June of 2005. This law had become widely used in the crackdown of criticism about the government or the exposure of unflattering truths about Turkey. As a consequence, many journalists, writers, and human rights activists were slammed with lawsuits. Among them was Turkish writer Orhan Pamuk for making statements about the Armenian Genocide, writer Perihan Magden for her article titled "Conscientious Objection is a Human Right," historian Taner Akcam who researched and wrote about the Armenian Genocide as well as many others. Even Hrant Dink's own son, also a journalist, would be convicted in 2007[63] for insulting Turkish identity by mentioning the word "Genocide."

Hrant Dink, who was known for his smiling eyes and bear hugs, accomplished with his death his lifelong wish of bringing Armenians and Turks together. His funeral was a historical event where hundreds of thousands of Turkish citizens holding signs that said, "We are all Armenian, we are all Hrant Dink," marched in protest of his assassination. He is probably turning in his grave now, considering how far from the days of hope for democracy Turkey has come (especially after the 2016 failed coup d'état against the government[64]).

In 2015, another Malatyazi[65], Garo Paylan, became one of the first Armenian parliament members in decades. He represents Dyarbekir as a member of the People's Democratic Party. In April of 2016, on the 101st anniversary of the Armenian Genocide, in a bold performance that was nothing short of herculean, he stood in the parliament and recounted the names of the 1915 Turkish Armenian politicians who were deported and killed in the Armenian Genocide. His efforts towards the recognition of the Genocide and his work against Genocide deniers have often spurred fights that have at times become physical and caused the parliament to be suspended. Even as he finds himself at the receiving end of constant racial slurs such as "Armenian Bastard," Paylan forges ahead, cognizant of and defying security threats to his life. He has been twice nominated for the Nobel Peace Prize.

---

63   C Onur Ant. "Son of Murdered Armenian Journalist Convicted." Guardian, October 12, 2007, https://www.theguardian.com/world/2007/oct/12/pressandpublishing.turkey.

64   "Turkey coup: Purge widens to education sector," *BBC News*, 19 July 2016. Retrieved 20 July 2016.

65   The Armenian "zi" suffix is used to form nouns indicating nationality or provenance.

Did You Know We
Were Cousins?

In 2004, I joined Homenetmen, the Armenian Athletic Union, and Scouts as a volunteer parent. As the years passed, I made the acquaintance of many volunteers such as myself. Many of them had started as scouts in their younger years and were now volunteering as parents. I participated in many general meetings where issues concerning the management and strategic planning of the organization were debated. Among some vocal members was Berj Bedoyan, a boisterous, dedicated, and very involved member.

By 2012, with my father's perseverance, we had located several additional relatives living in the United States. My parents were invited to dinner at one of these relative's home in California. They filled me in later, saying how warm of a person Mrs. Mary was. They had even met her son and granddaughter. My father explained to me how his grandfather and father had assisted in the settling of this branch of the family in Syria and Lebanon and that, in the course of the years, they had lost track of each other. Soon after, in July of 2012, I was volunteering at the annual Homenetmen Navasartian games and festival when Berj Bedoyan approached me with an amused look on his face and asked, without wasting time, "Did you know we were cousins?" It turned out that he was Mrs. Mary Tavitian Bedoyan's son! It was surreal!

All these years, we had no idea that we were related! Berj is the great-grandson of Nishan, my great-grandfather Garabed's younger brother, who was arrested along with their middle brother Manuel during the Genocide and killed by the Turkish authorities. The brothers that my great-grandfather had in vain tried to bribe the Turkish gendarmes to release, arriving too late at the karakol (police station) where they were first detained. And yet, here I was face to face with what Turkey had failed to eradicate: the lineage of a broken tree that succeeded to survive: a passionate patriotic grandson who would climb Mount Ararat with his lovely wife Christine two years later! Were it not for my father's inquiries, Berj and I would have continued working in the same nonprofit organization without knowing that we were the descendants of brothers who had lived thousands of miles across the Atlantic Ocean in a town called Malatya all those years ago. It makes one wonder; how many Armenians walk among their relatives without knowing them? Was it my father and my curiosity that led us to our relatives? Or was fate's hand being guided from above? Berj's mother, Mrs. Mary, would later become instrumental in my research about Nishan's lineage. She is the daughter of Khosrof, one of Nishan's sons who had survived after months of being forced to march on foot without any provisions and had lost his mother and his sisters Markrit and Satenig in the ordeal. Khosrof and his brother Meguerdich were the young orphans that my great-grandfather Garabed and great grandmother Varter had taken in, cared for, and brought with them on their long journey out of Turkey.

And just like a gift that keeps on giving, the orchestrators from above went at it again in 2019. My cousin Ilda and friend Siranush invited me to a Malatya cuisine night at a local restaurant. Siranush was the friend through whom I had found Ilda and her family. Thinking it would be a great opportunity to reunite, I attended the event with my husband. Siranush led me to her table, and I sat down next to Ari, a man I thought I had seen previously, although I could not recall where. We later established that he was Siranush's cousin, so it was probable that we had run into each other at some gathering. Ari and I struck up an effortless conversation about Malatya.

When I told him the story of how I had found my cousins through Siranush, he was thrilled and raised a celebratory toast to Siranush. As Ari found out that I was from Lebanon, he turned on his cell phone to share some old family pictures of his Yaya (grandmother) and relatives who had traveled from Lebanon to visit her in the early 1950s. "I had relatives in Lebanon, too," he said jovially. "Look at this picture of my Yaya Terfanda with her mother, who had come from Lebanon to visit her. Her mother had escaped to Lebanon during the Genocide and came once to see her. They took a family picture together during their stay." The world stood still for a moment because the photo he was holding up to me was a most familiar photo in my family's cherished collection! "Oh my God, I have a copy of that photo Ari!" I exclaimed. "The lady standing on the right of the top row is my grandmother Maryam, and the young boy next to your great grandmother is my father!" Ari looked at me with astonished eyes as I explained. The wheels in my mind started turning rapidly and aligning data I had harnessed through years of inquiries. Terfanda? Terfanda was the name of one of Manuel's daughters. I was surprised to discover that when my grandmother and father had visited Malatya in the early 1950s, they were accompanied by Manuel's widow (a fact that my father later acknowledged). I recited the names of Manuel's children in my head: Hagop, Hripsimeh, Avedis, Noyemzar, and Terfanda. While I had grown up knowing the families and whereabouts of Hagop, Hripsimeh, Avedis, and Noyemzar, I did not know anything about Terfanda. "Oh my God, Ari! You are the descendant of Manuel!" "Who?" asked Ari. "Ari, your great-grandfather and my great-grandfather were brothers! Your great-grandfather was killed during the Genocide, and his widow and children escaped to Lebanon with my grandfather's family!"

"Oh my God, I did not know any of this!" exclaimed Ari when I was done divulging all the details I knew. "My Yaya had not told us anything about her family, not even once. Did my Yaya's siblings survive? Did you know them?" "Of course, we knew them! They survived and formed large families. But why had your grandmother

251

stayed behind?" I inquired. Ari looked unsure and overwhelmed by all the information I was throwing at him. "A Tavitian from Malatya sitting next to a Tavitian from Lebanon!" he said as we drank another toast to that revelation. Strangers one minute, cousins the next! Over Manr Yaprak, a yogurt base soup with grape leaf-covered wheat squares specific to Malatya Armenians, and one of my grandmother's signature dishes whose recipe she had passed on to my mother, we made plans to investigate further and tie up all the loose ends that were unraveling in our family's history. "Ari, when I walked into the restaurant and Siranush led me to this table, there were several other vacant seats. I don't think that it was a coincidence that I took the one next to you," I proclaimed. Ari agreed that cosmic forces were bringing the fragmented pieces of our family together.

We wasted no time reaching out to a relative in France who had interviewed dozens of family members while working on a Tavitian family tree and found out from him that on the Atash Yildirim Night, when the Tavitians were attacked, a decision was made by the elders to leave Terfanda, one of Manuel's daughters behind because she was already betrothed to an Armenian man by the name of Krikor, Ari's grandfather. Ari was fascinated by all this. He was born in Malatya, but his family had moved from there when he was a child. He recalled his grandmother Terfanda being a very strong woman, "feared by all the daughters in law!" but had no knowledge about any of her family's Genocide experience, the killing of her father, or of the night of the attack. None of it. He was shocked by the fact that she had kept all that to herself, most likely to protect her family. The threat of persecution was still so real and the enforced suppression of the truth so overwhelming that in the aftermath of the Genocide, survivors had mainly resorted to burying their past and focusing on survival. "My Yaya had all these siblings, and yet she had stayed alone in Turkey!" exclaimed Ari, still trying to digest this revelation. I was sad that Ari had missed out on knowing his grandmother's large clan. "Well, Ari," I went on to tell him, "I am not surprised your Yaya Terfanda was a feisty woman! You should have known her sister Hripsimeh. She was one strong-willed lady!" I have since met more of Ari's and my relatives in California. My friend Siranush turned out to be Ari's relative from his grandfather Krikor's side!

The disruption of family trees and the theft of the knowledge of relatives make the Armenian Genocide an ongoing crime that affects every new generation. I was elated that I had found some of my great-grandfather's direct descendants, but what about his extended families, the uncles, aunts, cousins, and in-laws he must have had in Malatya? We know nothing about them. The Turkish Ottoman policy of separation of families and social and demographic engineering explains the high prevalence of family portraits in the era preceding and following the Genocide and the importance Armenians attached to them.

THE PICTURE FROM MY FATHER'S 1951 TRIP TO MALATYA THAT ARI SHOWED ME ON HIS CELLPHONE. BOTTOM ROW: KRIKOR, TERFANDA'S HUSBAND, MY FATHER STANDING NEXT TO MANUEL'S WIDOW, WHO HAD TRAVELED ALONG WITH MY GRANDMOTHER AND FATHER; HER GRANDDAUGHTER (STANDING NEXT TO HER) AND DAUGHTER TERFANDA, ARI'S GRANDMOTHER (SEATED FAR RIGHT). TOP ROW FROM LEFT: TERFANDA'S SONS (ARI'S FATHER IS IN THE MIDDLE) AND MY GRANDMOTHER MARYAM.

What Were Their Names?

I OFTEN REFLECT ON THE curious coincidences that brought the story of my paternal grandparents to me and wonder if the spirit of my grandmother has been guiding me and uniting me with her relatives. There is no doubt in my mind that she wanted me to know about her family and what they had gone through during the Genocide. Her fear of losing loved ones that I witnessed as a youngster was a clear manifestation of the trauma she had endured. PTSD was prominent among her generation, but so must also have been the guilt of having survived. Not knowing what had happened to her parents and brother must have been difficult to live with.

Memorabilia and photographs have played big roles in reconstructing my grandparents' story. Among treasured family heirlooms that we brought with us from Lebanon are my grandfather Sarkis' hand-stitched "kamarband," or waist sash, and a square exquisitely hand-sewn double-sided piece with strips of bright purple silk fabric that was the *Bokjah* bundle that carried my grandmother's dowry. A constant reminder of my grandparents, however, is a 4- foot by 6-foot Turkish (or Armenian) antique rug with crimson and royal blue oriental patterns that currently rests on the floor of our living room. I cannot miss it in my daily comings and goings. Among the many objects we had stuffed in our luggage when leaving Lebanon were three treasured rugs. They had belonged to my grandparents and were extremely special to my father. They were fairly small rugs that my grandparents had rolled up hastily and placed on their donkeys the night they escaped Turkey. I imagine they came in handy as the family camped outdoors in forests and on hills during their journey into Syria.

Later, they brought these rugs with them to Lebanon. My grandmother had told my father that they had been wedding gifts and that she had brought them all the way from their home in Turkey. In keeping with tradition, my parents, in turn, gifted one to me and another to my sister when we got married and kept the third to themselves. I often admire my precious rug with its beautifully woven floral patterns and vibrant colors that never fade no matter what kind of light hits them and wonder where in my grandparents' Malatya house it was placed. If only a rug could speak, what stories would it tell me? Was it lying at the entrance of their home? Did the Turks who attacked my grandparents on that fateful night walk over it? Did my grandfather run over it as he chased the intruders with his gun? Did grandma Varter sit on it in despair as her husband lay unconscious on the ground? Or was it hanging beautifully from a wall? This century-old rug has survived those tribulations and silently witnessed all those events.

One day in 2012, as Ilda and I were having one of our discussions, a question popped into my mind out of nowhere. I asked her if she knew the names of my grandmother Maryam and her grandfather Maynuel's parents; in other words, our Arpadjian great-grandparents. No one had mentioned the first names of these two individuals who were driven from their home in front of their children and taken with thousands of others from their town, never to be seen again. Who were they? What did they look like? How old were they when they were deported? Ilda confessed that she did not know their names and that she doubted that any of our Turkish Armenian relatives knew them either. She added that the pressure to assimilate, to forget in order to survive, made Armenians living in Turkey less inclined to inquire openly about their ancestry. I did not want to give up; there was surely a way to uncover their names. Instinctually, I picked up the phone and called my father while Ilda was standing next to me. My father, the ultimate record keeper, went silent for a moment, surprised that he did not know the names of his own maternal grandparents. Then suddenly, he said, "wait, I have my parents' Lebanese passports. Maybe their parents' names are mentioned in there." In the old days in the Middle East, people were identified as "son of" or "daughter of" so and so. I waited while my father went to locate the passports, once again marveling at his remarkable appreciation of record keeping! After a few moments, he came back to the phone. "Here is my mother's passport," he said. "Ok, let's see" "Mariame Tavitian, born in Malatya in 1898, daughter of Bedros and Elmas Arpadjian." "Oh wow, dad!" I exclaimed. It was so exciting to finally hear the names of my maternal great-grandparents!

"Their names were Bedros and Elmas!" I announced to Ilda. But one look at Ilda, and I knew something about this discovery bothered her. She downright looked distraught! I thanked my dad and hung up the phone. "What is it?" I asked. "Oh my God akhchig (girl in Armenian)!" she started. "Bedros is my eldest uncle's name, and Elmas is the name of his eldest sister!" she divulged. I paused for a moment to let her words register. Goosebumps ran up my arms when I finally digested what she was telling me. We both fought back tears! Maynuel, my grandmother Maryam's brother and Ilda's grandfather, once married and a father himself, had named his firstborn son after his father Bedros and his eldest daughter after his mother Elmas. Ilda, who had grown up amongst her uncles and aunts, was now finding out who her eldest paternal uncle and aunt were named after! When we recovered from this touching discovery, an idea crossed my mind. "Wait! What was your father's name Ilda?" "It was Krikor, right?" "Yes, Krikor," said Ilda. For a moment, I weighed a certain possibility. It was farfetched, but I went along with it anyway. "Ilda, do you think your grandfather Maynuel named his second son after his young brother who ran after his parents?" Ilda thought it was all too possible. We both drifted into our thoughts. Was my grandmother's younger brother's name Krikor? Was there any way for us to know… Or were we being told that it was?

REPUBLIQUE LIBANAISE   الجمهورية اللبنانية

MINISTERE DE L'INTERIEUR   وزارة الداخلية

SERVICE DU RECENSEMENT
ET DE L'ÉTAT CIVIL

مصلحة
الاحصاء والاحوال الشخصية

نذكرة الهوية

Carte d'Identité

№ 98/34

Délivrée à Mme *Mariame Bijradjian*

Taxe perçue : 5 P. L. S.   الرسم المستوفى : ٠ غ. ل. س.

Nom et prénoms *Mariame Arpadjian*

Prénoms du père *Bedros*

Nom et prénoms de la mère *Elmas*

Date et lieu de naissance *1848 Malatia*

Rite *Armen — orthodox*

Profession

Lettré ou illetré *Lettré*

Marié ou célibataire (enfants)

Domicile (1) *Bachoura*

District *Beyrouth* Caza *Beyrouth*

No. du registre *28/334*

LE GOUVERNEMENT LIBANAIS, CERTIFIE
QUE M *Mariame Arpadjian* EST LIBANAIS
EN FOI DE QUOI : NOUS LUI AVONS DÉLIVRÉ LA PRÉSENTE CARTE D'IDENTITÉ
LE *23 Mars* 19 *33*

LE CHEF DU RECENSEMENT ET DE L'ETAT-CIVIL   LE SECRÉTAIRE

(1) Pour les villes indiquer le quartier et la rue.

MY GRANDMOTHER'S PASSPORT FROM 1933: MARIAME ARPADJIAN (FRENCH
SPELLING), BORN IN 1898 MALATIA (AS SPELLED IN THE PASSPORT), FATHER'S
NAME: BEDROS, MOTHER'S NAME: ELMAS. FROM MY FAMILY'S COLLECTION.

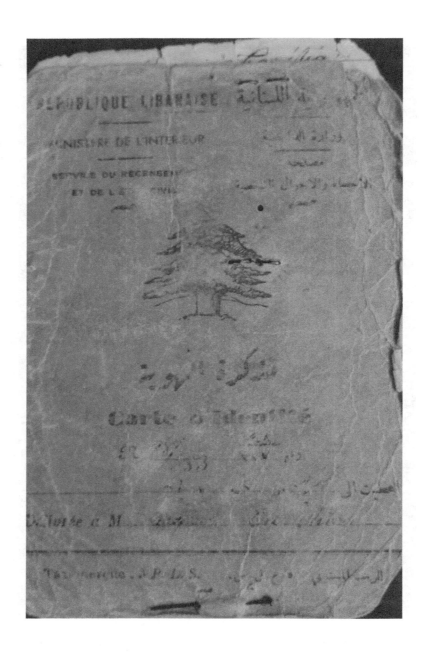

MY GRANDFATHER'S 1933 PASSPORT. SARQUIS TAVITIAN (FRENCH SPELLING), BORN IN 1890 MALATIA, FATHER'S NAME: GARABED, MOTHER'S NAME: VARTER. FROM MY FAMILY'S COLLECTION.

I Owe My Life to Turks?!

THE ARMENIAN GENOCIDE WAS ALMOST a perfect crime of annihilation. "Almost." As well planned and executed as it was in eliminating three-quarters of the Armenian population in Western Anatolia, it could not control a certain human element: compassion. As the different facets of the Armenian Genocide are further explored, it is my hope that more research and literary work will be dedicated to the Armenian Genocide's "Schindlers."

Many Greeks hid Armenians. Missionaries, such as Danish Maria Jacobsen, Amalia Lange, Karen Jeppe, and American Stanly Kerr,[66] as well as nurses and orphanage managers, saved thousands of orphans and thus many future generations. Turks and Kurds also risked their lives and their standing in society to save Armenians. The CUP had assigned Dr. Bahaeddin Shakir to head the Teskilat-i Mahsusa (Special Organization), a special government forces unit assigned to rid the Ottoman Empire of its internal "cancer." Shakir was notorious for enforcing the genocidal mission of the CUP. The CUP operated with a dual communication system: the official government announcements that spread incendiary lies about organized Armenian rebellion and rationalized the need to deport Armenians from areas of battle because they were traitors, and a clandestine network of communication where commands to

---

66 Stanley Kerr volunteered for the Near East Relief in Aleppo Syria during the Armenian Genocide. He published *Lions of Marash* in 1973, a first-hand account of the massacre of Armenians in Western Armenia. He was a professor at the American University of Beirut (AUB). Years later, his son Malcolm Kerr became president of the AUB. Stanley Kerr was also the grandfather of NBA player, broadcaster, and coach Steve Kerr.

starve and massacre the Armenians were delivered in person by so-called responsible "secretaries" or reliable "couriers" who destroyed written orders after reading them to the intended parties. Turkish Governors and government officials who did not follow these secret CUP orders or questioned them were subjected to demotion, brutal punishment, confiscation of property, and persecution. Many resigned their posts, citing the criminality and inhumanness of these directives. Several were killed as a consequence. Any Muslim who assisted or hid Armenians was "to be hanged in front of his house and his house burnt down."[67]

The fact that in an environment searing with visceral hatred, where the Muslim population as a whole participated in the plunder and killing of Armenians, some righteous and amazingly brave Turks and Kurds decided to uphold humanity and risk their lives by helping Armenians is enormously remarkable. These beings resisted getting swept away by the devious current of state-sponsored racism and impunity from homicide and criminal profiteering. Their humane acts of kindness were met with great resentment by nationalist Turks who considered them traitors. Their stories are not mentioned in Turkish history and have been deleted from the collective Turkish memory.

One of these governors, Celal Bey of Konya, had saved thousands of Armenian lives by the time he was removed from his post in October of 1915. In his memoirs, he described himself as "*a person sitting beside a river, with absolutely no means of rescuing anyone from it. Blood was flowing down the river, with thousands of innocent children, irreproachable old men, and helpless women streaming down the river towards oblivion. Anyone I could save with my bare hands, I saved, and the rest went down the river, never to return.*"[68] At times, the government allowed

---

67 John S. Kirakossian, *The Armenian Genocide: The Young Turks Before the Judgment of History* (Madison, CT: Sphinx Press, 1992), 169.

68 Orhan Kemal Cengiz, "1915: Heroes and Murderers," Cihan News Agency, November 2, 2012, http://www.armeniapedia.org/wiki/Orhan_Cengiz#1915:_Heroes_And_Murderers.

the Muslim population to take in Armenian women and orphans. At other times, it strictly forbade it in accordance with centrally devised demographic plans. Many of these women and children were unfortunately abused or used as slaves or concubines in harems. A majority were forever lost to their community as they were forcibly Islamized and Turkified.

Some Muslims, however, simply hid Armenians and helped them along without forcing them to convert. Such was the case with the couple who took in my grandmother and her siblings. Their selfless act has made my existence, as well as that of the descendants of my grandmother's siblings, possible. For them to have made a stop in Lebanon years later to visit my grandmother on their way to a pilgrimage to Mecca warms my heart. Holding a paper with directions given to them by my grandmother's brother Maynuel, the couple had made their way to my grandfather's fabric store in downtown Beirut. "We came to see our daughter," they had said, according to my father. In this, humanity is the same everywhere. There are good and bad players from every nationality and in every corner of the world. Evil and goodness define each other by their differences and will always coexist. There is a saying in Armenian: "*Asdvadz lav martou artchev haneh*," "May God send good people your way." Thousands of Armenians fell at the hands of bad people during the Genocide. Their cries went unheard, their experiences remain unknown, and their stories will never be told. Thankfully, my grandmother and her siblings, as well as hundreds of others, encountered good people. That was their destiny. We, the descendants of the Arpadjian kids, owe our lives to their heroic neighbors and the undeniable power of their one good deed!

Hatred and the dehumanization of those standing in the way of our materially defined successes, unfortunately, continue to plague our world. In our blind personal and national ambitions, we often hesitate to give less fortunate ones a chance and fail in tolerating those who do not look or think like us. As nations, we want to succeed at all costs, and in many ways, that entails putting our country, our ideals, our race, and our people ahead of all others. The fact is, however, that regardless of how powerful we get, we will still belong to the whole of humanity, and repercussions from actions we put out will eventually come around and affect us as well. No one nation's ambitions should overtake the world. Worse yet, no nation should advance itself by annihilating another.

The greatness and prosperity of nations lie in their courage to celebrate humanity as a whole. Had America not given refugees a chance, it would not have acquired many of the creative minds who have made America the great nation it is today. Actually, there would have been no America, period, since America is a nation of immigrants. Several inventions, for example, are credited to Armenian Americans. Christopher Ter-Serobyan invented the green color of the U.S. dollar bill, Hovannes Adamyan created color TV, Luther Simjian created the ATM, and Raymond Damadian invented the MRI machine. Currently, Nubar Afeyan, a Lebanese Armenian who migrated due to the Lebanese Civil War and co-founder of the biotechnology company Moderna, has become instrumental in the development of an mRNA Covid vaccine.

There would be no refugee and immigrant crisis if human life, dignity and safety were upheld above the material and expansionist ambitions of the ruling class. In a world becoming smaller every day thanks to technology and enhanced social interaction, one would think that primitive greedy tendencies and fanatical cultural elements would diminish to let everyone live in peace and harmony. Will there be a time where we no longer chant "America First," "Russia First," "England First," "Turkey First" etcetera and agree to instead put "humanity first"? Uncovering the stories of courageously compassionate Turks during the Armenian Genocide should be inspiring and enlightening to us all. Perhaps even more so to the Turkish people themselves, whose culture has been defined by the glorification of conquest.

Trip of a Lifetime

As it is with most Diaspora Armenians, visiting Armenia has been a dream of mine since childhood. That dream turned into reality and stumbled into my life in an unforeseen manner in May of 2017. Caught up in last-minute packing, I had no time to savor the fact that I was about to embark on the trip that I had longed for all my life. We were flying halfway around the world from Los Angeles to Moscow and, from there, to Yerevan, Armenia. I spent the long hours on the plane alternating between stretching, taking strolls down the aisles, and trying to find a comfortable position in my seat. On the last leg of the trip, I was sitting next to the window when the pilot announced that we had entered Armenia's airspace. Those words filled my heart with indescribable excitement. I was hovering over the land that, growing up, I sang songs and recited poems about! I was finally going to see Armenia, the land of my ancestors, the land that lived in my textbooks, so elusive in my childhood and miraculous in its current existence. A country whose independence was a dream none of us thought we would see in our lifetime! As the small plane descended in altitude and parted tall clouds, I braced myself for a first glimpse of my homeland.

The view that appeared through dissipating haze blew me away! Miles of green undulating landscape with dramatic parted gorges, like nothing I had ever seen before. It was stunning! My eyes met my husband's, and all I could manage was a huge grin while I pointed at the view outside the window! The plane veered to the left, preparing to land, and I turned my head just in time to glimpse a huge body of a mountain pass by the windows on the right side. "Oh, My God!" I thought to myself. As we filed into the airport, there they were, framed in the center of wall-to-wall windows, the holy twin peaks of Mount Ararat, the symbol of Armenia. For some crazy reason, whenever I saw a picture of Mount Ararat in the past, I used to think it was photo-shopped to make the mountain look unnaturally large compared to its surroundings! The realization that those photos were, in fact, untouched was quite humbling. Ararat was indeed quite large, with tremendous presence and breathtaking majesty. The glimpse we caught of Ararat was a short-lived gift because no sooner did we see it than it disappeared behind the veil of dusk. During the next 14 days of our stay, Ararat would play a game of peek-a-boo where some mornings we would wake up to find it completely exposed with its snowcapped twin peaks bright against the blue sky, and other times we could not even tell that it was there.

As our taxi ventured into town in the dark of night, I was mesmerized by the signs on the streets and up on the buildings. They were all in Armenian! We passed massive rectangular, poorly built, and mostly vacant grey buildings, and our driver explained that they were from the Soviet era. "Many have left through the years," he continued, hinting at innumerable hard times, "but I can't leave. This is our land!" he added. We swerved left from the Ararat Brandy factory, and we were suddenly in a wonderful city center that could have passed for any other modern-day European city, with beautiful architecture, water fountains, and pristine sidewalks; not a single piece of trash on them and not a single homeless tent! We settled in our hotel and woke up the next day eager to explore. What an exploration it turned out to be! I can honestly say that, even if I were not Armenian, I would have still found Armenia to be one of the most intriguing, ancient, innovative, adventurous, and inviting destinations to travel to!

I have to confess that deep down inside, I had previously harbored the thought that maybe as Armenians, we suffered from a bit of a superiority complex, similarly to, let's say, the Greeks who claim to have started everything. I was afraid that all the years of learning about our ancient history, the fact that we had out-survived so many ancient people who do not exist anymore, that we were the first nation to adopt Christianity, and so on would come crashing down in a heap of disappointment once I visited our homeland. What awaited me was the stunning and embarrassingly humbling realization that Armenia was actually much more than what I was taught at school; in fact, it was the material I was taught that was terribly lacking!

Considered by biblical scholars and theologians as the possible location of the Garden of Eden, Armenia is a uniquely mystical and earthy place. The formulated truths, that I had become attached to, seemed inept, and for the first time in my life, I was struck by the realization that everything I had learned growing up was painstakingly pieced together with the bits and pieces that the Diaspora was left with. I developed a newfound appreciation of what Diaspora Armenians had gone through in order to reassemble their history and retain their culture. A nation whose cream of the crop of leaders, journalists, writers, politicians, physicians, historians, and theologians were taken out all at once, whose priceless libraries, ancient manuscripts, artifacts, illuminated gospels, archeological treasures, churches, and antique relics were destroyed, had done their best to gather the torn pieces of their culture to resurrect their national identity with whatever they had salvaged on their way to exile.

Even though thousands of priceless manuscripts were burned during the Turkic and Mongol invasions, Armenia had apparently succeeded in retaining a sizeable repository of manuscripts and scrolls that are now on display at the Mesrob Mashdotz Institute of Ancient Manuscripts, the Matenadaran. Most of these manuscripts were retrieved or saved from ancient monasteries and churches. Others were donated by individuals or missionaries who had found them or were entrusted with them during the Genocide. One of the oldest complete volumes, the Lazarian gospel, dates from the year 887. Between the Matenadaran and numerous historical museums, there is so much for visitors to discover and so much for archeologists to unearth in this newly accessible Armenia!

In no time, I was bit by the *"Hoghe kez geh kasheh,* earth will draw you in" bug, a phenomenon that I had heard of many times but had brushed aside with skepticism. Armenia does pull you towards it! I wanted to take it all in, but no matter how long I stood at the entrance of St. Gayaneh church and read about its founding in year 630, or strolled in the bustling streets of the capital Yerevan founded in year 782 BC, or stared into the gaping entrance of the cave in Areni where the 5,500-year-old leather shoe (world's oldest) as well as the most ancient tools of winemaking were found, or stood in the ray of light streaming through the opening in the cupola at the medieval monastery of Geghard where legend says the spear that pierced the side of Christ was kept, I was not able to take my fill of the country. I was drawn by the medieval monasteries in remote areas the most. Their ageless architecture and humble, pew-less, minimally decorated interiors take you back to the rise of Christianity, and you sense the holiness of the grounds. These UNESCO heritage sites were nothing like I had ever experienced in my life. Like time machines, they transported us back in time as we walked in the footsteps of the song weaving bard Sayat Nova and stepped over the burial stones of monks who elected to be buried inside the churches to continue serving their parishioners after death.

It is said that these monasteries, erected in the most precarious places at the edge of a gorge or high up at the side of a mountain, are built at the crossings of energy lines where previous pagan Armenian temples were built. As sanctuaries, they were also constructed in strategic locations that provided excellent vantage points from which to spot invading enemy armies. A case in point is Tatev monastery, built on a mountain plateau 2,344 meters above sea level. Today, it is easily accessible by a newly built state-of-the-art aerial tramway that holds the world record for the longest non-stop double track cable car. The ten-minute ride provides an out-of-this-world experience. True to its name, *Wings of Tatev*, it makes you feel like a bird flying over deep valleys, breathtaking hills, flowing waterfalls, and ancient moss-covered ruins. The pivotal role that Christianity has played in the history of the Armenians is unmistakable. The church was revered and intertwined with governance and national defense. It defined our destiny. We fought and died upholding our faith. At Tatev, we ran into many European tourists, some visiting with theology tours intently studying all the rich details of the church complex.

Now that it is open to the world, Armenia has also piqued the interest of archeologists who have flocked to it to uncover the treasures of its ancient civilization. My husband and I became fast friends with Rudik, the tour guide/driver we hired, a tall, elegant, light-complexioned army veteran. He played beautiful folkloric music in the car while he told us that Armenian citizens loved their land and were willing to endure any hardship if only the corrupt government would change. The three of us went all over the country: Lake Sevan, Lori, Dilijan... We even drove to the disputed area of Artsakh (Karabakh) bordering Azerbaijan. Many a time, we had to wait for shepherds to guide herds of fat sheep and cows away from the road. Miles and miles of sparsely populated stunning views rushed by between quaint villages. Artsakh, nestled in its stunning hilltops, greeted us through a dissipating fog. Liberated after a hard-won war, it felt like it held the heartbeat of the Armenian nation. Some of the oldest Armenian Christian monuments are at Artsakh, some from as old as the 4th century AD, such as Amaras monastery! We were so impressed to see the city of Stepanakert destroyed by heavy shelling during the 1990s war, developing beautifully in defiance of Azerbaijani tyranny.

Even though its newly refurbished airport stood unused because of Azerbaijan's threats of shooting down civilian planes landing there, we were pleased to encounter many European and Russian tourists who had not minded taking the eight-hour bus ride from Armenia to come and discover the beauty of Artsakh. Everywhere we went, I noticed how attentive to cleanliness Armenians were. Old grandmas and grandpas sweeping in front of their modest abodes or planting flowers in tourist destinations, fragrant laundry wafting from balconies that took me back to Bourj Hammoud, Lebanon. The warm embrace that I had felt in Bourj Hammoud returned, this time enveloping me in more robust arms. And those eyes, those Armenian eyes... Especially of those of 17-, 18-year-old beautiful boys in military uniform strolling in the streets of Shushi, one of the hardest-fought areas of Artsakh, made me lower my own eyes to the ground in shame. These beautiful, young people were sacrificing their lives to defend this patch of homeland while the majority of us Armenians lived in the Diaspora. I will forever cherish our visit to the historic Ghazanchetsots Cathedral of Shushi, and the delicious *Zhengyalov Hats*[69] *we* munched on in a bakery on the ground level of the building across from it. Walking around in the misty town that sits atop an impressive rocky plateau, I said a quiet prayer for the thousands of Armenians slaughtered there by the Azeris in 1920, but I mostly wanted to reimagine the brave 1992 "Wedding in the Mountains" operation that liberated it.

Rudik drove us all the way to Tigranakert, five miles away from the border with Azerbaijan proper. We were so close to the border that our cell phones reverted to Baku time. On our way there, we came upon an entire area of abandoned destroyed homes. I asked Rudik about it, and he informed us that these were Azeri neighborhoods that were evacuated during the war that ravaged the area. I thought the site was as sad as the destroyed Armenian quarters, churches, and monuments, in Shushi, Baku, Nakhichevan and elsewhere. I consoled myself with the thought that at least the displaced Azeris were not subjected to massacres and pogroms like the Armenians were.

This was the city of Agdam. Built in the 19th century in Artsakh's Askeran province, it was within the so-called "seven Azeri territories

---

69 A traditional Artsakh and Syunik flatbread, stuffed with finely diced local herbs and vegetables, cooked on a special griddle called Saj or in a Tonir oven.

occupied by the Armenians." During the 1990s Karabakh war, the Azeri forces were viciously shelling Artsakh's capital Stepanakert from Agdam, which left the Armenian fighters with no other recourse but to organize an offensive and occupy the area to safeguard Karabakh and place it out of range of artillery and Grad rockets. The city would not have been destroyed and its inhabitants would not have fled if, instead of launching a war, Azerbaijan had respected Nagorno-Karabakh enclave's original wish to peacefully secede and rejoin Armenia. And yet, when we arrived in Tigranakert past Agdam, the absurdity of the whole matter became evident. The area was recognized as part of Azerbaijan proper, a country of a mere 100 years of history, while, in fact, we were within the ancient Armenian province of Utik. The land itself told the story of Turkic people settling in the lowlands of Karabakh, changing the demographics and creating a new country over an ancient one. It was an out-of-this-world feeling to stroll among the uncovered city walls of the ancient city Armenian King Tigran the Great had built in the first century BC! The excavations had also unearthed the silhouette of the foundation of a 5th-century Armenian basilica. While we rested in the shade of a mulberry tree, Rudik reached out and plucked from the fruit, and my husband and I followed suit. As I savored the sweet white berry extending my hand to plumper ones on higher branches, I suddenly discerned a small church, perfect in its symmetric beauty, high up on the very edge of a mountain above the excavation site. The day had been long, and we had to head back, so I promised myself to visit that church on my next trip. I asked Rudik for the church's name: "*Vankasar* church from the 7th century." "And this area is considered Azeri land?" I thought to myself, marveling at Stalin's sloppy distribution of territories.

Back at our Hyatt hotel in the capital Yerevan, we enjoyed fantastic western hospitality. The city of Yerevan is replete with unique and trendy restaurants, with terrific cuisine that marries the simple peasant *Khorovadz* (Kebab) to Middle Eastern favorites like Shawerma and Taboule that have become more prominent in the city with the recent influx of Armenian refugees from war-torn Syria. And, oh, how delicious are the organically grown fruits and vegetables sold in the produce markets! I almost had tears in my eyes smelling the tomatoes! I had forgotten what real tomatoes smelled like! Apricots, sour plums, and figs were sold in the streets in the most present- able and neatly plastic-wrapped baskets. What also struck me about Yerevan was how cosmopolitan and cultured it was! Even the young seemed to appreciate the museums, the opera, and art galleries. It was as if everyone had a keen understanding of how precious of a gift this holy land and our existence as a nation were.

We were sitting in front of Hyatt hotel sipping on "*ourdz*" (thyme) tea when I overheard a group of American ladies having a conver- sation on the couches next to us. When they stood up and started walking towards us, I approached them and asked where they were visiting from. They informed us that they were with some cultur- al organization from Arizona of all places! They were pleasantly surprised when we informed them that we were from California. A blonde blue-eyed lady pulling a poncho-type shawl around her asked if we were Armenian. We confirmed that we were and that this was our first time visiting our homeland. This captured the interest of the ladies who now accorded us their full attention. The blond lady asked me what part of Armenia my family was from. The question took me off guard, and for a few seconds, I was awkwardly lost for words. As I contemplated my answer, my eyes darted away and skimmed the activity in the city center, looking for something to help me explain; maybe a pair of snowcapped peaks. I gave the ladies the best answer I could come up with. "You see Mount Ararat, right?" I asked. "Oh yes, so amazing!" they gushed. "Well, my an- cestors are from behind Mount Ararat, the part of Armenia that is part of Turkey now," I responded. The ladies oohed and aahed and gave us looks full of regret and sympathy. "We understand," said a couple of them, "we saw the movie *The Promise*." "What a great movie that was!" added another, "It is unfortunate that it did not do as well at the box office. People are not interested in history and genocide stories…" "So, how does it feel to be in Armenia for the first time?" added a middle-aged brunette. "It feels like… meeting my biological homeland," I answered. Yes, in many ways, visiting Armenia was like getting to know a biological parent after years of being at foster homes. A motherland about whom I had heard and studied but had turned out to be completely different in a familiar yet totally foreign and fascinating way.

At the airport, on our trip back home, we sat staring at Mount Ararat. We could not get our fill of it. Growing up in Gemmayze Lebanon in the middle of a civil war and yearning for an unattainable homeland in the refugee neighborhoods of Bourj Hammoud, I never thought I would see the day when Eastern Armenia was independent again, let alone stand in front of the majestic spread of the twin-peaked Armenian Holy Mountain. If only this mountain could speak of all that it had witnessed unfold in this ancient land! Byzantines, Persians, Romans, Arabs, Seljuks, Mongols, khans, tsars, kings, and caesars have all looked at its expanse and passed, and yet it remains there as unshakable as the will of the Armenian people. I wondered how it would feel to visit the towns on the other side of the mountain where generations of my ancestors had lived. "Maybe one day I will visit Western Armenia," I thought to myself, unwilling to call it by its current designation as "Eastern Turkey." I looked past the twin peaks of Ararat, beautifully visible on that bright morning. My gaze slid down the dip into the lowest area of the valley between the two peaks. In my mind's eye, I saw myself climbing up then down to the other side into the unknown land that I originated from, traveling northbound to Kars and Ardahan, then turning south towards Erzurum, Mush and Lake Van, the cradle of the Armenian people, towards my father's Malatya, walking through the bristling apricot groves, then continuing further southeast towards the Cilician plain, inhaling the familiar smells and feeling the warm embrace of my mother's Adana.

The trip back was difficult. I struggled to reengage in normal life. I made mental notes of what bills I had to pay when I got back home. I prepared myself for the long freeway ride to work on Monday morning, past Little China, Little Thailand, Little Armenia, and homeless tent cities and franchise restaurants. I half-heartedly attempted to catch up with the current affairs of America, my adoptive country that I loved and owed so much to. A weird feeling in my gut kept on interrupting my thoughts and messing with my mood. The sad predicament of generations crept up on me! As one of the oldest surviving people, we sure had been dealt a terrible hand! "The Black Dog of Fate," as writer Peter Balakian would call us. The 2016 American elections had concluded six months prior. They were particularly abrasive and had resulted in a billionaire businessman, who had never held public office, rising to the presidency of the most powerful nation in the world. But I had just left Yerevan, a city preparing to celebrate its 2,800th birthday! I had walked on the grounds where Jesus' apostles Thaddeus and Bartholomew had brought Christianity! I had stared at intricately engraved Khachkars (cross-stones) resting against monasteries so old that the ground had grown around them through the centuries! I had lit a candle in the Armenian Vatican, Etchmiadzin, founded in the year 303! "That's 1,714 years ago!" And now I was headed towards a 300-year-old baby of a nation that is trying its hand as a modern-day empire, dictating the fate of nations that have survived from the antiquities.

Trump, Hillary, Putin etc....modern-day Pharaohs and Caesars who decide the fate of nations! What is America but a medley of people who have escaped persecution, war, discrimination, bigotry, racism, and poverty whose loyalties are torn between their homelands and the "great experiment" of a nation that offers them peace, freedom, and the pursuit of happiness? What will become of America if its efforts to retain geopolitical and economic power uproot more and more foreigners from their lands and bring them to its shores and borders, vying for the safety and prosperity it promises? Immigrants and refugees are the residue that rivers of the stormy whims of powerful nations toss here and there when the rushing floods of wars and economic upheaval settle on distant foreign shores. The Ottoman Turks needed to create a country called Turkey by massacring indigenous nations they were ruling over and stealing their lands. The orphans and survivors of these nations escaped to nearby countries like Syria and Lebanon. The Germans used what the Turks did to the Armenians as a blueprint to eliminate six million Jews. The Jews, discriminated against and persecuted for centuries, wanted their promised land back, so they took over Palestine. A war with the Arab nations broke out, which resulted in thousands of Palestinian refugees settling in Lebanon. This caused a civil war to erupt, which forced thousands of Lebanese to flee to America, a country that western-bound pioneers and persecuted Europeans created out of the lands of the indigenous Native Americans. And that was how I, grandchild of Arpadjians, Tavitians, Bchakjians, and Torossians from the center of the Armenian Highlands, today called Eastern Turkey, had ended up in California! I couldn't help but wonder what was going to become of Armenia, landlocked and surrounded by hostile neighbors.

The long flight carried me further and further away, but I could not extricate from my mind the miles of beautiful land covered with red poppies that had rushed by as we drove through the countryside; the antique air, and the ancient whisper of the land that had pulled at my heartstrings! It felt as if I had left my heart lying amongst the red poppies in the fields of Armenia.

A side note:
The following year, in 2018, I took a DNA test, just for the fun of it. The results indicated that I was of Armenian ethnicity and that a whopping 89% of my genetic makeup originated from Eastern Turkey! Turkey, a country that I have never set foot in, and neither have my parents or my maternal grandparents! In the map of my results, big circles were placed over Malatya and other cities where my ancestors lived long ago! While men try to alter history, redraw maps, rename places, and concoct false narratives, nature has its way of uncovering the truth. The truth is always there, eternal and

unchangeable. Although DNA test kits are currently prohibited in Turkey, ancestry testing has apparently become the rage for Turks who purchase the kits abroad. Most are finding out that they are related more to the indigenous people who were Turkified than their revered ancestors who migrated from the Steppes of Asia.[70] The Turkic expansions have absorbed the DNA of the nations they overcame. Current Turkish DNA is a medley of genetic material from conquered people, mostly Armenians and Greeks who preexisted in those lands.

ARMENIA'S CAPITAL CITY OF YEREVAN WITH MOUNT ARARAT WITH ITS TWIN PEAKS IN THE BACKGROUND. PHOTO BY SEROUJ OURISHIAN, APRIL 18, 2016, NO CHANGES WERE MADE TO THE PHOTO. HTTPS://EN.WIKIPEDIA.ORG/WIKI/EN:CREATIVE _ COMMONS HTTPS://CREATIVECOMMONS.ORG/LICENSES/BY/4.0/DEED.EN

---

70 Akhilesh Pillalamarri, "The Epic Story of How the Turks Migrated From Central Asia to Turkey," *The Diplomat,* June 5, 2016, https://thediplomat.com/2016/06/the-epic-story-of-how-the-turks-migrated-from-central-asia-to-turkey/

Armenophobia with Impunity

Oil pipelines, strategic locations, and economies driven by geopolitics fuel Turkey's and Azerbaijan's caviar diplomacies. To their credit, their leaders know how to manipulate Western systems and weaknesses very well. Turkey, for example, exploits Europe with continuous threats of shipping Syrian refugees there, which works magically as Europe hurries to pay up exorbitant amounts so that Turkey can "take care of its refugees." Azerbaijan has even been bribing members of the Council of Europe into campaigning for the Aliyev regime and portraying it in a favorable light. The Council of Europe that is mandated to uphold human rights expelled 13 of its members in 2018 for having accepted gifts and bribes from Azerbaijan in a money laundering "cash for votes" scheme worth $2.9 billion dollars. These members helped cover up Azerbaijan's abysmal human rights record and certified that it held clean elections when ballots have essentially listed only one presidential candidate for the past eighteen years! Aliyev, in turn, cites these assessments as proof that his country has no issues in human rights and democratic freedoms![71] [72] In a world where everything seems to have a price tag, how can small nations afford to acquire justice?

71 Jennifer Rankin, *Council of Europe Members Suspected of Corruption, Inquiry Reveals,* The Guardian, April 22, 2018

72 Jesse Chase-Lubitz, *Council of Europe Body Expels 13 in Azerbaijan Bribe Case,* OCCRP, July 3, 2018

Early 2000s to 2018.

MORE THAN TWO DECADES AFTER the 1994 Karabakh ceasefire, emboldened by the momentum of its anti-Armenian propaganda, and banking on fading memories concerning the genesis of a war that it itself waged and lost, Azerbaijan, not only started working counter the OSCE agreements in finding a peaceful resolution to the conflict, but it constantly violated the ceasefire at the border in order to taunt the Karabakh forces into another war. Armenian soldiers in the line of defense were constantly taken down by sniper bullets, and villagers were subjected to sporadic random shelling. The Azeri government threatened to shoot down civilian planes if the airport at Stepanakert (Karabakh's capital) was used, obstructing the economic progress of blockaded Karabakh. Azeri children were thought to hate Armenians, and anti-Armenian racism and Armenophobia were indoctrinated in the country. Yet leading nations in the world had no problem investing in and dealing with Azerbaijan.

Azeri soldiers who committed atrocities against Armenians were celebrated as heroes. An example is Ramil Safarov, an Azeri lieutenant who, in 2004, murdered a sleeping Armenian counterpart with an ax while participating in a NATO Partnership for Peace program in Hungary. Safarov was sentenced to a lifetime of imprisonment. However, after six years of incarceration, he was extradited to Azerbaijan with assurances by the Azeri government that he would serve the remainder of his sentence there. The minute he landed, however, President Ilham Aliyev issued him a pardon, commuted the rest of his prison term, and promoted him to the rank of major, and the world did not bat an eye.

In addition, Azerbaijan committed historical theft and cultural genocide by promoting as its own Armenian archeological sites, inscriptions, excavated treasures, traditional rugs, and even popular music while actively destroying ancient Armenian monuments and cemeteries. By late 2006, it had erased all trace of Armenian existence and culture in its exclave of Nakhichevan by systemically destroying 89 Armenian churches, over 5,800 Khatchkars (cross-stones), and 22,000 tombstones, including the UNESCO-protected ancient Armenian cemetery of Djulfa.[73] The Azeri government barred the European Parliament from investigating the destruction of 10,000 Armenian Khachkars in the Djulfa historic cemetery, an act condemned by UNESCO and the International Council on Monuments and Sites (ICOMOS) and described as cultural genocide.[74] However, no criminal case was opened by the West against Azerbaijan. Instead, President Aliyev made large donations to UNESCO, and the matter was not only put to rest, but in 2004, UNESCO made first lady Mehriban Aliyeva a UNESCO ambassador! Since 2012, the Heydar Aliyev Foundation has even made large donations towards renovations at the Vatican, garnering in return Pope Francis' accolades about Azerbaijan being a religiously tolerant nation, although no Christian Armenians from anywhere in the world are allowed to travel there and the Azeri leadership continues to destroy Armenian churches and monuments!

The millions the Azeri government invests in bestowing extravagant gifts and expensive getaways in Azerbaijan upon politicians and leaders from around the world keep returning dividends (policy known as Caviar Diplomacy). In a stunning development in 2008, the United Nations passed resolutions declaring that the territorial integrity and internationally recognized borders of Azerbaijan must be respected and that the Armenian forces should withdraw from "all occupied Azeri territories"! When first announced, the

---

73 Dale Berning Sawa, "Monumental Loss: Azerbaijan and 'the Worst Cultural Genocide of the 21st Century,'" *Guardian*, March 1, 2019, https://www.theguardian.com/artanddesign/2019/mar/01/monumental-loss-azerbaijan-cultural-genocide-khachkars.

74 "By analogy, other tragic events or threatening processes are designated today by Armenians as 'cultural genocide' (for example, the destruction by Azerbaijanis of the Armenian cemetery in Julfa)." Yulia Antonyan and Konrad Siekierski, "A Neopagan Movement in Armenia: The Children of Ara," chap. 17 in *Modern Pagan and Native Faith Movements in Central and Eastern Europe*, ed. Kaarina Aitamurto and Scott Simpson (London: Routledge, 2014), 280n17.

Azeri propaganda of the Armenians "occupying seven Azeri regions around the enclave of Nagorno-Karabakh" was received with outrage and ridicule by Armenian communities around the world, who consider those liberated Armenian lands. The majority, if not all of the territories in question, are the lowlands of Karabakh, which, in 1923, were carved away from its highlands and absorbed into Soviet Azerbaijan in order to isolate the remainder of the "enclave" deeper within Azerbaijan.[75] They contained in them ancient Armenian monuments and churches; hundreds, if not thousands of years older than the country of Azerbaijan. Additionally, the Armenian side needed these surrounding regions as buffer zones from Azerbaijan's inhumane bombardments and genocidal ambitions. With constant repetition, however, the petrodollar-funded propaganda about Armenians occupying Azeri land succeeded in eclipsing Karabakh's liberation movement from the oppressive Soviet Azeri regime, and turned the truth on its head by instead depicting Armenia as the aggressor nation! The United Nations described Azerbaijan's borders as "internationally recognized", when in fact they were drawn by the Soviet regime and are not backed by any legitimate international measure of demarcation. Ironically, the United Nations' predecessor, the League of Nations, had, in 1920, described the same Karabakh as being part of Armenia's historic lands in the Caucasus! The leading Western nations were now protecting the borders drawn by Stalin that, at the time, the United States had considered to be illegal and had refused to recognize! In fact, the League of Nations had rejected Azerbaijan's 1920 membership application, with an unfavorable report stating that Azerbaijan "had never formally constituted a state" but was part of Mongol or Persian territories incorporated into the Russian empire, that they were not sure about the authority or the legitimacy of its then government, that the name it chose for itself was the same as that of the Persian province to the south, and that its territorial disputes

---

75 Rouben Galichian, *Clash of Histories in the South Caucasus: Redrawing the Map of Azerbaijan, Armenia and Iran.* Nov 5, 2012, Bennett & Bloom

with established neighboring states Armenia and Georgia made its boundaries hard to ascertain. Moreover the United States had refused to recognize Azerbaijan as a country![76] [77] By contrast, their report on Armenia pointed out that by signing the Treaty of Sevres, the Allied nations had de jure recognized the Armenian Republic. It is stunning what time and changing dynamics do to humanity's collective memory!

The West's reluctance in recognizing Karabakh's independence was puzzling not only because one would expect the West to advocate for democracy and freedom, but also because Nagorno-Karabakh was already, by definition, a semi-independent region, an "autonomous enclave" run by its indigenous Armenian population, a detail noticeably missing in news stories and avoided on media platforms. The narrative, instead, seems to insinuate that Karabakh was an official part of Azerbaijan, when in truth it was nothing more than a region "contested" by Azerbaijan and placed in it illegally by the Soviet Union. Karabakh had always held its separate political entity and had never been part of an "independent" Azerbaijan to now be described as a "separatist" region (as Azeri propagandists often refer to it). More importantly, Karabakh had voted democratically to rejoin Armenia, and had seceded from the Soviet Union based on the legal framework of the 1990 Secession Law. Azerbaijan had no legal ground to launch a war on independent Karabakh, where the people had voted on a referendum for independence from the Soviet Union. Additionally, the international community did not consider, and the Armenian side failed to point out that while gaining its independence in 1991, Azerbaijan had announced that it was seceding from the Soviet Union "as the successor of the 1918 Independent Azerbaijan" which included neither Nakhichevan nor

76   Edita G. Gzoyan: *Nagorno-Karabakh in the Context of Admitting Azerbaijan and Armenia to the League of Nations*. The Armenian Review Journal, Spring Summer 2017, vol 55 issue 3-4

77   Edita G. Gzoyan (2017): The admission of the Caucasus states to the League of Nations: the role of Soviet Russia, Caucasus Survey, DOI: 10.1080/23761199.2017.1342412, pg 6

Karabakh with its surrounding lowlands (See chapter: Where is Karabakh?). By denouncing the Soviet regime as an "occupying" force, Azerbaijan had by default also delegitimized all the decisions made by that regime, including the transfer of Nakhichevan and Karabakh from Armenia to Azerbaijan. Most astonishingly, the UN neglected to enforce its genocide prevention protocols and did not take into account Azerbaijan's human rights violations, its anti-Armenian pogroms, its historic and ongoing ethnic cleansing of Armenians, its record in Nakhichevan, or its indoctrinated Armenophobia. Based on the clear existential threat it was living under, as well as its right to self-determination, Karabakh should have been accorded remedial sovereignty and allowed to reunite with Armenia. Instead, Europe, the UN, and NATO acted in sync with Western economic and geopolitical interests that seemingly favored strategic partner Turkey and oil-exporting Azerbaijan over truth, justice, democracy, and the freedom of an indigenous people. Russia, on the other hand, wanted to uphold the Soviet-era borders and their corresponding territorial disputes that kept the countries of the region dependent on its influence as a "mediator." To its defense, the UN described only the seven surrounding regions as "occupied" and made no recommendations <u>against</u> the recognition of the Republic of Nagorno-Karabakh. It has simply spoken against further advancements by the Armenian forces during the 1990s Karabakh war, and has asked for Armenia to use its influence on Nagorno-Karabakh to help deter such advancements.

In order to combat Armenia's historic rights to Artsakh (Karabakh), the Azeri leadership either destroys Armenian monuments or comes up with historical revisionism to mischaracterize and falsify their origin. For example, it has come up with the creative hypothesis that Azeris (who are overwhelmingly Muslim) are the descendants of Christian Caucasian Albanians and that the Armenian churches in Artsakh are, in fact, Albanian! This theory was first floated in the 1950s by controversial Azeri academic Ziya Bunyadov, who has been accused of reprinting antique and medieval sources where he had the words "Armenian state" replaced by "Albanian state."[78] Many international scholars have dismissed his claim that Armenian churches were Albanian as unfounded. British expert on the Caucasus Thomas de Waal has even called it "rather bizarre."[79] Artsakh has been described as part of Armenia in the works of ancient geographers and historians whose works have mentioned that the border between Armenia and Caucasian Albania was the Kura River, and Artsakh and Utik are in the west and south of the Kura River. Ironically, most of what is known about the short-lived Caucasian Albanian Kingdom comes from the writings of ancient Armenian historians Movses Khorenatsi (Late Antiquity) and Movses Kaghankatvatsi (Medieval) where it emerges in history as a vassal state of the Armenian Kingdom (321BC to 428AD). The borders of Caucasian Albania shifted at different times. After the collapse of the Armenian Kingdom that was ruling over it, with the help of the Sasanid Persians, for a time it expanded west and seized Artsakh and Utik. Movses Khorenatsi has also written about a certain Aran, "descendant of the Armenian Patriarch Hayk", who ruled as governor from the Arax River (Araz) to the Kura River, and that the region's Armenian name *Aghuank* was named after Aran who was described by Armenians as *Aghu* (soft, amiable).[80] Movses Kaghankatvasi referred to Aran as the founder of the first Caucasian Albanian dynasty, the Aranshahiks.[81] The region was in fact known as Arran (or Aran) by the Persians and Arabs. Culturally related to Armenia, Caucasian Albania did not have a unique ethnicity but was rather comprised of 26 tribes. Its King Urnayir was baptized to Christianity by the Armenians, and Albanian churches

78 "Albanian Myth" (in Russian) / V.A. Shnirelman, "Voyni pamyati. Mifi, identichnost i politika v Zakavkazye," Moscow, Academkniga, 2003

79 Thomas De Waal. *The Caucasus: An Introduction*. Oxford University Press, USA. 2010, p. 107

80 Moses Khorenats'i (1978). *History of the Armenians*. Translated by Thomson, Robert W. Cambridge, Massachusetts & London: Harvard University Press. pp. 139–140.

81 *The History of the Caucasian Albanians by Movses Dasxuanci*. Translated by Charles Dowsett. London: Oxford University Press, 1961, pp. 3–4, 7, 24

were consecrated under the jurisdiction of the Armenian Mother Church of Etchmiadzin (in other words, they belonged to/were affiliated with the Armenian Church). Even the Caucasian Albanian alphabet, from which the Udi dialect was later derived, was created by the Armenian monk Mesrob Mashtots, the inventor of the Armenian alphabet. While their cultural affairs were highly influenced by the Armenians, politically, the Caucasian Albanians elected to be more loyal to the Sasanid Persian power. In the 8th century, Caucasian Albania adopted Islam under the rule of the Arab Caliphate, assimilated into the Arab and Persian communities, and disappeared three centuries prior to the migration of the Turkic ancestors of the Azeris, while the Armenians in Artsakh and Utik continued to thrive under different Armenian kingdoms and princehoods *(melikdoms)* and built many more churches in the region. Until recently, when this theory has again been revived, Azeris were harassing the tiny community of Christian Udis (Caucasian Albanian tribe) who still survive in Azerbaijan; and now they use them to further this politically motivated propaganda. Many Udis were, in fact, thrown out of Azerbaijan in the late 1980s along with the Armenians.[82] While Caucasian Albanians were cited briefly, Armenians have been mentioned as inhabitants of the Caucasus throughout history. On the other hand, no internationally known ancient or modern-day historian, geographer, historical record, or relic (Christian or Muslim) has ever mentioned or attributed the terminology or ethnicity of Azeri or Azerbaijani to the Caucasus above the Araz River prior to 1918. The fact is that the majority of Azeris are descendants of Oghuz Turks, identify as Turks, and have nothing to do with Caucasian Albanians whose remnants they simply Turkified.

Russia and Azerbaijan denied the Karabakh Armenians their human rights by declining their democratic petition to rejoin Armenia and by dismissing their right for self determination. While the West

---

82 Avetisyan, Armine. "Fading - On Being Udi in Armenia". *Chaikhana*

was supporting NATO ally Turkey, landlocked and surrounded by genocidal foes, the 1991 independent Republic of Armenia, on its part, had no choice but to sign energy and military agreements with regional power Russia.

In 2009, the OSCE Minsk group prioritized Azerbaijan's territorial integrity in its Madrid Principles. Karabakh's status was to be determined in an undefined future only after the surrounding "occupied regions" were returned to Azerbaijan, during which time Karabakh would be given an "interim status" with guaranteed security and self governance. By comparison, Azerbaijan was allowed to continue to occupy parts of the east Martuni and east Martakert regions of the enclave of Nagorno-Karabakh proper. The Madrid Principles were not well received by the Armenians. One can imagine a people's trauma in dealing with lands bearing physical proof of its ancient history and containing the cemeteries of its ancestors being constantly described as lands it "occupies" from another country. These were territories of Khachen liberated with the blood of the Armenian people from 70 years of Soviet and Azeri rule. In the absence of an independent status, losing them as a security belt, would put Karabakh's priceless ancient historical monuments and its vulnerable population in serious peril once again.

In 2017, the Armenians renamed the Republic of Karabakh by its historical name of Artsakh. Due to their own baggage of interests, the Minsk partners, Russia, France, and the U.S., brought the conflict to a convoluted impasse by upholding both Azerbaijan's "territorial integrity" and a "people's right for self-determination." For starters, why would a people, that is already living in its ancestral lands, need to claim the right for self-determination? And how can its right to self-determination be implemented, when the same land, that was an autonomous enclave for the past 70 years, is now being presented as part of the country it was placed in illegally? A country that was artificially created over the historic lands of the people in question! The reference to "self-determination" itself became problematic, considering the issue was not "separation" (Karabakh was never part of an independent Azerbaijan), but rather liberation and the rejoining of mainland Armenia. With every skirmish initiated at the border by Azerbaijan, the OSCE undermined the importance of truth and accountability by following a policy of false parity and an appearance of even-handedness with an unethical call for "both sides to refrain from violence." This constant appeasement and the lack of decisive condemnation served to further embolden the Azeri leadership and destabilize the region. Reassured by the success of his caviar diplomacy and the impunity everyone offered him in return, Aliyev cranked up his warmongering and vocal plans for solving the Karabakh conflict by force, dismissing the Minsk group's mandate for a peaceful solution. The outnumbered and blockaded Armenians, on the other hand, failed to invest time and effort to tell their story and educate the world about the root cause of the conflict. They failed to leverage their 1994 victory to secure Azerbaijan's acknowledgement of Artsakh as part of Armenia (based on its people's referendum) within a peace treaty, instead of simply agreeing to a ceasefire meant to give Azerbaijan time to prepare for another war. By all accounts, Armenia saw its military victory in the first Karabakh war as final, and relied on the Minsk group to resolve the political side of the matter peacefully.

Over the course of the years, the UN Committee on the Elimination of Racial Discrimination, the European Commission against Racism and Intolerance, and the Council of Europe Advisory Committee on the Framework Convention for the protection of National Minorities and other international organizations reported on and confirmed on many occasions the extreme systemic racism and xenophobia against Armenians in Azerbaijan. The country blacklisted many journalists, politicians, and celebrities for having visited or planning on visiting Artsakh. The Human Rights Watch Report continuously alerts about freedoms of association, expression, and assembly being severely curtailed in Azerbaijan, where, according to its assessments, homosexuals, dissent, opposition, and critics are regularly targeted, tortured, and jailed without due process.

Europe, Russia and the U.S. could have solved the conflict by recognizing Artsakh's independence as an existential necessity for its survival, sustainability, and the safety of its citizens. However, interests embedded in a regional power play, oil and arms sales were, it seems, overriding factors in keeping the conflict alive.

THE DECISIONS OF THE FIFTH COMMITTEE OF THE LEAGUE OF NATIONS ON THE MEMBERSHIP APPLICATIONS OF THE REPUBLICS OF ARMENIA, AZERBAIJAN AND OTHERS , 2ND SECTION ON RIGHT MENTIONS THE REJECTION OF AZERBAIJAN'S APPLICATION. (JOURNAL OF THE FIRST ASSEMBLY OF THE LEAGUE OF NATIONS, GENEVA 1920, P. 139, CITED IN THE ISSUE OF *NAGORNO-KARABAKH IN THE LEAGUE OF NATIONS*, ARMENIAN WEEKLY, JULY 2, 2020)

The U.S. Congress Recognizes the Armenian Genocide!

In the 1980s, on occasion, I would share with American friends, details about atrocities committed against Armenians during the Genocide. I would test the waters, careful not to divulge too much about the sacred martyrdom of my people to folk for whom it meant nothing. The reactions I would get ranged from skepticism to disgust and horror to unapologetic disinterest. After all, the crimes inflicted on my ancestors were so barbaric that they did not jibe with the late 20th century and, frankly, sounded more like things out of a fictional horror movie. The Kardashian phenomenon was still years away, and most Americans I met were not familiar with "Armenian" as a nationality, let alone know about the Armenian Genocide. But then ISIS (the Islamic State of Iraq and the Levant) came along, and the same atrocious crimes that the Ottoman Turks had committed against the Armenians, from beheadings to selling of women as slaves to the destruction of monuments, were repeating in the 21st century for the entire world to witness on social media!

THE SO-CALLED ARAB SPRING THAT had erupted in 2010 with anti-government protests against oppressive regimes across the Middle East reached Syria's doorsteps, where instead of toppling the leadership of President Bashar Al-Assad, it flung the country into a civil war. It was then that ISIS, an offshoot of Al Qaida, re-emerged as part of the rebellion against President Assad's regime. The rebels against Assad were being supported by the United States. Downplayed at first by President Obama as the "JV team" in contrast to Assad's brutal regime, ISIS became the deadliest global terrorist network within two years' time. The devastating war, in addition to the violence Isis committed against Christians and other Muslim factions, led to a massive refugee migration crisis. As if it was 1915 all over again, hundreds of exhausted families, marching with bundles, pushed against the borders of European countries to let them in. Family members were separated, and people drowned in the seas in their attempt to flee for their lives. In all this chaos, Christian minorities were attacked, forced to convert to Islam, churches and cultural sites were destroyed, and Christian Yazidis and Assyrians were massacred by the thousands. And just like in 1915, nothing much was done about this new genocide. The fate of Christians in the Middle East does not seem to be of major concern to world leaders. As a matter of fact, this unsavory subject was barely covered by American news channels. Eastern Christians simply do not fit the current narrative of the Western media where Muslims are often portrayed as the victims and Christians are the villains. Analysts have also observed an underlying indifference or racism against non-white Middle Eastern Christians in that Western Christian nations do not consider them part of their brotherhood. In 2014, when the Armenian Syrian town of Kessab at the border with Turkey was attacked by anti-Assad militant rebels and Islamic State forces backed by Turkey, ironically, it was President Assad and the Syrian army that came to the rescue and thwarted them.

On September 22 of the same year, Armenians woke up to the news that the elegant Armenian Genocide memorial church and museum complex built in 1990 in Deir Zor, Syria, was bombed and destroyed. ISIS was blamed for this bombing. This news was very chilling because of what the church stood for and what the act could possibly be implying. Was the persecution of the Armenians restarting? In 1915, Ottoman Turkey deported its Armenian population to Deir Zor in the Syrian Desert, where the majority of the 1.5 million victims were killed. As a matter of fact, Deir Zor is considered the Auschwitz of the Armenians. The Genocide Memorial complex housed actual remains of victims gathered from its surroundings. ISIS's caliphate dream seemed to involve the same old plan of clearing the Christian minorities to make way for a homogeneous Islamic bloc. A year later, in 2015, the 100th anniversary of the Armenian Genocide was marked by a massive march in Los Angeles where over 160,000 Armenian Americans, among them my family and friends, walked to the Turkish Embassy demanding that Turkey acknowledge the Armenian Genocide. Special centennial commemorations took place in Armenia, Lebanon, and elsewhere in the world. While Armenians were still waiting for justice, their grassroots political activism had succeeded in raising worldwide awareness of the crime committed against their nation. Over 30 countries and almost all U.S. states had officially recognized the Armenian Genocide. The Federal government, however, was still electing not to upset Turkey.

That the Armenian Genocide has shaped the course of human history is undeniable. As the 20th century's first mass extermination act of its kind, its atrocities have inspired the coinage of the word "genocide," while the fact that it has gone unpunished has set a treacherous precedent of impunity for crimes against humanity. Many genocides following in its aftermath bore no consequences, while others, such as the Jewish Holocaust and the Bosnian Genocide, have borne the brunt of the United Nations General Assembly and the international criminal courts. Selective justice and inequities in the enforcement of international law continue to undermine the United Nations Genocide Convention and precipitate new atrocities. The demise of masses of innocent victims, whose communities or countries are not geopolitically prioritized by the leading nations of the world, is often treated as an inconsequential footnote of "inevitable" world unrest, and the culprits are never brought to justice.

The once ghost town of Gemmayze, Lebanon, where I was born and where my family lived, became one of the trendiest districts in Beirut after the civil war ended in 1990. Full of high-end bars, nightclubs, and bohemian restaurants carved into refurbished historic buildings, it was dubbed "Greenwich village" and "Soho." Once the target of snipers, Gemmayze Street that my sister and I crossed apprehensively on our way to school became notorious for its jam-packed traffic on the weekends. No expense was spared in cleaning up and rebuilding downtown Beirut, although it never regained its prewar vibrancy. Nightlife in Lebanon was yet again unmatched, and famous artists and celebrities from all over converged there and had their clothes made by world-famous Lebanese designers such as Elie Saab, Zouheir Mourad, and Reem Acra. Currently, however, Lebanon is going through its own revolutions. Government corruption, sectarian rule, and a collapsed economy have brought the country to the brink of a humanitarian crisis.

During what became known as the Four Day War in April of 2016, Azerbaijan attacked and took back some villages on the border with Artsakh, where Azeri fighters and hired Afgan mercenaries beheaded captured Armenian soldiers, murdered and cut off the ears of elderly Armenian villagers. The perpetrators paraded pictures of their deeds on social media a la ISIS-style, and the world did not care. Europe, the U.S., and Israel were focused on Azerbaijan's oil production and its strategic proximity to Iran. It was also the first time military drones were used by Azerbaijan against the Armenians, a foreshadowing of things to come. Since losing the war in 1994, Azerbaijan had advanced its oil production, projected an outward image of a modern country, promoted investments in high-rises and international hotels (including Trump towers), and erased the memory of bloody anti-Armenian pogroms from its streets. Starting in 2014, it launched a vigorous militarization campaign spending billions on arms and military technology in particular from Russia, Turkey and Israel. It had also hired international PR companies and lobbying firms to enhance its image, cover up its human rights abuses and disseminate anti-Armenian slander and historical revisionism.

Suddenly, fake articles started popping up in the United States and elsewhere about a supposed invasion of Azerbaijan by Armenia in the 1990s and the resulting occupation of Azeri territories by Armenians. Ads were gushing about Azerbaijan, a country that is currently 96% Muslim and where Armenians are barred from traveling, as being a secular multi-cultural tolerant country! It mattered not that Armenia was a burgeoning democracy and Azerbaijan was a dictatorship, oppressing freedoms and promoting violent racism and hatred against Armenians. Azerbaijan was vilifying the Armenians, enlisting the help of entities who stood to profit from the reoccupation of Artsakh by Azerbaijan. The world ran on money, oil, and guns. And while it worked hard to advance its tech sector, landlocked Armenia continued to mostly run on history and culture. In other words, it still had nothing to offer to the world in order to receive the privilege of sitting at the table of nations and be worthy of defending.

Since liberating their homeland, the Armenians were focused on peace and prosperity while Azerbaijan was getting ready for war. It used the Turkic signature modus operandi of instigating an unprovoked attack and then blaming the other side for having started it when the operation did not go as planned. When they were successful in regaining territory, the Azeris celebrated without qualms about the success of their offensive and the might of their army. From their part, the OSCE Minsk Group co-chairs, Russia, America and France, deviated from their mandate to keep the military balance and find a non-use of force resolution by openly selling/sending weapons to Azerbaijan. Influenced by their national and regional interests, they undermined the credibility and authority of the Minsk Group by addressing both sides evenhandedly during flare-ups caused by Azerbaijan, instead of unequivocally condemning its continuous ceasefire violations and war crimes. The Armenian side agreed time and again to place international monitors at the border to identify which side was breaking the ceasefire in the line of contact, while Azerbaijan refused. Armenia wanted all parties who had signed the original Bishkek ceasefire accord in 1994, Russia, Armenia, Azerbaijan, and Artsakh to be active parts of the peace process. Azerbaijan had since once again refused to acknowledge Artsakh as a political entity to deal with, dismissing the human rights of the Armenians who live there, and disregarding their very existence. The nuance that the world seemed to miss was the fact that Azerbaijan was not only asking for the return of the seven "occupied territories" around the enclave of Nagorno-Karabakh but that it wanted the whole region without its indigenous Armenians. It had successfully shifted the narrative to that of its "compromised territorial integrity" and its right "to defend itself." Had Azerbaijan recognized the Karabakh Armenians' right for self-determination, there would have been no war or so-called occupied territories.

In 2018, our Armenian driver Rudik's dream of a change of government in Armenia seemed to come true. What became dubbed the "Velvet Revolution" toppled the existing government without a single shot being fired and ushered in the hope of full democratization for Armenia, a country going through the pains of shedding Soviet-era corruption and redefining itself within the ever-shifting politics of the region. In 2019, it registered an economic growth of 7.6% and was considered one of the fastest-growing countries within the Eurasian Economic Union. Export of goods, real estate construction, and tourism were booming, and advances, especially in its IT technology sector, caught the attention of international markets. It remained landlocked, blockaded on the East and West by Azerbaijan and Turkey, and mostly reliant on Russia for fuel, energy, and security.

In 2019, President Trump prided himself in having defeated the ISIS caliphate in a war coalition where the American-backed

Kurdish Democratic Forces (SDF) in northern Syria emerged as the most effective fighters in freeing a majority of ISIS-held territory. The Turks, who sabotaged war efforts, argued that the SDF had ties with the terrorist Kurdistan Workers Party (PKK). Since the 1970s, the PKK in Turkey has been fighting against discrimination and for the sovereignty of Kurdistan, whose historical lands extend from northern Syria and Iraq into Eastern Turkey. In October 2019, after a call from Turkish President Erdogan, President Trump announced his sudden decision to withdraw the U.S. troops from northern Syria. The move prompted the resignation of Secretary of Defense General Mattis and was denounced from all sides. Trump was accused of betraying Kurdish allies and leaving them to be massacred by the Turks. Republican Senator Lindsay Graham called the decision a "stain on America's honor," the worst mistake of Trump's presidency, which will ensure the comeback of ISIS. In a tweet, Republican Senator Marco Rubio observed, "at request of this administration the Kurds served as the primary ground fighters against ISIS in Syria so U.S. troops wouldn't have to." He said Trump "then cut (a) deal with Erdogan allowing him to wipe them out. Damage to our reputation & national interest will be extraordinary & long lasting."[83]

When he hosted Erdogan at the Oval Office in Washington DC a few days later, Trump, who was being investigated for abuse of power and obstruction of congress, blurted out what that deal entailed as he told reporters, "We are keeping the oil. We have the oil. The oil is secure. We left troops behind only for the oil."[84] When a powerful nation is at the top of the food chain, it has the authority to assassinate undesired foreign political figures, award

---

83 Natasha Turak, "Trump Defends Allowing Turkish Offensive Against Kurds: 'They Didn't Help Us in the Second World War,'" CNBC, October 10, 2019, https://www.cnbc.com/2019/10/10/trump-defends-allowing-turkish-offensive-on-kurds-in-syria-they-didnt-help-us-in-ww2.html.

84 Ishaan Tharoor, "Trump's Perplexing Insistence on 'Keeping' Middle Eastern Oil," *Washington Post*, November 14, 2019, https://www.washingtonpost.com/world/2019/11/15/trumps-perplexing-insistence-keeping-middle-eastern-oil/.

the lands of one country to another, and invade and put its hands on other nations' natural resources with impunity. All it has to do is enlist some righteous reason for its actions and have it repeated a few times on national TV, et voila, the people will approve of it. But a weak country without anything to offer is called a terrorist when it defends itself and an occupier when it frees its homeland, and calculated lies are publicized about it on platforms it cannot afford to reach or is simply barred from.

As anticipated, Turkey attacked swiftly and took over an entire so-called "safe zone" in Northern Syria, claiming plans to settle Syrian refugees there. Ironically, an additional 300,000, mostly Kurds, were displaced from the area as the Turkish offensive pushed the SDF forces out amidst rumors of excessive force and war crimes.[85] Most experts viewed this exercise as new demographic engineering and ethnic cleansing aimed at crushing the Kurdish prospects for a sovereign Kurdistan. A century after WWI, all involved parties seemed to be picking up from where they had left off, pursuing the same objectives and gains. The same Turkey that decried the buffer zone the Armenians of Artsakh had carved out to defend themselves from Azeri aggression had no issues convincing the United States to let it occupy a security zone from northern Syria. No one, of course, talked about the breach of Syria's territorial integrity. During his Oval Office meeting with Trump, Erdogan addressed yet another subject. In the midst of these developments, the House of Representatives had introduced a resolution to officially recognize the Armenian Genocide. Between striking deals, Erdogan had lobbied Trump against the house resolution and warned of dire consequences if it were to pass. He would later threaten to shut down the U.S. Injirlik base in Turkey and accuse the U.S. of having committed genocide against the indigenous American Indians.

To the Armenian community's delight, House Resolution 296, recognizing the Armenian Genocide passed on October 29 with

---

85 "Damning evidence of war crimes by Turkish forces and allies in Syria". *Amnesty International*. 18 October 2019.

an overwhelming 405 to 11 vote! In turn, Senators Bob Menendez and Ted Cruz introduced a similar bipartisan resolution in the Senate. Armenians around the world held their breath week after week as the vote came to the floor of the Senate three times and, each time, was blocked by a Republican senator at the request of President Trump, claiming it was not the right time to pass such a resolution. Interestingly, all three Republican senators who vetoed the vote, Lindsay Graham, David Perdue, and Kevin Cramer, made a point of saying that they were objecting on behalf of the Trump administration but would not do so again. It is worth noting that Trump's predecessor, Barack Obama, who as a candidate had promised to recognize the Armenian Genocide, not only reneged on his promise as president, but he outright prohibited Congress from passing any such resolutions. On December 12, 2019, a fourth attempt for a unanimous vote by the Senate went unchallenged, and Senate resolution 150 passed, making it official U.S. policy to commemorate the Armenian Genocide! The state of Mississippi and the U.S. executive branch remained the only two entities yet to officially recognize the Armenian Genocide. Finally, 104 years after American ambassador to the Ottoman Empire Henry Morgenthau Sr. telegraphed Washington DC, sounding the alarm about what he described as "race extermination," it was politically expedient for the American Congress to formally acknowledge the Armenian Genocide.

The resolutions came during a time of heightened tensions between the United States and Turkey, not only over its invasion of Syria but also its purchase of Russian S-400 missile systems. Analysts said that the resolutions passed as a show of Congress's disapproval of Trump's abrupt decision to withdraw American forces from Syria and to deter potential Turkish atrocities against the Kurds. Although I was elated, deep down, I felt a curious uneasiness about the passage of the resolutions. They obviously had no political teeth, but they made me remember what I had read in my research about Turks striking Armenians down after each political gain the latter made.

Six days later, on December 18, the House of Representatives approved articles of impeachment against President Trump. Soon, the country was engrossed in the impeachment trials, and the Turkish invasion of Syria was all but forgotten. The same media that had gone to great lengths to denounce the Assad regime's bombings of civilians went completely mum about the massive Turkish bombardments of the Kurds and Syrians.

President Trump's outwardly isolationist foreign policy was, in effect, focused on isolating Iran and weakening Russia with the aid of sanctions and proxy wars. For their part, Russia and local players were competing to reassert their powers in the absence of an American presence. Trump has, on many occasions, expressed his admiration towards Erdogan and called him a friend. He waved Section 907 of the U.S. Freedom Support Act that prohibits U.S. aid to Azerbaijan. In the 2018-2019 fiscal year, the Trump administration proceeded to raise U.S. military aid to Azerbaijan to a whopping $120 million (previous aid did not exceed $3 million), providing support with military technology for the security of its southern border with Iran and for "human rights training." [86] The motive and integrity of the latter part of the aid statement were questionable to the very least, considering the U.S. was arming a dictatorship with one of the worst human rights records and a genocidal policy against Armenians.

Despite its military alliance with Armenia, a member of the Collective Security Treaty Organization (CSTO), Russia also upheld a close relationship with Azerbaijan and dramatically increased its arms sales to it. Instead of reacting to the fact that Russia was selling weapons to their enemy and adopting alternate measures, the Armenians stayed true to their alliance by not buying weapons from the West, and America in particular, in fear of Russian retaliation. With the support of powerful friends and continued appeasement

---

86 Emil Sanamyan, "US Allocates $100 Million in Security Aid to Azerbaijan 2018–2019," USC Dornsife Institute of Armenian Studies, July 17, 2019, https://armenian.usc.edu/us-allocates-100-million-in-security-aid-to-azerbaijan/.

by the Minsk group, Aliyev's enhanced confidence was becoming evident in his increasingly belligerent announcements of resolving the Karabakh conflict with force. Feeling emboldened, he went as far as claiming that the entire country of Armenia, with its 3,500 years of written history, belonged to Azerbaijan, a country with a mere 100 years of history! It was a stunningly dumbfounding statement being tossed at a disengaged world crippled by fake news and a deficiency and disinterest in historical knowledge! While Aliyev expressed impatience with the OSCE Minsk peace process, which insisted that the Karabakh conflict could not be solved militarily, the Armenian side squandered its 1994 victory and sat on its laurels instead of getting ready for the worst-case scenario.

GEMMAYZE STREET, THE WAY IT CURRENTLY LOOKS (OCTOBER, 2022).
PHOTO TAKEN BY MY COUSIN, TALINE TAVITIAN TERZIAN.

American Interests?

"Where the hell are YOU from?" The question asked to me by the pharmacy customer I had helped all those years ago still rings in my ear. Yes, where am I from and why am I in America? A Lebanese Armenian in a tapestry of White Caucasians, African Americans, Mexicans, Chinese, Persians, and every other nationality you can think of. Why are any of us here?! Many interviews with new and old relatives, astounding family secrets revealed, and hours of research later, I came to discover that I was the daughter of one of the most continuously persecuted nations on earth, an ancient people with a most unfair and unjust fate, but a fate not necessarily unique among small nations trampled by so-called big nations vying for power at all cost.

EVER SINCE WE MOVED TO America, we kept hearing about Armenian Genocide Recognition resolutions being debated in the halls of the U.S. Congress. Most were stopped by the powerful Turkish lobby and its allies in Washington. Some passed the House but were denied a Senate vote, even though that was the next step in the legislative process. Year after year, American congressmen speaking against these resolutions would cite the same two reasons: "Not the right time" and "against American interests." And year after year, the number of Genocide survivors brought by the Armenian community to these hearings would dwindle. This was not President Woodrow Wilson's America. It was an America that had Turkey as a close ally, supporting it monetarily and militarily. Justice for the Armenians needed to wait.

As a new country founded on the mantra of "life, liberty and the pursuit of happiness," for a while, America followed an isolationist policy and did its best to adhere to its principles of small government and government "by the people for the people" until the end of World War I, when lured by the post-war arms race and the emerging world currency of oil, it was drawn into the woes of geopolitics. To stay in the game of superpowers means leading in humanitarian, innovational, and environmental fields. Inevitably and in spite of the most honorable intentions, however, it also entails developing monopolies in leading industries which suck jobs and opportunities away from less resourceful countries. It means using weaker nations as bargaining chips and luring them into your sphere of influence and installing puppet regimes in the name of "building nations with advanced values," often in order to access strategic geographic locations as well as local natural resources in return. It means exploiting and inflaming divisions to advance your country's agenda and fueling proxy wars to weaken the competition. As timeless as these activities have been in the history of powerful nations, most do not mesh well with American values of freedom, equality, and justice. When a country's "interests" are not in sync with its values, they risk eroding its credibility and diminishing its respect and authority in the world. Once a country's principles are on shaky ground, its entire national structure becomes unsound. The bulk of the burden to fund foreign policy endeavors has fallen on the American middle class that often works two jobs to make ends meet and has mostly no say in where its hard-earned tax dollars are spent. Ironically, for a country that defines itself as the beacon of freedom, democracy and human rights have become the least prioritized areas in these transactional foreign relations that emphasize strategic partnerships involving military, intelligence, energy, and trade contracts. Allowing an ally country to get away with genocide because of national interests is not very American.

Siding with oppressive regimes instead of fighting for the rights of the oppressed is not very American. Upholding corrupt dictatorships instead of supporting fledgling democracies is not American. Allowing the federal government to be run by the powerful lobbies of authoritarian countries who learned to align themselves with "American interests" in order to receive military and economic aid, as well as extricate impunity for their crimes and human rights abuses, is not American. However, these are the challenges and complexities facing today's American foreign policy. One wonders how American interests in Transcaucasia would have best been served instead if, in 1920, America had been able to place a mandate over Armenia, the only country aligned with Western democratic values in the region today. It will, however, be remiss not to mention here, that since its independence, Armenia has received millions in U.S. aid for economic development and democracy programs. The U.S. has one of the largest Armenian Diasporas, and maintains friendly relations with Armenia and Artsakh.

In March of 2020, the world became overrun by the pandemic of the novel Coronavirus, COVID-19. Cities were put under lockdown to slow transmission, economies went into manmade semi-recessions, millions urged to stay home lost their jobs, and hundreds of thousands of infected people died. In May, the killing of a Black man named George Floyd by a White police officer in Minneapolis, Minnesota, brought revolution to America's doorsteps. In major cities, violent rioters mingled amongst the peaceful demonstrators of the "Black Lives Matter." Businesses were looted, properties set on fire, police officers attacked and killed, districts occupied, and historical monuments and statues from the era of slavery toppled. Pouring gas on fire was the constant barrage of polarizing political viewpoints, mingled with fake news, being spewed from media platforms.

Overnight, old wounds were forced open, and mistrust and hatred spread at an alarming speed. Suddenly, capitalism was being vilified and socialist ideals promoted by the same America that was vehemently against socialist regimes, notably the USSR, Cuba, and China. One side was building walls while the other was building sanctuary cities. America was no longer a new country. It was following in the familiar steps of aging countries, where humanism and nationalism collide. The only exception is that, in America, the land historically belongs to none of the parties currently in dispute.

With each cycle of worldwide ups and downs, different groups have risen with new ideas of revolutionary socioeconomic and governing systems. Clans, tribes, kingdoms, feudalisms, dynasties, dictatorships, democracies, communism, capitalism, socialism, Marxism, and so on and so forth, have been tried and recycled, often within the same given society. The rule of the jungle is always clashing with the human mind's aspirations of achieving a more dignified existence. These societal models invariably come with shelf lives because of evolving and changing socioeconomic dynamics and the human mind's innate need to compete. It is to be seen if America, the greatest human experiment, with its ingeniously crafted Constitution of checks and balances will be able to reinvent itself yet again and become a better union, or will it tumble down the historic path that every maturing empire has ultimately fallen into?

Throughout the ages, man has known that power lies in numbers and structured assembly. Unions and empires were formed for the common goals of sustainability and power. Each was started with great convictions in the new model it was built around. But as it has matured, more often than not, the central governing power has grown too large for oversight, giving way to corruption. Its bureaucracy has become too complex to manage, its debts too overwhelming to recover from, its economic ambitions too grand, and its military too overstretched. With the weakening of the governing body, the rule of law and the quality of its institutions have deteriorated. Underlying divisions and existing prejudices have resurfaced. Pride in a shared national identity has eroded. Different sectors have risen up to perpetuate identity politics that have given way to divisiveness, violence and unrest. In turn, the resulting lawlessness has, in many instances, paved the way to the rise of authoritarianism.

In order to keep their standing in the world and boost economic revenue with military, trade, and development contracts, many empires and unions at the brink of collapse have gone to desperate lengths of creating wars or unrest in different parts of the world. Civilizations have risen and fallen along these predictable patterns. There was once a Roman Empire, a Persian Empire, a Russian Empire, an Ottoman Empire, a British Empire, a Soviet Union... Even the current European Union is faltering with Britain's exit. With the inevitable shifts in economic, political, and military powers come the waves of migration. People leaving war-torn countries and collapsing economies to new unions promising safety and prosperity, and the cycle repeats.

The challenge lies in maintaining a delicate balance between government authority and individual freedoms, between competitiveness and dominance, and between rule of law and authoritarianism. While a healthy desire to compete pushes the envelope in innovation and knowledge, the concept of dominating emanates from the desire to attain power and risks being divisive, racist, hurtful, and unfair. Imperialism, colonialism, expansionism, industrial monopolies, and economic and military powers have never produced perfect peace and harmony. They have created most of the world's unrest and instability. One of the principal victims in these interactions has been "the truth," often manipulated, covered up, or denied in order to achieve certain ends. Truth matters. Truth is what gives life meaning. Without truth, civilization is in detrimental peril; therefore, it is imperative that truth be upheld, safeguarded, and communicated.

It remains to be seen if humanity will ever find a way to come up with an international structure of checks and balances that will eliminate inequities in quality of life. A system that will hold no nation above the law, where human rights violations are apprehended equally and without exceptions or favoritism, and where evil receives zero tolerance. You may say that the law of the jungle is what nature has intended in order to control population growth. Human beings cannot help the way they behave because that is how they were created. Their passion is to give meaning to their existence and leave their mark on earth. Their mistrust of each other and their fear of failure push them into new adventures as well as troubles and wars. However, by the same token, we cannot deny all the good that the human mind and spirit have also achieved in enhancing quality of life and elevating human dignity.

The American dream is one such accomplishment. The United States of America will remain the world's unique experiment, where people from all over the world have fled the troubles of their homelands and assembled to coexist as equals, putting their humanity above their differences in race, sex, religion, and creed. This great experiment needs to be saved from the precipice of the ways of an "empire." It needs to return to the roots of its inception and its promise to be governed "by the people for the people." Regardless of which party is in power, Americans have to remain the owners of their destiny and remember that the freedoms they enjoy also empower them to learn from past mistakes and build upon advances made. This cannot be achieved unless every denomination is listened to, the past is allowed to be examined, and changes are implemented while everyone commits to the rule of law, compromise, individual responsibility, mutual respect, and celebration of diversity.

America has come a long way from the days when signs in windows in Fresno, California, read "No Armenians or Dogs Allowed," and every new arriving group, from Jews to Scots to Italians, was discriminated against in New York and other major cities. It has come a long way in correcting the treatment of African Americans whose ancestors were brought over as slaves and abused for centuries. Yes, there are racial inequalities as well as racists in American society, just as there are in all societies. However, there are also elements that strive to make it nonracist, including its written law, which allows for freedom of speech and civil recourse. In fact, there are laws against discrimination based on race, color, religion, sexual orientation, national origin, disability, or age. While systemic racism is still embedded in the layers of society, the American legal system does not have laws that legalize racist acts. For example, schools do not openly teach young kids to hate a certain minority group. Criminals who kill people just because they belong to a certain race are not celebrated as national heroes. Politicians, journalists, writers, scientists, professors, and artists are not jailed for expressing certain views. Citizens belonging to a vilified minority are not allowed to be tortured, beheaded, and burned alive with impunity. Minority civilian populations are not bombed by the government. Ethnic languages and cultural traditions are not forbidden. Places of worship are not desecrated and destroyed. Yet, America is far from being perfect. It behooves the American people to uphold and safeguard its founding principles and strive to keep the American dream alive. I will always love America and be grateful for the second chance it has given me; it had me at "have a nice day!"

2020, Annus Horribilis

"So everything is fake news," Orla Guerin, BBC news correspondent interviewing Aliyev November, 2020, regarding the indiscriminate Azeri shelling of civilians and the use of cluster bombs documented by BBC journalists and Human Rights organizations.

"Of course," Ilham Aliyev responds. "Why not. We are facing these fake news for decades."[87]

The Ten Stages of Genocide by Dr. Gregory Stanton, President of Genocide Watch: 1.Classification, 2. Symbolization, 3. Discrimination, 4. Dehumanization, 5. Organization, 6. Polarization, 7.Preparation, 8. Persecution, 9. Extermination, 10. Denial

THIRTY-SIX YEARS HAD PASSED SINCE the day I waved goodbye to family and friends standing in the middle of the street in a neighborhood of Bourj Hammoud, Lebanon. That image is still the last one I carry with me, as I never went back for a visit. Someday, I will for sure. Based on updates, the neighborhoods in Bourj Hammoud were no longer as crowded as we remember them. More and more of its residents are migrating due to the country's economic hardships and renewed political instability. California had also changed. Once

---

87 Siranush Ghazanchyan, *Aliyev Accuses the BBC, Human Rights Watch of Spreading Fake News*, November 9, 2020, Public Radio of Armenia,

pristine sidewalks are now full of homeless tents and piles of trash. The political divisiveness in the country is a far cry from the civilized American governing system we had admired as new immigrants.

It was also hard to believe that three decades had elapsed since I first embarked on the journey to uncover my family's past and to understand how the Armenian Genocide had gone unpunished for this long. In the absence of a statehood, the disbursed Armenian Diaspora's rights continued to be unrepresented on the world stage and its demands for justice ignored. In 2019, I came across a photograph from the early 1930s of my grandmother's brother Maynuel. Getting to see what he looked like, after having researched about him for the past several years, pushed aside the last fold in the curtain of my window, looking into the past of my father's side of the family. The photograph was of him, his wife, and his two young sons. Little Krikor standing at Maynuel's side reminded me of his daughter, my newfound cousin Ilda. Even more precious, was Maynuel's handwritten message on the back of the postcard photo. It was in Armenian cursive. He was sending the photograph to his sister, my grandmother Maryam, in Lebanon, as a memento until they met again. He had signed his name "Maynuel Arpadjian," the family name from a long time ago in old Malatya, where thousands of Armenians lived their lives, raised their families, tended to their gardens, and grew their businesses. There are very few Armenians in Malatya now. Most of them do not speak nor write in Armenian. Many are hidden Armenians. The Arpadjian name no longer exists either. It was changed in 1934, soon after Maynuel's family portrait was taken, by the so-called Surname Law that mandated that all ethnic-sounding names be changed to Turkish ones. The first president of Turkey, Kemal Ataturk, was Turkifying the remaining Armenians, Greeks, and Assyrians in the old provinces of the country, completing the ethnocide of these minorities. And yet Maynuel's handwritten message had survived through the decades and landed in my hands as if in defiance of that law! The old postcard reconnected the broken family branches that I had stumbled upon and brought my journey to a gratifying closure. Two years prior, in 2017, I had visited and fallen in love with the current Republic of Armenia. I had also visited wondrous Artsakh, whose struggle for independence had unraveled in real time in the background of my personal journey in researching my family's story. Artsakh inspired us all. Fate seemed to be finally smiling at my people. We were still here, and we were moving on. None of us expected that the green-eyed, hundred-year-old monster was about to be reawakened in the 21st century!

> *"The aim of all Turks is to unite with the Turkic borders. History is affording us today the last opportunity. In order for the Islamic world not to be forever fragmented it is necessary that the campaign against Karabagh* be not *allowed to abate. As a matter of fact drive the point home in Azeri* circles that *the campaign should be pursued with greater determination and severity." Kazim Karabekir, Speaker of the Grand National Assembly of Turkey (1946-1948).*[88]

Something woke me up early in the morning of Sunday, September 27th, 2020. Chiming and vibrations on my cell phone caught my attention. Curious, I turned on my phone and noticed several news alerts and postings on Facebook. Through the dissipating fog of my interrupted sleep, the words I deciphered I wished I were not seeing. Azerbaijan, with the full assistance of Turkey, had launched an all out massive invasion of the entire border of Artsakh! It was happening! The Armenian Genocide had entered yet another active phase. This time, under the excuse of "restoring Azerbaijan's territorial integrity." A world ruled by geopolitics was upholding Azerbaijan's Soviet-era illegal borders above the threat of ethnic cleansing facing the indigenous Armenians of Artsakh,

---

88   Kazim Karabekir, Istiklâl Harbimiz/n.2/, p. 631

thus enabling Azerbaijan's dishonest and criminal strategies and bringing the conflict to yet another boiling point.

Turkey and Azerbaijan, who call themselves "one nation, two states," had decided that this was the most opportune time to derail Armenia's progress and, from all indications, reignite their age-old dream of Pan-Turkism. Just as World War I had offered the perfect cover to perpetrate the Armenian Genocide, the Covid pandemic presented the ideal opportunity to invade while Armenia was struggling with a high number of cases and the world was paralyzed by lockdowns. Billions spent on weapons, intelligence, military training, and technological support had given Azerbaijan the decisive military advantage it was seeking over the Armenian forces that in the past had proven to be more strategic and motivated compared to their Azeri counterparts. Trump's isolationist policies and close relationship with Erdogan seemed to also offer a narrow window of opportunity for Turkey and Azerbaijan to make their move prior to the takeover of a possible Biden administration. The timing of the invasion during the American presidential elections was suspect, as if intended to drown it in the news cycle. Most notably, internally, Armenia was at its most vulnerable as it was transitioning to a new parliamentary government system fresh out of its 2018 popular Velvet Revolution.

A couple of months earlier, on July 12, 2020, in what many believe was a skirmish orchestrated by Azerbaijan,[89] a flare-up had erupted in Armenia's northern Tavush region, where in the absence of world condemnation, killings of Armenian civilians and military targets by constant Azeri sniper fire had become the norm. When the Azeri offensive that involved heavy artillery and drones was pushed back in self defense by the Armenian units, Azerbaijan pulled its predictable tirade against supposed "Armenian aggression," reminiscent of its gaslighting reaction when the Armenian side won the first Karabakh war that Azerbaijan itself had started. Dozens of Armenian homes,

---

89 The Nagorno-Karabakh Conflict: A Visual Explainer. International Crisis Group. Retrieved 15 April 2021

a school, and even a factory producing Covid-19 masks for health-care workers were hit by Azeri shells.[90] The ongoing Azeri strategy of intentionally taunting the Armenians at the border in order to start a war was not evolving favorably, hence the Azeri President's restlessness and more drastic measures. The plummeting oil prices in the wake of Covid-19 lockdowns and domestic dissatisfaction with the oligarchic dictatorial regime had reinvigorated the opposition movement, and President Ilham Aliyev seemed to be under pressure to assert his power. The Armenian side had been on high alert following a belligerent statement he had made a week prior on July 6, describing the OSCE Minsk group's mediation efforts as "pointless" and threatening to solve the Karabakh conflict by military force, as if that was an acceptable or legal option in opposing a people's right of self-determination.[91]

To the dismay of Armenians all over the world, the same Western media that was sympathetic to the Karabakh independence movement in the 1980s, now adhered to the line of "renewed unrest between the two countries" instead of reporting the truth about Azerbaijan's aggression and continuous violation of the 1994 cease-fire. On July 16, as the clashes abated, Azerbaijan threatened to strike Armenia's nuclear power plant if Armenia dared to target its oil pipelines that run close to Armenia's Tavush region where the skirmish took place. This reeked of propaganda aimed at fueling anti-Armenian sentiment and escalating the unrest by enlisting the support of countries that rely on Azeri oil. It was hard to believe, that having liberated Artsakh, the Armenians would suddenly desire to start a new war with Azerbaijan, a country with three times

---

90 Emil Sanamyan, "Armenian, Azerbaijani Forces Tussle for High Ground on Tavush Border," USC Dornsife Institute of Armenian Studies, July 13, 2020, https://armenian.usc.edu/armenian-azerbaijani-forces-tussle-for-high-ground-on-tavush-border/.
91 Mushvig Mehdiyev, "Azerbaijan President Criticizes OSCE Minsk Group Inaction on Armenia's Illegal Activities," Caspian News, July 9, 2020, https://caspiannews.com/news-detail/azerbaijan-president-criticizes-osce-minsk-group-inaction-on-armenias-illegal-activities-2020-7-7-39/.

the population and a much superior arsenal. Aliyev amped up his war-mongering, ignoring the March 2020 UN Secretary General's appeal to a global ceasefire and worldwide focus on combating Covid-19 which Armenia had endorsed and Azerbaijan had refused to sign. To the shock of Armenians around the world, thousands of Azeris took to the streets in throngs chanting "death to Armenians," asking for Covid restrictions to be lifted so that they rush to the border at Tavush to fight! This was coordinated with unrest in Lebanon, France, Russia, and the United States. Turkish sympathizers in the Muslim sector of Beirut took to the streets, vowing to massacre the remaining Armenian community there. Azeris in Russia attacked and beat up Armenians and vandalized their businesses. In Lyon, France, Turkish and Azeri mobs took to the streets at night "looking for Armenians." In San Francisco, California, an Armenian elementary school was vandalized with hate-filled racist graffiti bearing the Azeri flag, an Armenian church was set on fire, and a household was marked with a red cross, similarly to what was done to Armenian homes that were attacked in the Sumgait pogroms in Azerbaijan! All this racial hate crime was taking place out in the open in the year 2020!

In a shockingly brazen move, under the orchestrated pretext of coming to its brother Azerbaijan's defense against "Armenian aggression," Turkey transferred American F16 fighter jets, military units, and high-tech weaponry to Azerbaijan, and on July 29, the two countries launched a two-week large-scale military drill at the conclusion of which Turkey conveniently left the F16 fighter jets, military equipment, and personnel behind in Azerbaijan. Rumors circulated that more weapons were being rushed from Turkey and Israel and that thousands of enlisted mercenaries from Syria, among them Isis terrorists, were heading to Azerbaijan. Logic dictates that none of this momentous activity involving thousands of military personnel and equipment could have materialized on a whim without months, if not years, of preparation. By all accounts, Armenia, did not anticipate that NATO would allow Turkey to transfer NATO weapons to Azerbaijan and launch a massive attack on a small peace-ful population whose only crime is wanting to live free in its home-land. Erdogan, however, emboldened by the green light he received in invading Syria, was on a roll, destabilizing Europe, the Middle East, North Africa, and the Caucasus. In fact, a few weeks prior, he had hinted at rekindling Pan-Turkism and basically acknowledged the Armenian Genocide by vowing, without qualms, to finish what his "ancestors had started in the Caucasus" and get rid of the "rem-nants of the sword," an old insult traditionally directed at Christian Armenians, Greeks and Assyrians who have survived massacres by Turks, and are thought of as enemy leftovers unworthy to be alive.[92]

America's distraction with its own internal unrest, and Trump's isolationist policy and announcements about not involving America in any foreign wars, seemed to have reawakened traditional ex-pansionist policies in the Caucasus. For her part, Lynne Tracy, the American ambassador to Armenia, was lulling the Armenians with the perplexing proposal of reassigning American dollars from a life-saving demining program in Artsakh to efforts of "preparing Armenia for peace"! This was in stark contrast to the unprecedented $120 million in military aid that the Trump administration had just sent to Azerbaijan by waiving section 907 of the 1992 Freedom Support Act that prohibits American aid to Azerbaijan pursuant to its blockade of Armenia and Karabakh during the first Karabakh war.[93] In 2001, against calls from the Armenian American com-munity and the Republic of Armenia to keep the policy as is, the American Senate, under pressure by the U.S. State Department, had adopted an amendment to section 907 that allows the president to waive it, if he/she determines that aid:

---

92 Genocide Watch, *Turkey: Erdogan uses "Leftovers of the Sword" anti-Christian hate speech,* May 11, 2020

93 Ara Khachatourian, "How Do You Prepare 'Populations for Peace?: You Kill and Maim Them," Asbarez, May 23, 2020, https://asbarez.com/194322/how-do-you-prepare-populations-for-peace-you-kill-and-maim-them/.

1. *Is necessary to support the operational readiness of United States Armed Forces or coalition partners to counter international terrorism; or*

2. *Is important to Azerbaijan's border security; and*

3. *Will not undermine or hamper ongoing efforts to negotiate a peaceful settlement between Armenia and Azerbaijan or be used for offensive purposes against Armenia.*[94]

Every U.S. administration since has waived Section 907.

Incomprehensibly, however, the conditions of the waiver seemed to now be breached, yet the Trump administration did not admonish the Aliyev regime! Azerbaijan, where American tax dollars were sent "to prevent terrorism" in accordance with one of the conditions of the waiver, was itself now rumored to employ Isis, Pakistani and Syrian mercenaries in its invasion of Artsakh![95] The American aid that was not supposed to be used for "offensive purposes against Armenia, or hamper efforts in negotiating a peaceful settlement" was deployed to a country engaged in an active invasion of Armenians! And yet, no unequivocal condemnation of Azerbaijan's actions was being articulated by NATO, the UN, the U.S., and the OSCE!

The Armenian Diaspora knew in its gut that the September 27 invasion was an attempt to finish the Armenian Genocide. In a united front, Armenians all over the world took to the streets, blocking freeways, demonstrating in front of American PR and lobbying firms hired by Turkey and Azerbaijan, as well as military drone parts exporters and news outlets, raising the alarm about the impending genocide in Artsakh. Their efforts were up against the millions spent

---

94 The Federal Register, The Daily Journal of the United States Government, National Archives, *Extension of Waiver of Section 907 of the Federal Support Act with Respect to Assistance to the Government of Azerbaijan,* A notice by the State Department, May 5, 2021

95 Pierre Balanian, *Turkey sends 4,000 Syrian ISIS mercenaries to fight against the Armenians,* Asia News, Sept 28, 2020

by Turkey and Azerbaijan in silencing Western media or, worse yet, having it repeat their lies and misleading propaganda. The demonstrations against weapons technology firms bore some fruit as some companies in the U.K., the U.S., and Canada stopped sending drone technology to Turkey, but these were futile steps being taken after the fact, as Bayrakdar and Harop drones were decimating the Armenian units from the air. Turkey had taken over the military command and was fighting the war of its client state Azerbaijan. Most distressing for us Armenian Americans was the realization that, we had ourselves, with our tax dollars as American citizens, funded the American jets and NATO weapons attacking our brothers and sisters in our homeland unprovoked! Azerbaijan was also using a barrage of internationally forbidden illegal weapons from cluster bombs to heavy missiles along with unmanned Kamikaze drones on Artsakh's schools, hospitals, homes, transportation, ambulances, communications, electricity and gas facilities, and all civilian infrastructure, including the Ghazanchetsots Cathedral of Shushi that my husband and I had visited three years prior!

Among the men, women, and children injured on the Armenian side were French and Russian journalists who were reporting from Artsakh, while Azerbaijan had blocked entry to all international media. As Armenians demonstrating in the streets of Los Angeles, Washington DC, New York, Paris, London, Buenos Aires, and elsewhere urged the world to recognize Artsakh's rightful independence to grant it international security, cargo planes kept on rushing more drones and missiles from Israel to Baku. As if in a trance, Armenians watched helplessly as Armenia's neighbor to the north, Georgia, restricted all flights from Russia and elsewhere to Armenia, barred Georgian Armenians from crossing the border into Armenia to enlist in the fighting, and instead accommodated Turkish planes and military trucks to use its air and land to transport weapons and possibly mercenaries to Azerbaijan. Next, Azerbaijan used white phosphorus bombs to burn the ancient sacred forests of Artsakh where Armenian fighters and civilians were hiding. The gruesome flesh-eating burns victims sustained from this incendiary carcinogenic chemical were inhumane! With the impossibility of viable replenishments through roads that were at the mercy of drone strikes, Artsakh was set to run out of ammunition. Armenia's military ally, Russia, contended that its alliance responsibilities were limited to the territory of Armenia alone and did not apply to Artsakh! Raising suspicions of foul play, Putin added that Russia had close ties with both Armenia and Azerbaijan. The Armenians knew what was coming. Beheadings, rape, torture, dismemberment, desecration of cemeteries and ancient monuments, and the loss of their homeland of millennia... Protest, march and scream as they did in the U.S. and around the world, they could not rouse the conscience of civilized nations enough to perpetuate any major politically viable repercussions. Instead of calling out Azerbaijan and Turkey for their use of force, condemning their breach of the OSCE diplomatic process and their disregard of the UN Secretary General's call for a ceasefire during the Covid pandemic, world leaders used instead calculated evenhanded remarks calling for "both parties to stop the fighting" and return to the negotiating table when one side was clearly the aggressor and committer of terrible war crimes, while the other was defending itself and hanging on for dear life.

Artsakh's limited air defense was said to have been eliminated within the first week of the war, and Azeri forces were now relentlessly taking out 18- to 20-year-old Armenian soldiers with satellite-guided precision strikes of unmanned drones. Resigned to a fate of constant persecution by Turks, these young troops had answered the call of yet another war with bright eyes and smiles on their faces. In true Armenian fashion, they had held spontaneous *shourch bars*, Armenian traditional line dance and posted them on social media in defiance of tyranny. These beautiful young soldiers, raised with so much care in the aftermath of pogroms and massacres that their parents had lived through 26 years prior, were now dying by airstrikes from superior technology they did not possess without getting to fight in man-to-man combat. As the Armenian Defense

Ministry put out daily lists of casualties and footage of massive destruction of civilian infrastructure flashed on social media, we all anxiously prayed that the obscenely violent David versus Goliath quandary would be halted by a timely ceasefire. The total disregard for humanitarian and international laws of warfare was a glaring example of "might is right," the ultimate abuse of power, a 21st-century version of the genocide of Christians as expressed by the organization of International Christian Concern, Persecution.org. A nation that has suffered from massive losses of population and homeland and that has been denied justice for so long was being allowed to be struck yet again, this time by an incredible coalition of several countries and paid terrorist mercenaries headed by the perpetrator of the 1915 Genocide, and it was facing all this power all by itself! We couldn't help but wonder what Armenia had ever done to any of these countries? Was this about Armenia or some new regional grand plan?

> *Flashback to a propaganda piece from Azerbaijan where a teacher in an elementary classroom asks the students, "Who are our enemies?" The young voices respond loudly, "The Armenians." The teacher asks, "What are we going to do?" "Take back Karabakh," the students respond. "Why?" the teacher continues. "Because we have gold there," the students respond.*

Judging by the world's inaction, it was evident that Azerbaijan had won the propaganda war. The massive revenue from its oil industry now proved to be a decisive edge over landlocked and blockaded Armenia's service-based poorer economy. Appeased and enabled by everyone, Aliyev, usually prudent in hiding his xenophobia on media platforms, proceeded with newfound confidence, using shockingly racist remarks with abandon as he vowed to kick the Armenians out of Karabakh "like dogs," dismissing everything the Armenian side put out as "fake news" coming from "liars and rats."

[96] Genocide Watch issued a Genocide Alert of stage 9: Extermination and 10: Denial, warning about signals it picked up from Azerbaijan indicating that the country was poised to commit genocidal activity against the Armenians. Similarly, the International Association of Genocide Scholars put out the following statement: *"History, from the Armenian Genocide to the last three decades of conflict, as well as current political statements, economic policies, sentiments of the societies and military actions by the Azerbaijani and Turkish leadership should warn us that genocide of the Armenians in Nagorno-Karabakh, and perhaps even Armenia, is a very real possibility. All of this proves that Armenians can face slaughter if any Armenian territory is occupied, consequently, recognizing of the independence of the Republic of Artsakh is the way to save Armenians of Artsakh from extermination now or in the near future."* [97] Armenians around the world did not need these warnings; they already knew what was coming for Artsakh. PTSD, anxiety, fear, and depression gripped our communities as the Turkish and Azeri forces advanced into several of the buffer territories and were now moving into the enclave of Nagorno-Karabakh proper! And like the cliffhanger of a horror film, nauseatingly predictable images of Azeri soldiers showing off decapitated Armenian soldiers' heads and cut-off ears started emerging on social media. A 19-year-old Armenian soldier was said to have been skinned alive, and an elderly lady who had barely managed to evacuate from her village described witnessing Azeri soldiers decapitating an Armenian civilian man in the middle of her street. Horrific videos of torture, decapitation, and persecution were surfacing on Facebook, Instagram, and Twitter as if they were acceptable social pastimes. Azeri and Turkish aggression and racism had also spilled over onto social media in the form of threats by bots against any Armenian sympathizers, including

96 Joe Nersessian, "The Mixed Messaging of Ilham Aliyev," EVN Report, October 22, 2020, https://www.evnreport.com/politics/the-mixed-messaging-of-ilham-aliyev.
97 Ewelina U. Ochab, "Shortly Before Ceasefire, Experts Issue a Genocide Warning for the Situation in Nagorno-Karabagh," *Forbes*, November 11, 2020, https://www.forbes.com/sites/ewelinaochab/2020/11/11/shortly-before-ceasefire-experts-issue-a-genocide-warning-for-the-situation-in-nagorno-karabakh/?sh=4dc502e9d005.

several American celebrities. Facebook later took down the pages of a massive number of 8,000 Azeri trolls disseminating lies, hatred, and propaganda.[98]

As we agonized over the increasing number of casualties, it became evident that our nation was abandoned yet again. The monstrous invasion by Azerbaijan with the full backing of Turkey had all the markings of a premeditated and meticulously planned operation. Captured mercenaries confessed that they were promised a salary of $2,000 a month and an additional $100 per decapitated Armenian head! Yet, if you heard the international media's coverage of the story, you would think that it pertained to a legitimate war! Artsakh, with a population of 150,000 of whom 100,000 had evacuated, and the rest were in bunkers, and Armenia, with its population of 3 million, were up against a combined population of almost 100 million between Turkey and Azerbaijan, in addition to the military command of the Turkish forces which constitute NATO's second-largest army, and imported mercenaries! The world's powers could have easily stopped this blatantly criminal aggression against the Democratic Republic of Artsakh by imposing severe sanctions and deploying UN military measures against aggression, an illegitimate conduct by international standards. As the assault continued unabated, one couldn't help but wonder if it had the blessing of major players in the region. Conspiracy theories trying to explain the unraveling calamity were abound. Many thought that with its inaction, the West was handing over Artsakh to Azerbaijan in exchange for Azeri oil and strategic cooperation while letting Turkey's involvement and growing influence undermine Russia in the Caucasus, and that Russia was handing over Artsakh in the hopes of forming a coalition with Turkey and Azerbaijan to lead them away from the West. All theories sounded plausible. The one sure thing, however, was the vulnerability of the Armenian nation, where the age-old tug of war between the West and the East and the ominous specter of

---

98 Isaiah Alonso, Tech Times, *Facebook Removes Azerbaijan's Massive 8,000 Troll Pages, Thanks to Whistleblower Shophie Zang's 'Political Manipulation' Leaks,* October,8, 2020

Pan-Turkism seemed to converge, yet again. While French President Macron was vocal in his condemnation of the direct involvement of Turkey, a NATO and OSCE country, and the use of terrorist mercenaries, the Trump administration ignored its Minsk responsibilities and stayed mostly mum as long as it could.

According to analysts, the ferocity of the assault with its fleets of drones was unprecedented in modern-day warfare, and the operation was most likely presumed to wrap up in a matter of days. However, the Armenian fighters, from the lowlands to the snow-covered positions, were not giving up and were giving it their all, despite their tremendous disadvantage. Many heroic tales of individual 18-year-old soldiers taking out several enemy tanks all by themselves were being relayed from the battlefield.

It was only after Armenian Americans' loud turnout at Trump's presidential campaign rallies that Trump commented that he found "the Armenian flags to be beautiful, that Armenians were great businessmen and that he will be helping them." The perfunctory ceasefire agreement he brokered, however, failed just like its predecessors brokered by France and Russia simply because while the Azeri representatives would agree to stop the fighting, Turkey, which was in command of the war, would continue the fight on the ground. Getting the media to tell the truth continued to be a struggle. In fact, the couple of instances of the Armenian side retaliating by bombing the city of Ganja in Azerbaijan seemed to get disproportionately more coverage than the overwhelming Azeri war crimes, Turkey's overt abuse of power, and the massive daily shelling of Artsakh's towns, including the capital of Stepanakert.

The war lasted 44 days, culminating with the sudden fall of Shushi. Our beloved fortress town that was liberated with the legendary "Wedding in the Mountains" operation was relinquished with a final Armenian wedding performed in the bombarded Ghazanchetsots Cathedral, just a few days prior. The bride in her traditional Armenian garb held on to the hands of her groom in military uniform surrounded by more than a dozen local and international reporters in safety gear, as the bishop conducted the ceremony. The ceasefire that Russian President Vladimir Putin brokered turned out to be a devastating capitulation of the Armenian side. The trilateral statement signed by Putin, Aliyev, and Pashinyan created shock and havoc in Yerevan, Armenia, where accusations of treachery ran rampant and outraged citizens broke into the government building demanding Prime Minister Nikol Pashinyan's resignation, as a rebuke to the outrageous declaration! According to the deal, all forces were to stay in the positions they were in, meaning the Azeri forces were going to stay where they had advanced within the territories belonging to the enclave of Nagorno-Karabakh, including the towns of Hadrut and Shushi, which overlooks Artsakh's capital of Stepanakert! In other words, the Azeris were being allowed to occupy additional parts of what constituted the Autonomous Enclave of Nagorno-Karabakh proper. Yet in complete contradiction, in its next paragraphs, the statement dictated that the Armenian forces were to retreat from the remaining areas of the "seven occupied regions" that they still hung on to and that were, in fact, twice as larger than the areas the Azeris had advanced into! These areas were to be handed over to Azerbaijan without a single shot fired! The Armenian civilian population living in these regions was given a few weeks' time to abandon their homes! The situation reeked of a programmed defeat of the Armenian side and renewed ethnic cleansing of Armenian villages! The lowlands of Karabakh were once again being transferred to Azerbaijan! Prisoners of war, hostages, and the bodies of the dead were to be exchanged, and a Russian peacekeeping force of 2,000 was to move in and stay in place for a minimum of five years, protecting, among other areas, the critical Lachin corridor that links Armenia to Artsakh. But this was not all. Armenia was also to guarantee the safety of transport links and the construction of new infrastructure through its southern territory of Zangezur (Syunik) that will link Azerbaijan to its autonomous exclave of Nakhichevan and from there to Turkey, as well as link all three nations to Russia eastbound! For the Armenians, this part exposed what the war was truly about: the reinstatement of the Pan-Turkic ideology. It had all the markings of Erdogan's influence and Putin's attempt to secure an economic and geopolitical coalition with Azerbaijan and Turkey, by sacrificing Armenian land yet again. Transport routes through the southern part of Armenia had nothing to do with the Karabakh conflict, especially since transport between the countries could be reinstated by the mere opening of the closed Turkish and Azeri borders. Aliyev's description of these routes as a "corridor" through the southern province of sovereign Armenia, pointed to Turanic joining of Turkey with Azerbaijan and gradual plans of annihilating the Armenian nation "completing what their ancestors had started in the Caucasus" as Erdogan had put it. A hundred years later, they were picking up from where their ancestors had failed. They were going for Zangezur (see: Where is Karabakh?). Nowhere in the agreement was the status of Nagorno-Karabakh addressed, even though it has been the key issue of the entire twenty six year conflict! Armenia had suffered a humiliating defeat by an obscenely superior force and was yet again forced to sign, "at gunpoint," an illegal agreement to benefit the Azeri, Turkish and Russian sides, at the cost of priceless ancestral lands soaked with the blood of its people. After all that was said and done, 75% of the Republic of Artsakh was lost, hundreds of civilians and upwards of 4,000 Armenian soldiers were killed, hundreds were captured as POWs or were missing in action, thousands more were injured and maimed, and about 100,000 Armenians from Artsakh were displaced and were now refugees in Armenia. Soon enough, videos of Azeri soldiers shouting "Alahu Akbar" off the top of vandalized Armenian churches and the planting of the Azeri flag over Vankasar church's cross surfaced. Vankasar was the church I had glimpsed high atop a mountainside over the ruins of the 2nd century BC Tigranakert.

Footage after footage of Azeri soldiers desecrating and vandalizing Armenian homes, cemeteries, and churches, demonstrated yet again why the Armenians wanted their independence from

Azerbaijan in the first place. It is simply treacherous for Armenians to live under Azeri rule because Azeri citizens are indoctrinated by their state to demonstrate open and unapologetic hatred towards Armenians. In an immediate violation of the agreement, instead of "stopping at their current positions," Azeri forces continued advancing into Nagorno-Karabakh proper, occupying additional land from the region of Hadrut, where they took dozens more Armenian POWs! The areas in question were assigned to the jurisdiction of the Russian peacekeepers who were on their way there! Under the pretext of reinstating its borders, Azerbaijan advanced, snatching land from Armenia proper as well, including half of the gold mines at Sodk, a village in the Gegharkunik Province of Armenia. Instead of protecting CSTO member Armenia's territorial integrity, as the terms of its alliance call for, Russia's nonchalance seemed to be enabling the Azeri transgressions! Together with Turkey, it marked the opening of a "peacekeeping center" in Karabakh to monitor the ceasefire! The aggressive party that launched the war and committed war crimes is apparently to be trusted with keeping the peace!

According to international norms defined by the UN Charter, an agreement between two countries achieved by the use of force that has not been ratified by the involved governments is not legally binding.[99] However, aside from a few statements made by the French about the illegality of the November 9, 2020 statement signed by the Armenian side under duress, and implemented unilaterally by Russia outside of the mandated Minsk process, no other Western power challenged the legality of the announcement! According to Artsakh's Human Rights Ombudsman, more than 100 videos of torture, humiliation, and beheadings of Armenian servicemen and civilians by Azeri and Turkish soldiers and terrorist mercenaries have surfaced, and 1,452 overwhelmingly Armenian monuments, including the renowned monasteries of Dadivank and Tsitsernavank, the

---

99 Article 52, Coercion of a State by the threat or use of force. Vienna Convention on The Law of Treaties Signed At Vienna 23 May 1969, Entry Into Force: 27 January 1980

archeological sites of Tigranakert and the Azokh Paleolithic caves, architectural monuments of ancient castles and bridges, museums and galleries with 19,311 exhibits have passed into Azeri hands, in addition to essential water power plants, agricultural fields, wineries, and private businesses. As the Azeri forces were moving into Artsakh, we all agonized over the fate of the Armenian monuments passing under their control.

Twenty-six years of celebrated democracy and freedom in Artsakh were coming undone! Armenian communities all over the world were devastated and in shock! The Turkish and Azeri aggression and racism have rehashed old anxieties of persecution with impunity. The current generations experienced the same traumatizing loss as the generation of the Genocide survivors who were thrown out of their ancestral lands in Western Armenia. Startling footage was next released of Aliyev and his Vice President First Lady, clad in military fatigues, taking a victory tour of the "returned territories," even stepping into the shelled Ghazanchetsots Cathedral in occupied Shushi, where, only a few days earlier, Armenian women and children had taken refuge from Azeri bombs! Seizing Shushi, where the Azeris had suffered a major defeat in the first Karabakh war, was apparently of top priority for Aliyev!

During the days of war, as with most Diaspora Armenians, my mind was consumed by the events in my homeland, the homeland that I had just discovered and was looking forward to keep on visiting and exploring. At work, I feigned normalcy and presented a happy façade to coworkers, while at breaks I glimpsed at beheadings on my cell phone. One beheaded kid with arms frozen in their grip for life still had his backpack on. I could not imagine what his family was going through. Some Azeri soldiers called the relatives of the captured Armenian soldiers on the soldiers' cell phones and had them witness the execution of their son, daughter, husband, brother, and father. What kind of hatred was this? The numbered days passed quickly as thousands of Armenians, packed in cars and trucks stuffed with all their livelihoods, left the regions to be relinquished.

Many were so distraught that they burned down their own homes in order not to leave them to the Azeris! Through social media, we bore witness to the sad goodbyes of the Armenians who visited their beloved monastery of Dadivank in Karvachar for the last time on their way out of the area. The songs they sang, holding hands in a large circle in the courtyard of the church complex, will haunt us forever! (Dadivank is the 9th-century monastery where several of the Meliks of Khachen are buried). Karvachar (or Kelbajar, its Azeri name) was one of the seven so-called "Azeri territories occupied by Armenians." A region snatched from the first Republic of Armenia in 1923, it was now being claimed by a country that was created in 1918, more than 1,000 years after the construction of the Armenian monastery of Dadivank there! A journalist friend of mine braved a last glimpse of the ruins of the 2nd century BC city of Tigranakert ahead of the arrival of the Azeri forces in Agdam. She also posed for a last shot with the sign at the entrance of Artsakh that we had all come to cherish. It said in Armenian, "The Independent and Free Artsakh Greets You"! Its dismantling by Azeri bulldozers, as well as that of the sign at the entrance of our beloved city of Shushi, was broadcast on social media a week later. Images of the exodus of our people from yet another piece of our homeland left us dumbfounded and numb.

Almost exactly 100 years after Ataturk had bargained for Armenian lands from Lenin and Stalin with the illegal Moscow and Kars Treaties, Erdogan was doing the same with Putin, and once again, the West was standing aside. Even though logically, the Armenian side did not stand a chance against the massive invasion, introspection and self-criticism were nevertheless prevalent reactions. Why didn't Armenia use the leverage of the 1994 victory and honor the petition of the Armenians of Artsakh by officially reannexing it? Why did we not use the maps and documents in our possession to make the case that Artsakh historically and legally belonged to Armenia and that the equally historically Armenian seven region buffer zone was essential for its security? Why did we not secure a remedial sovereignty for Artsakh in the face of Azerbaijan's proven genocidal intent? Why didn't Armenia, once independent, reinstate its pre-Soviet 1918 internationally recognized borders, thus delegitimizing the usurpation of its lands by the Soviets, Turks, and Azeris? Why did we not point out to the West that they were upholding the illegitimate borders of Stalin?[100] Most of all, why did we, as a nation, fail to be ready, diplomatically and militarily, for what we knew was sure to come?

Following the 44 day war, Azerbaijan held a victory military parade in Baku where Aliyev and Erdogan oversaw from their balcony a procession of tanks and equipment captured from the Armenians, further demoralizing the Armenian side (Aliyev would later build a military trophy park replete with the helmets of killed Armenian soldiers, and ugly mannequins depicting Armenian troops in agony and defeat). Aliyev, boasting of a victory handed to him by Turkey, announced that Yerevan, the 2,800-year-old capital of Armenia, was historic Azeri land where Azeris would return and that with the Azeri raised iron fist, he had "crushed the enemy's spine and crushed the enemy's head," while Erdogan praised the marching Turkish and Azeri detachments and said, "Today, may the souls of Nuri Pasha, Enver Pasha, and the brave soldiers of the Caucasus Islam Army, be happy!"[101] A brazen celebration of Turkic ethnic cleansing of Armenians as Enver Pasha was one of the architects of the Armenian Genocide, and Nuri Pasha was his brother. In 1918, they had brought their Army of Islam to the Caucasus and, with the help of the Azeris, had massacred thousands of Armenians in Baku in order to secure it for a second Turkic nation. These statements

---

100   It was only in 1933, that President Roosevelt finally acknowledged the Soviet Union for geopolitical reasons.

101   "At Baku Victory Parade, Aliyev Calls Yerevan, Zangezur, Sevan Historical Azerbaijani Lands and Erdogan Praises Enver Pasha," *Armenian Mirror-Spectator*, December 11, 2020, https://mirrorspectator.com/2020/12/11/at-baku-victory-parade-with-erdogan-aliyev-calls-yerevan-zangezur-sevan-historical-azerbaijani-lands-erdo-gan-praises-enver-pasha/.

reinforced the Armenian side's paranoia about the impending annihilation of their homeland at the hands of its mortal enemies.

Azerbaijan's most shocking violation of the November 9, 2020,
trilateral statement was the taking of dozens more Armenian POWs
as its forces advanced further into Karabakh by the time the Russian
peacekeepers arrived. No one in the world cared to punish this unethical breach of the so-called trilateral statement, and the Russians
who are there to enforce the terms of the ceasefire did not impose
on the Azeris to return those POWs, as well as the villages in question to the Armenian side and retreat to the positions they had
reached leading up to the ceasefire. Despite Azerbaijan's agreement
to exchange POWs, most of the Armenian prisoners are still held
in its jails, and videos of torture continue to surface to the chagrin
of their families. (Armenia, on the other hand, has immediately
returned all the POWs it held). This is a blatant violation of all human rights Geneva Conventions, and yet aside from international
calls to release the POWs and detained civilians, no concrete puni-
tive steps have been taken so far against Azerbaijan's war crimes.

To manipulate the truth and disseminate misinformation in
order to demoralize and discredit the Armenian side, the Aliyev
regime continues to engage in traumatizing psychological warfare
unfortunately all too familiar to Armenians. He constantly gaslights
the Armenian side assigning to it that which Azerbaijan commits
in symmetrical propaganda. This mind game aims at confusing
the world and discouraging calls for accountability. Aliyev was also
quick to pick up the new trend of discrediting the media as fake.
As such, when BBC correspondent Orla Guerrin insisted that BBC's
own reporters had personally witnessed Azeri drones and cluster
bombs target the civilian areas while reporting from Artsakh, Aliyev
said those reports were not reliable because they were fake!

The blood of the young soldiers had not dried yet when the U.S.
and British ambassadors to Baku congratulated the Azeri government for having restored the country's territorial integrity with
the liberation of the "occupied" territories! Historically Armenian

territories that were reclaimed by the Armenian side in direct consequence to Azerbaijan's own act of war and attempt of ethnic cleansing! One can't help but wonder since when have aggression and force against a peaceful population electing freedom become praiseworthy by Western countries that preach democracy, freedom, and human rights? Since when does the West approve of war crimes, the use of illegal weapons, and terrorist mercenaries? The U.S. ambassador's statement was particularly disconcerting, given the fact that the U.S. is one of the co-chairs of the OSCE Minsk Group with an international mandate to come up with a peaceful resolution to the conflict!

A century after the 1920 Shushi massacre, oil contracts and a gold mining company seemed to prevent the British parliament from taking sides again. Following Azerbaijan's independence, the British Petroleum Company (BP) had entered the Azeri market in 1992. On the other hand, the Anglo Asian mining company, the only business listed on the London Stock Exchange that operates exclusively in Azerbaijan and owns 49% of the gold share in Azerbaijan, at the conclusion of the 44-day war, announced its plans for prompt commencement of mining in the newly "liberated" Zangilan territory! Anglo Asian's non-executive director is none other than U.S. lawmaker Republican John Sununu, former chief of staff to President George W. Bush. Apparently, the company was anxiously monitoring the progress of the war as it announced that "once secure, the Company plans to immediately start work at Vejnaly. The Company will update its shareholders with further developments!"[102] Interests and priorities!

Armenians who contribute to their adopted communities all over the world found out the hard way that neither historical truth nor their human rights mattered. The UN can preach about human rights, the right to self-determination, prevention of genocides, and

---

102 Alison Tahmizian Meuse, "Azerbaijan's Victory Carves Path to a Gold Mine," *Asia Times*, November 9, 2020, https://asiatimes.com/2020/11/azerbaijans-victory-carves-path-to-a-gold-mine/.

peaceful resolution of conflicts all it wants. World leaders prioritize economic and military empowerment and recognize another nation's right to independence and even its right to exist only if it suits their country's interests. However, it is not up to earthly powers to grant liberty. Liberty is a God given unalienable right. Being the only democracy in the region, one would have expected that protecting Armenia's territorial and human rights would have been of strategic import to Western nations. Their tacit silence, however, stunned Armenians all over the world. For his part, Erdogan announced that Armenia could stop being isolated (Turkey and Azerbaijan are the ones who have closed their borders and blockaded Armenia) and even prosper economically if it "behaves" and makes the correct decisions. In other words, if Armenia acknowledges the Soviet-era illegal Turkish and Azeri borders as final, forgets about the Genocide, lets go of its rights for land and material reparations, recognizes Western Armenia as being part of Turkey, and gives up Artsakh and its own southern province so that Turkey and Azerbaijan are joined by land.

The American elections that eclipsed the war in faraway Karabakh did not turn out as President Trump had hoped, and his opponent Joe Biden won. On January 19, 2021, literally in its eleventh hour, the Trump administration signed a surreal bilateral U.S.-Turkey Memorandum of Understanding that formally grants Turkey legal rights over all archeological, historical, and religious monuments within its lands. In other words, this understanding will make it very difficult for all the indigenous people of Turkey to be able to access or rescue their cultural artifacts away from a regime known to appropriate or destroy every last trace of its Christian Armenian, Greek and Assyrian heritage, a truly beguiling and unethical parting gift from an outgoing American President who branded himself as a Christian Conservative and protector of religious rights. Erdogan has been on an open mission to destroy Christian churches. In July 2020, he converted the ancient Christian Orthodox Cathedral of the Haghia Sophia from a museum back to a mosque, put an ancient Armenian church up for sale, and bulldozed another, while others were converted to theatres, libraries, and mosques. The timing of the agreement showed how intent Erdogan was on extricating the very last drop of benefit from his "friendship" with Trump. With this corrupt agreement, Erdogan was perhaps also hoping to mitigate any future legal reparations imposed on Turkey for material and cultural losses of Christian minority heritage.

2020 has earned its reputation as one of the worst years ever. It will be mentioned in history books as the year of the devastating Covid-19 world pandemic that has so far taken the lives of over 5 million people worldwide. On August 4th, 2020, approximately 2,750 metric tons of ammonium nitrate unsafely stored in the port of Beirut ignited and exploded in a blast considered one of the largest in modern history, resulting in a massive mushroom cloud and a seismic shock wave ripping through the city destroying everything in its path. Hundreds were killed, thousands were injured, and hundreds of thousands became homeless in a blink of an eye. Because of its proximity to the port, Gemmayze's many old historic buildings came tumbling down. My heart was broken. After all, that is where I was born.

For me, as with most Armenians, the icing on the cake was Azerbaijan's shocking war of aggression and the open Armenophobia exhibited by Azeris, which made us realize that the Armenian Genocide had never stopped. Our generation was also living through it. In a matter of six weeks, our Artsakh of millennia that we had liberated against all odds, and that we wanted the entire world to see, was mostly lost to us, and its priceless cultural heritage was in grave danger of destruction. Similarly to Armenians in Armenia who glance helplessly at the neglected ruins of the city of Ani across the Akhurian river and yearn for Mount Ararat so close and yet unreachable, Armenians in Artsakh are now glancing at the Ghazanchetsots Cathedral of Shushi a mere few kilometers from the outskirts of Stepanakert, and Tsitsernavank (in Kashatagh) and Dadivank (in Karvachar) monasteries so close to the new demarcation line that places them in Azeri hands.

THE 9TH CENTURY MONASTERY OF DADIVANK FROM AFAR.
PHOTO REPRINTED WITH PERMISSION © VAHAGN GRIGORYAN

A close-up of Dadivank Monastery in Artsakh's Karvachar region, where Armenian Melik princes from the Kingdom of Khachen are buried. After the 44 day war, once again in Azeri held territory. Photo © David Karamian, reprinted with permission from *Armenia-The Lone Stone*

A Last Word

Under Article 81 of the 1907 Hague Convention and Article 54 of the 1899 Hague Convention, an arbitral award, duly pronounced and notified to all the agents of the parties in dispute, settles the dispute definitively and without opportunity for an appeal.

On July 22, 1920, acting as the legitimate ruler and representative of the Ottoman Empire, Sultan Mehmet VI agreed to grant President Woodrow Wilson the arbitration to draw the frontier between Armenia and Turkey, in accordance to the Constitution of the Ottoman Empire of 1876 and 1909.

On September 28, 1920 the committee headed by professor Westerman submitted to the U.S. State Department the report that defined the border between Armenia and Turkey-guaranteeing Armenia access to the Black sea via Trabizon as well as 103,600 square kilometers of land (including Bitlis, Van and Erzrum).

On November 22, 1920, President Wilson signed the report and issued his Arbitration Award to Armenia. The award bore the great seal of the United States and was sent to the US ambassador in Paris, Hugh Campbell Wallace. On December 6, 1920 Wallace delivered the document to the secretary general of the peace conference for submission to the Allied Supreme Council.[103]

I REMAIN CONVINCED THAT FINDING my grandmother's relatives was not a random occurrence. The coincidences involved were simply too perfectly aligned to be considered haphazard. Many Armenians mention having experienced the same phenomenon, where relatives separated by the Genocide ended up finding each other under fascinating circumstances. It is as if our ancestors are leading us to each other and want to speak their truth through us. The hundreds of thousands deported and killed just for being Armenian were not mere statistics. They were human beings. They were our families. Their stories and the story of every other victim of ethnic cleansing and genocide need to be told in order to expose the dark side of humanity and help curtail it.

As relatives kept on appearing and the puzzle pieces kept on falling in place, I realized that not only had my family's story found its way to me, but it was also leading me down the intriguing path that had beckoned to me throughout my childhood. The research I conducted in order to put the events of my grandparents' ordeal into a historical perspective, ended up unveiling the many compelling truths I was chasing all my life! It led me to a world that I had always wanted to explore. It led me to Armenia. The unattainable country that growing up in Beirut I had sang songs about. The land that my ancestors were subjected to genocide for. The homeland that I was deprived of. The more I read, the more I became overwhelmed with the realization of how much was taken from us as a people! From antiquities, to large swaths of ancestral lands, to priceless monuments, to millions of lives; the loss was staggering! And as I finally formed a clear picture of where my roots were from and why my life was dealt with its particular set of circumstances, the dormant

103 Michael Sosikian, "Summary of Events Leading Up to the Establishment of Wilsonian Armenia," Asbarez, August 14, 2020, https://asbarez.com/196202/summary-of-events-leading-up-to-the-establishment-of-wilsonian-armenia

tempest that had torn Armenia apart reawakened, threatening to destroy the precious little that remains of it!

That the Armenian Genocide would resume in the 21st century under a new guise was inconceivable yet not shocking. Openly racist authoritarian leaders who remain unrepentant and deny, cover up, and justify the crimes of their predecessors are bound to continue the same crimes. The crimes never stop. They simply transition from active phases to denial phases. The perpetrators evade justice by finding ways to align themselves with the interests of leading nations that turn a blind eye to their crimes in exchange for so-called strategic alliances, oil, and military contracts. Just like Ataturk was allowed to violate the terms of the Treaty of Sevres and occupy Western Armenia, awarded by arbitration to the Armenians by the President of the United States, Azerbaijan has violated the 1994 Karabakh ceasefire, upended the Minsk peace process and invaded the democratic republics of Artsakh and Armenia, so far, without any noteworthy repercussions.

Several months have passed since the official ceasefire of the recent Karabakh war. The trilateral statement was just a ruse. The invasion continues. It has moved from all-out combat to incursions, occupation, and terrorism, and none of it is being covered by the international media. The Armenian side has lost more land in the aftermath of the ceasefire than it had during the war! The central issue of the conflict, the status of Nagorno-Karabakh, has yet to be addressed. The courageous Artsakh refugees have returned to a much smaller and more confined Artsakh, where Russia has now installed a military base. No foreign journalists were at hand to report on the challenges they faced (as many have lost their homes), or ask about the loss of their loved ones in the war, or how they felt now that they were completely surrounded by Azeri armed forces. Another 30,000 refugees are still in Armenia.

The seven region buffer zone is gone, and the Soviet-era Azeri abuses are back, even in the presence of Russian peacekeepers. Civilians have been kidnapped and tortured. Shepherds are harassed and beaten, their cattle are confiscated, and their pastures taken over. Reports of random shootings and shelling of Armenian towns, even Artsakh's capital of Stepanakert, as well as intentional arson of fields and homes, have become commonplace. A priest was dragged and beaten! The Azeri forces are regularly shooting at Armenian farmers to prevent them from harvesting their crops. World dignitaries and humanitarian organizations are prevented from entering Artsakh which keeps the world from seeing the plight of the Armenians there. Sadly, while the American government sent $120 million in military aid to Azerbaijan, it has yet to send any humanitarian aid to Artsakh or Armenia. This is the same America that, a hundred years ago, organized the largest foreign aid in its history in order to assist the Armenians and prevent their extinction.

As I write these last words, about 1,000 Azeri forces penetrated Armenia proper at different points in its Gegharkunik and Syunik provinces (May 2021). They even captured Armenian soldiers as hostages on Armenian soil! Their aim is to take over, by force, a corridor going through southern Armenia, linking Azerbaijan to Nakhichevan and Turkey while dividing Armenia in two. Such a corridor will be a death sentence for Armenia, cutting it off from its only open border in the south. Its southern portion will then be at risk of occupation and annexation by Azerbaijan, hence the realization of the Pan-Turkic dream. It came as no shock, when Armenia's official request for intervention by the CSTO[104], in light of the Azeri invasion of its sovereign territories, was also declined, with the excuse that the situation can be peacefully resolved with the demarcation of borders and the implementation of the terms of the ceasefire! After all, not only is Russia one of Azerbaijan's main arms suppliers, but in Putin's own words, Russia also has close ties with Azerbaijan. Legitimizing Azerbaijan's Soviet era borders will mean losing the lowlands of Artsakh for good. It will also isolate the rest of Artsakh within Azerbaijan, and put it in serious risk of

---

104 CSTO: Collective Security Treaty Organization, a Russian-led intergovernmental military alliance in Eurasia that Armenia is part of.

ethnic cleansing. Currently, however, Azeri forces have penetrated beyond the Soviet era borders and hold positions deep within sovereign Armenia!

Azeri soldiers keep on advancing with the pretext of reinstating borders, methodically taking over critical water sources and strategic military heights within Armenia proper! Based on reports, they are currently occupying all of Armenia's Lake Sev, of which only 10% was given to a former so called "Red Kurdistan" that Soviet Azerbaijan had created in 1923 from the territories it carved out of Karabakh's lowlands including Karvachar, Kashatagh (Lachin), Ghubatlu, Zangelan, and part of Jibrayil! I was stunned to learn about "Red Kurdistan" whose formation was, apparently, collaborated with the Soviets to secure a land separation between Armenia and the enclave of Nagorno-Karabakh, in order to isolate the enclave deeper within Azerbaijan and make it harder for it to rejoin Armenia! It appears that subsequent to the forceful displacement of Armenians from these areas, the remaining population consisted mostly of Kurds settled there in the 16th and 17th centuries, and not enough Azeris lived there to afford Azerbaijan a majority Azeri demographic presence, which prompted Soviet Azerbaijan to create the *Uyezd* (Soviet administrative unit) of Red Kurdistan out of those lands! In the late 1920s, Red Kurdistan complained that it did not have enough water sources to irrigate its agricultural lands and negotiated to take over parts of water sources in bordering Armenia. It later secured more pastures from Armenia, as well as small enclaves sitting on Armenia's major north south highway linking it to Georgia in the north and Iran to the south, even though there were no Kurds or Azeris living in those areas! The intention could have been to access or control Armenia's major trade artery. All this land loss was imposed on Armenia in the name of Communist brotherhood since, after all, the whole region had become part of the USSR. Objections by the Armenians were simply ignored. In order not to damage its relations with Turkey and Iran by upholding Kurdish nationalism, Azerbaijan ended up dissolving Red Kurdistan in 1929.

However, it kept to itself the enclaves, pastures, water sources, as well as all of the territories (Karabakh lowlands) that fell between Soviet Armenia and the enclave of Nagorno-Karabakh that made up the short-lived Uyezd of Red Kurdistan. The Kurds of the area were then displaced by the Soviet Azeri leadership to other regions in the USSR or were assimilated into Azeri society. During the first Karabakh war, the Armenians liberated these lowlands and reattached the majority of historic Artsakh back to Armenia. Ironically, these territories became known as "Azeri regions occupied by Armenians!" Currently, the Azeri forces are basically reinstating the territories of Red Kurdistan (and then some), calling them their "returned territories," and Western diplomats are congratulating them for it!

Not only have they retaken the Red Kurdistan enclaves on Armenia's major Armenia-Iran Goris Gapan highway, but they are sabotaging the flow of goods by setting up checkpoints and harassing freight workers or shutting down the highway altogether to cut off this major trade route. The Armenian side is currently scrambling to look into potential alternate freight routes! The aim seems to be to prevent the sustainability of Armenia.

Russia is downplaying all this usurpation of Armenian land by calling it "demarcation and borderization." Suffice it to say that in the civilized world, demarcation and borderization between two countries are never accomplished by invasion and violence! They involve a lengthy diplomatic process and mutual cooperation. Perhaps by pushing for the implementation of the terms of the trilateral statement, Putin's hope is to finally realize Stalin's dream of a Russian-Turkish union. The Turkish government, in turn, is praising Russia's cooperation, while citing the Turkish-Russian historic brotherhood! While it continuously pushes the Armenian side to adhere to every single term of the trilateral statement, Russia keeps giving Azerbaijan full leeway to violate all of those terms (or is simply unwilling/unable to stop the Azeri transgressions). Aliyev continues to break Geneva Convention international humanitarian laws by not only retaining the Armenian POWs, but by dragging them through sham trials and using them as hostages to be exchanged for more territorial concessions from Armenia, as well as the release of mine maps! He has declared that the conflict of Nagorno-Karabakh is resolved. An announcement that rings like a reverberation from a hundred years ago of the Armenian Genocide mastermind Talaat pasha's statement that the Armenian Question (i.e., the independence of Western Armenia) had been solved.[105] "What on earth do you want? The question is settled; there are no more Armenians." Talaat had responded to German ambassador Johann von Bernstorff's inquiries.[106] Aliyev has even gone as far as announcing that Artsakh no longer exists and will never exist, and the "few" Armenians living in Artsakh will become Azeri citizens. Citizens that he sees as sub-human, who were only recently subjected to massive shelling and all sorts of atrocities by his armed forces. He continues his psychological warfare by claiming that all of Armenia is "Western Azerbaijan" and vows to take over a corridor through Armenia's Syunik (Zangezur) "whether the Armenians like it or not." Aliyev pushes concocted narratives derived out of context from the days of Persian rule in promoting his expansionist goals. He masterfully puts into practice the philosophy that if a state repeats a big lie frequently enough, people will come to believe it.[107]

As a nation, we are tormented with the realization that the world is allowing the continuation of the Armenian Genocide in the 21st century. Neither the West nor the East seem to want to lose their foothold in the Caucasus. Therefore, they continue to stall the conflict's only just resolution: respecting the will of the people of Artsakh, and offering it remedial sovereignty to save it from Azerbaijan's ethnic cleansing. Although hope never dies, many of

---

105 Travis, Hannibal (2010). *Genocide in the Middle East: the Ottoman Empire, Iraq, and Sudan*. Durham, N.C.: Carolina Academic Press. p. 219. ISBN 978-1594604362.

106 A., Bernstorff (2011). *Memoirs of Count Bernstorff*. Kessinger Publishing. ISBN 978-1-169-93525-9.

107 Tom Stafford, BBC Future, *How Liars Create the Illusion of Truth. Repetition makes a fact seem more true, regardless whether it is or not. Understanding this effect can help you avoid falling for propaganda, says psychologist Tom Stafford*. October 26, 2016

us are showing signs of combat fatigue and numbness. This 130-year ongoing persecution has affected generations of our families, each time taking more innocent lives and more pieces of our homeland, while we are continuously denied justice because of geopolitics and power games. The 160,000 km² Wilsonian Armenia was reduced to the 70,000 km² 1918 first Republic of Armenia, which was shrunk to 43,000 km² and then 31,000 km² when it joined the USSR and the Moscow and Kars Treaties took effect, and further down to 29,743 km² when additional enclaves, pastures and bodies of water were given to Azerbaijan, and the Azeris have currently advanced tens of kilometers (41 km²), at different points of contact, within the current Republic of Armenia!

I now have a new appreciation for the words my father uttered while leaving Lebanon: "I want my children to be the citizens of a big and powerful nation." Small nations, especially those surrounded by hegemonic authoritarian leaderships, run the risk of being killed and annihilated. Had Armenia's neighbors respected its right to exist and world powers upheld its rights, it would have been more than five times its current size. With its democratic values, its culture, history, and innovative character it would have contributed to humanity at the potential it was meant to possess. The number of Armenians walking the face of the earth would have been closer to 40 million instead of the current 11 million. A large gene pool lost to the world. The crime of genocide is a crime against all of humanity. It robs humanity of a part of its own diverse cultural, historical and creative treasure.

Coverage of the continued Azeri war crimes, ongoing ethnic cleansing, daily human rights abuses, and destruction of cultural monuments in the aftermath of the 44-day war is in large part missing in Western media. So far, there has been no condemnation of or mobilization against the Azeri invasion that has come anywhere close to the magnitude of the international reaction to Iraq's 1990 invasion of Kuwait, where the UN Security Council authorized the use of force in ousting the Iraqi forces and liberating Kuwait from occupation. The UN charter that describes the framework within which the UN can take enforcement measures against any "threat to the peace, breach of the peace, or act of aggression" does not differentiate or discriminate between victim countries! According to the UN, every citizen, regardless of his/her country's status, has the same human rights, starting with the right to exist. And yet Artsakh's status remains in limbo, when Azerbaijan's policy of ethnic cleansing alone should have by now garnered it remedial sovereignty. While world leaders upheld Azerbaijan's "territorial integrity," we are yet to see a similar stance in regards to Armenia's territorial integrity, as well as UN resolutions ordering Azerbaijan to retreat from the lands it is currently occupying in Armenia and Artsakh. This double standard is doubly outrageous, considering it applies the concept of "territorial integrity" to Azerbaijan's illegally drawn Soviet-era borders while ignoring Armenia's and Artsakh's indigenous territorial integrity within historical borders recognized as such by the League of Nations, prior to the take-over of the Soviet Union!

Second only to Armenia's independence in 1991, the 1994 heroic liberation of Artsakh was a most uplifting event in a series of detrimental catastrophes for the Armenians. It had restored our people's dignity and instilled confidence in our nation's ability to defend itself and forge a viable future. This hard-earned victory and the safety Artsakh Armenians were finally enjoying have now been taken away by an obscenely aggressive force. If nations who believe in the values of democracy and freedom do not intercede on behalf of Artsakh, its future will remain bleak as it is once again at the brink of being blockaded. Armenia, on the other hand, finds itself once more at the epicenter of clashing Eastern and Western values and goals. A fragile new democracy in a sea of authoritarian regimes. Advanced nations will do well to remember that racism and fascism have an unlimited appetite. They do not respect borders, and if unchecked, what is happening in faraway Armenia and Artsakh will fast affect the rest of the region and the world.

Artsakh Armenians suffered greatly. However, they were not the only ones affected by the war. Many in the Armenian Diaspora have also lost their investments in Artsakh's roads, infrastructure, health care, hospitality, and agriculture, as well as cultural and business developments. During the past 26 years, generations of Armenian youth visited Artsakh from abroad and forged a bond with their homeland. Archeologists from all over the world were uncovering amazing artifacts of Armenian history from pagan to early Christian dates, and Artsakh was continuously registering increases in tourism.

Invoking its donation-backed "mutual agreement of cooperation" with UNESCO, Azerbaijan is currently barring UNESCO officials from visiting Artsakh's religious and cultural sites that have fallen under its control. President Aliyev has announced plans of defacing Armenian letters and symbols from these sites, while footage of terrible vandalism and destruction of churches, museums, and ancient cemeteries keeps surfacing on social media and via satellite imaging. Azerbaijan is demolishing Armenian churches even after claiming that they are Caucasian Albanian or simply "renovating" them to look Albanian! Woven on a conspiracy theory involving an extinct kingdom, this horrific cultural genocide against ancient and priceless Armenian churches and monuments is directed against the whole world, as these early Christianity relics and historic treasures belong to all of humanity.

During the victory parade in Baku, Erdogan had also recited a controversial poem that laments the separation of Azeri-speaking people by the river Araz and hints at claiming parts of northern Iran. This prompted the Iranian government to remind Erdogan that today's Azerbaijan, previously known as Arran, was a territory of the Persian empire and that there was no country of Azerbaijan prior to 1918. It is to be seen how world leaders will heed Turkey's and Azerbaijan's expansionist overtures.

No one can predict what the future holds for Armenia, Artsakh, and their neighbors. Since the end of the recent war, ten states in the U.S. and many cities and parliaments around the world have officially recognized Artsakh and acknowledged its self-determination as being fundamental for its survival. Simply put, the recognition of Artsakh's independence remains an urgent matter of life and death for the Armenians.

Many have also called for Turkey's expulsion from NATO in light of its increasing economic and political ties with Russia and, more importantly, its purchase of Russian weapons in direct conflict with NATO's security (Russia is also building Turkey's first nuclear power plant). The U.S. government has, in fact, imposed sanctions on Turkey over its purchase of Russian S-400 missiles. The European Union, the United Nations, and the Organization for Security and Cooperation in Europe (OSCE), as well as hundreds of American and European politicians, have called on Azerbaijan to return the Armenian hostages and POWs it continues to detain in violation of the November 9, 2020, trilateral statement, and international humanitarian laws. Aliyev, however, is not complying. In fact, he continues to show total disregard to the rule of law and to apply pressure on the Armenians with the threat of brute force.

With millions spent on PR and international news platforms, Turkey and Azerbaijan continue to wage their information warfare. Their often-deployed strategy of "mirror propaganda" replicates in no time every legitimate grievance made by the Armenian side with fabricated or misconstrued similar complaints of their own to discredit the Armenians and create a smokescreen to blur the truth, such as property destruction they point at in their newly "returned lands" to counter the decimation of infrastructure and cultural genocide the Armenian side accuses them of. For starters, the magnitude of Azeri destruction of Armenian structures and heritage is massive, and cannot be compared to war related destruction of Azeri property by the Armenian side. If the Armenians caused damage it was because of a war that was imposed on them by Azerbaijan and not because of a culture of hate against Azeris. Thousands of historic Armenian structures, medieval churches, ancient cemeteries, and monuments from the antiquities, including UNESCO-protected ones, were and continue to be deliberately destroyed, altered or misappropriated by Azerbaijan, mostly during peaceful times, in order to erase all trace of Armenian existence and prevent Armenians from ever returning (an example of misappropriation is the Armenian Church of the Holy Virgin in Baku that was destroyed and a section of it converted to a restaurant). It is worth mentioning here that Artsakh had recently allocated its meager resources to the renovation of the mosque in Shushi in an effort to protect cultural diversity. In stark contrast, during the 44-day war, Azeri forces used precision strikes to shell the Ghazanchetsots Armenian Apostolic Cathedral not far from that mosque twice on the same day while civilians and journalists were taking refuge within. Recent satellite images have shown that the Armenian Green Church, also in the vicinity of the Ghazanchetsots Cathedral, was destroyed after the city was surrendered to the Azeri forces, along with several surrounding residential buildings that have since been razed to the ground.

In response to Karabakh people's democratic vote to live in freedom and democracy on its ancestral lands, Azerbaijan had blockaded Karabakh in the first war, cut off its gas and electricity (the current logistics make the cutting off of electrical power and gas a renewed threat), and shelled it daily, bombing every building in its capital Stepanakert by warplanes and Grad missiles which resulted in the deaths of thousands of civilians. This inhumane blockade (which was also extended to Armenia) that prevented civilians from escaping or accessing food and medicine and had surgeons operating under candlelight prompted the U.S. government to adopt Section 907 of the 1992 Freedom Security Act banning any type of direct American aid to the government of Azerbaijan. Besides its cultural genocide, the billions in damages inflicted by its massive shelling of civilian targets and infrastructure during both Karabakh wars, highlight Azerbaijan's hypocrisy in decrying destruction of property!

Understanding where we come from enriches our lives. This journey has done just that. My newfound relatives' and my family's lives are so much richer now that we have found each other. Although intergenerational trauma continues to be part of us as Armenians, and nothing can fill the void in the gaping hole that genocide and exile from our homeland have caused in our lives, research and understanding of the past have taught us the importance of knowing where we come from and what we have gone through in order to understand the events of today. Looking back, I now realize that the closest I have ever come to experiencing Western Armenia, my ancestral homeland, was in the streets of Beirut, walking among my grandparents' generation of survivors and refugees. My homeland was in the twinkling eyes of boisterous grandpas playing *Shesh Besh*[108] and the sharp looks of busy grandmas shouting orders to their children, then crossing themselves with prayers for everyone's safety. They look at me now from afar, oblivious as always of the deep creases in their faces, with fiery eyes that have seen so much, reassuring me with fervor that, in them, I always had a homeland and that, through them, I will continue to.

As we move further away from the generation that suffered from the Armenian Genocide, revisiting lessons learned and keeping survival stories alive become more and more valuable. Knowledge of history is of particular importance for the young generations who are poised to become the leaders of tomorrow. A nation that does not know its history and the socio-politics that drove it is bound to fall into the same traps, make the same errors, and gamble with its very existence. And a world that does not eradicate criminal behavior and uphold human rights and dignity will only enable more anarchy and human suffering, which will adversely affect everyone on this ever-shrinking earth.

As for me, I drift along within the melting pot of America with a renewed understanding of my existence on this planet. I am the

---

108 Turkish Backgammon

daughter of one of the most continuously persecuted nations on earth, the grandchild of refugees who fled through mountains running from genocide, the child of immigrants who flew over oceans escaping from a civil war, and the citizen of a mighty nation that is yet to prove that all men are born equal.

I am a piece of the Armenian nation's dispersed and unrepresented majority. Communities of descendants of orphans shipped to faraway lands. The overwhelming living, breathing body of evidence of an unpunished crime against humanity: the Armenian Diaspora. And the Armenian Diaspora is, in turn, part of a larger quilt made up of many other ethnic Diasporas spread around the world because of economic and sociopolitical currents and movements created by the ruling elite and power-obsessed leaders.

And, together, we are the good, the bad, and the ugly of humanity.

On April 24, 2021, President Biden became the first American President to officially recognize the Armenian Genocide in the annual White House statement on Armenian Genocide Remembrance Day, making the recognition a government-wide policy in the United States. Prior to making his official statement, he called Erdogan, the leader of the denying and unrepentant country to warn him about the announcement. It took 106 years for America to finally reject complicity in Turkey's denial and stand up to the Turkish leadership's bullying and blackmail. Although the carefully worded statement reeked of an agenda of safeguarding Turkey's impunity with words such as "Ottoman-era genocide" and "we do not cast blame," this was nevertheless a historic moment for Armenians, Greeks, and Assyrians around the world and for all of humanity. Against great odds, the Armenian Diaspora's unwavering resilience and grassroots activism had at last succeeded in fulfilling the vow of generations in getting recognition for what happened to their grandparents and exposing an unpunished crime that, shockingly, continues to this day. Will this confirmation ever translate into justice? Did America finally play the Armenian Genocide card to contain an openly belligerent Turkey? Is it trying to whitewash having waived Section 907 of the Freedom Support Act and in doing so risked placing American weapons in the hands of terrorist mercenaries and Armenian-hating Azeris in the 2020 Artsakh war?

Immediately following President Biden's acknowledgement of the Armenian Genocide, the U.S. State Department quietly waived Section 907 of the Freedom Security Act once again in order to send more military aid to Azerbaijan![109]

In 2021, Russia proposed a "3+3" economic alliance with Turkey, Azerbaijan and Iran (also including Georgia and Armenia). On February 22, 2022, Putin and Aliyev signed an alliance to deepen their military and diplomatic cooperation. Two days later, on February 24, the war between Russia and Ukraine erupted. A world that did not make a peep about Azerbaijan's invasion of Armenia, now roared (as it should), about Russia's invasion of Ukraine. The extent and pace at which Azerbaijan is building roads, bridges and infrastructure in its "liberated lands" attest to prearranged plans. Large swaths of Armenia and Artsakh remain occupied by Azeri forces and in the hands of Russian peacekeepers whose imminent five year exit looms ahead...

---

109 Daniel Larison, *Biden arms waiver is 'slap in the face' of Armenian-Americans,* Responsible Statecraft, May 20, 2021

Resources Used

Robert Fisk, *Pity the Nation: Lebanon at War,* 3rd ed. (Oxford, UK: Oxford University Press, 2001), 382–83.

Thomas Friedman, *From Beirut to Jerusalem* (New York, NY: Macmillan, 1995), 161. From there, small units of Phalangist militiamen, roughly 150 men each, were sent into Sabra and Shatila, which the Israeli army kept illuminated through the night with flares.

The American mission in Adana estimated 195,200, but Armenian estimates were closer to 400,000. "The Pre-War Population of Cilicia," 1920, MS Toynbee 44, Stats, Bodleian Library, Oxford.

Rouben Paul Adalian, *Historical Dictionary of Armenia* (Lanham, MD: Scarecrow Press, 2010), s.v. "Adana Massacre."

Robert H. Hewsen, *Armenia: A Historical Atlas* (Chicago: University of Chicago Press, 2001), 74, 168.

Encyclopaedia Britannica, 9th ed. (1878), s.v. "Anni."

Stanford Shaw, *History of the Ottoman Empire and Modern Turkey* (Cambridge, UK: Cambridge University Press, 1976), 1:13.

Encyclopaedia Britannica Online, s.v. "Fall of Constantinople," accessed April 10, 2021, https://www.britannica.com/event/Fall-of-Constantinople-1453.

ArchNet, s.v. "Hagia Sophia," accessed April 10, 2021, https://web.archive.org/web/20090105062813/http:/archnet.org/library/sites/one-site.jsp?site_id=2966.

Encyclopaedia Britannica, *9th ed. (1878), s.v. "Anni."*

 slâm Ansiklopedisi (Türk Diyanet Vakfı, 2003), s.v. "Malatya," 468–73.

Isidor Wallimann and Michael N. Dobkowski, eds., *Genocide and the Modern Age: Etiology and Case Studies of Mass Death* (Syracuse, NY: Syracuse University Press, 1987).

Hooman Peimani, *Conflict and Security in Central Asia and the Caucasus* (Santa Barbara, CA: ABC-CLIO, 2009).

Raymond Kévorkian, *The Armenian Genocide: A Complete History* (London: I. B. Tauris, 2011), 382.

Erzurum, a city in Turkey in the northeastern part of Anatolia, was once known by its Armenian name of Karin.

Astrig Tchamkerten, *Calouste Sarkis Gulbenkian: The Man and His Work* (Lisbon: Gulbenkian Foundation Press, 2010).

Benny Morris and Dror Ze'evi, *The Thirty-Year Genocide: Turkey's Destruction of Its Christian Minorities, 1894–1924* (Cambridge, MA: Harvard University Press, 2019), Rural Decline.

Morris and Ze'evi, *Thirty-Year Genocide*, A Rural Community Under Siege.

Kévorkian, *The Armenian Genocide.*

Taner Akçam, *The Young Turks' Crime Against Humanity: The Armenian Genocide and Ethnic Cleansing in the Ottoman Empire* (Princeton, NJ: Princeton University Press, 2012), 129.

Akçam, *Young Turks' Crime*, 131

Morris and Ze'evi, *Thirty-Year Genocide*, 156, 157.

Akçam, *Young Turks' Crime*, 248.

George A. Bournoutian, *A Concise History of the Armenian People (From Ancient Times to the Present)*, 2nd ed. (Costa Mesa, CA: Mazda Publishers, 2003).

Henry Morgenthau, *Ambassador Morgenthau's Story* (1918; repr., London: Forgotten Books, 2015), 339.

Morgenthau, *Ambassador Morgenthau's Story*, 333, 334.

Morgenthau, *Ambassador Morgenthau's Story*, 347.

Morgenthau, *Ambassador Morgenthau's Story*, 309.

Sabrina Tavernise, "A Devastating Document Is Met with Silence in Turkey," *New York Times*, March 8, 2009.

Zack Beauchamp, "Germany Just Voted to Recognize the Armenian Genocide. Turkey Is Furious," Vox, June 2, 2016, https://www.vox.com/2016/6/2/11839830/germany-vote-armenian-genocide.

Lebanon was part of the Ottoman Empire until the end of World War I, when it was put under a French mandate.

"Robert Fisk: Living Proof of the Armenian Genocide," *Independent*, March 9, 2010, https://www.independent.co.uk/voices/commentators/fisk/robert-fisk-living-proof-armenian-genocide-1918367.html.

Vartkes Yeghiayan, comp., *Vahan Cardashian: Advocate Extraordinaire for the Armenian Cause* (Glendale, CA: Center for Armenian Remembrance, 2008), 99.

Razib Khan, "What It Means to Be a Turk," *Discover*, June 4, 2009, https://www.discovermagazine.com/health/what-it-means-to-be-a-turk.

Akhilesh Pillalamarri, "The Epic Story of How the Turks Migrated From Central Asia to Turkey," *The Diplomat*, June 5, 2016, https://thediplomat.com/2016/06/the-epic-story-of-how-the-turks-migrated-from-central-asia-to-turkey/.

U ur Hodo lugil and Robert W. Mahley, "Turkish Population Structure and Genetic Ancestry Reveal Relatedness Among Eurasion Populations," *Annals of Human Genetics* 76, no. 2 (2012), https://doi.org/10.1111/j.1469-1809.2011.00701.x.

Rouben Galichian, "A Brief History of the Maps of Armenia," accessed April 10, 2021, http://roubengalichian.com/2015/06/24/a-brief-history-of-the-maps-of-armenia/.

"7000 Year Old DNA Found in Artsakh Cave Matches Genes of Modern Armenians," Asbarez, November 22, 2016, http://asbarez. com/157371/7000-year-old-dna-found-in-artsakh-cave-matches-genes-of-modern-armenians.

Encyclopaedia Britannica, 9th ed. (1878), s.v. "Anni."

Rubina Peroomian, *Literary Responses to Genocide, The Second Generation Responds* (Yerevan: Armenian Genocide Museum-Institute, 2015), pg. 26

"The Turco-Mongol Invasions," Rbedrosian.com, accessed May 22, 2012, http://rbedrosian.com/atmi4.htm.

Samuel S. Cox, *Diversions of a Diplomat in Turkey* (New York: Charles L. Webster, 1893).

"Pope Francis in Turkey Urges Faiths to Combat Fanaticism," BBC video, 2:17, https://www. bbc.com/news/av/world-europe-30251197/ pope-francis-in-turkey-urges-faiths-to-combat-fanaticism.

Akçam, *Young Turks' Crime*, 242–48.

Joseph L. Grabill, *Protestant Diplomacy and the Near East: Missionary Influence on American Policy, 1810–1927* (Minneapolis: University of Minnesota Press, 1971).

"New Historical Novel on Armin T. Wegner Launched at Frankfurt International Book Fair," *Armenian Weekly*, November 4, 2014, https://armenianweekly.com/2014/11/04/new-historical-novel-armin-t-wegner-launched-frankfurt-international-book-fair/.

DiPublico.org, Derecho International, *The Treaty of Sèvres, 1920 (The Treaty Of Peace Between The Allied And Associated Powers And Turkey Signed At Sèvres August 10, 1920)* Oct 22, 2010.

The 1917 Bolshevik Revolution led by Vladimir Lenin put an end to czarist imperial rule by violently toppling the Romanov dynasty.

Mark Malkasian, *Gha-Ra-Bagh! The Emergence of the National Democratic Movement in Armenia* (Detroit, MI: Wayne State University Press, 1996), 22.

In Armenian, *Nakh* means "first," and *Ichevan* means "descent." According to Armenian tradition, Nakhichevan was where Noah first settled after his ark landed on Mount Ararat.

Mary Kilbourne Matossian, *The Impact of Soviet Policies in Armenia* (Leiden: E. J. Brill, 1962), 30.

Richard G. Hovannisian, ed. *Foreign Dominion to Statehood: The Fifteenth Century to the Twentieth Century,* vol. 2 of *The Armenian People from Ancient to Modern Times* (New York: St. Martin's Press, 2004), 417.

Rubina Peroomian, *And Those Who Continued Living in Turkey after 1915, The Metamorphosis of the Post-Genocide Armenian Identity as Reflected in Artistic Literature* (Yerevan: Armenian Genocide Museum-Institute, 2008, 2012)- p. 192

Treaty of Peace Between the Allied and Associated Powers and Turkey Signed at Sèvres, August 10, 1920, accessed April 10, 2021, https://wwi.lib.byu.edu/index.php/Section_I,_Articles_1_-_260.

Taner Akçam, *Armenien und der Völkermord: Die Istanbuler Prozesse und die Türkische Nationalbewegung* (Hamburg, Germany: Hamburger Edition, 1996), 185.

Shevket Sureyya Aydemir, *Enver Pasha*, vol. 3 (Istanbul: Remzi Kitabevi, 2000), 468.

Rudolph J. Rummel, "1,883,000 Murdered: Turkey's Suicidal Purges," chap. 10 in *Death by Government* (New Brunswick, NJ: Transaction Publishers, 1994), *233*.

"Turk's Insane Savagery: 10,000 Greeks Dead," *The Times*, May 5, 1922.

J. J. Norwich and B. Henson, *Mr. Five Percent: The Story of Calouste Gulbenkian* (Home Vision, 1987), VHS video.

"Human Rights Watch World Report 1993 – The Former Soviet Union". Hrw.org. Archived from the original on 18 February 2015. Retrieved 28 April 2014.

De Waal, Thomas (2004). *Black garden: Armenia and Azerbaijan through peace and war.* ABC-CLIO. p. 172. ISBN 0-8147-1945-7. Archived from the original on 3 June 2016.

Margaret C. Tellalian Kyrkostas, "U.S. Media Coverage," University of Minnesota: Center for Holocaust & Genocide Studies, https://cla.umn.edu/chgs/collections-exhibitions.

Grabill, *Protestant Diplomacy.*

Joan George, *Merchants in Exile: The Armenians of Manchester, England, 1835–1935* (London: Gomidas Institute, 2002), 184.

Simon Vrastian, "How Armenia Was Sovietized, (Part V)," *Armenian Review* 2, no. 1 (1949): 123.

Esra Özyürek, "A Turkish 'I Apologize' Campaign to Armenians," *Los Angeles Times*, January 5, 2009, https://www.latimes.com/la-oe-ozyurek5-2009jan05-story.html.

Robert Tait, "Turkish PM Dismisses Apology for Alleged Armenian Genocide," *Guardian*, December 17, 2008, https://www.theguardian.com/world/2008/dec/18/armenian-genocide-apology-turkish-rebuttal.

Tait, "Turkish PM Dismisses Apology."

Paul Antonopoulos, "Greek and Armenian 'Terrorists'! Wild Comments by Erdoğan, but Is He Greek Himself?," *Greek City Times*, May 6, 2020, https://greekcitytimes.com/2020/05/06/greek-and-armenian-terrorists-wild-comments-by-erdogan-but-is-he-greek-himself/.

"Soyadi Kanunu," accessed April 10, 2021, https://web.archive.org/web/20170107165807/http:/www.nvi.gov.tr/Files/File/Mevzuat/Nufus_Mevzuati/Kanun/pdf/soyadi_kanunu.pdf.

Anastasia Lekka, "Legislative Provisions of the Ottoman/Turkish Governments Regarding Minorities and Their Properties," *Mediterranean Quarterly* 18, no. 1 (Winter 2007): 135–54, https://doi.org/10.1215/10474552-2006-038.

Akçam, *Young Turks' Crime.*

Uğur Ümit Üngör and Mehmet Polatel, *Confiscation and Destruction: The Young Turk Seizure of Armenian Property* (New York: Continuum Publishing, 2011).

Ali Çaksu, ed. *Balkanlarda slam Medeniyeti II. Milletlerarası Sempozyumu Tebli leri: Tiran, Arnavutluk, 4-7 Aralık 2003* [Proceedings of the Second International Symposium on Islamic Civilization in the Balkans, Tirana, Albania, 4–7 December 2003] (Istanbul: Research Center for Islamic History, Art and Culture, 2006).

Harun Tunçel, "Türkiye'de İsmi Değiştirilen Köyler" [Renamed Villages in Turkey], *Fırat Universitesi Sosyal Bilimler Dergisi* 10, no. 2 (2000): 23–34.

Kerem Öktem, "The Nation's Imprint: Demographic Engineering and the Change of Toponymes in Republican Turkey". *European Journal of Turkish Studies,* 7. (2008). doi:10.4000/ejts.2243. Retrieved 18 January 2013.

Hovann H. Simonian, ed., *The Hemshin: History, Society and Identity in the Highlands of Northeast Turkey* (London: Routledge, 2007), 161.

Corry Guttstadt, *Turkey, the Jews, and the Holocaust* (Cambridge, UK: Cambridge University Press, 2013), 75; Andrew G. Bostom, *The Legacy of Islamic Antisemitism: From Sacred Texts to Solemn History* (Amherst, NY: Prometheus Books, 2008), 124.

Sargis Serobyan, "More Than Half of 4–5 Million Islamized Armenians Confess That Their Ancestors Have Been Armenian," ArmRadio.info, November 5, 2013,

Oliver Baldwin, *Six Prisons and Two Revolutions: Adventures in Trans-Caucasia and Anatolia, 1920–1921* (Fresno, CA: Meshag Publishing, 1944), 122.

Moses Khorenats'i (1978). *History of the Armenians*. Translated by Thomson, Robert W. Cambridge, Massachusetts & London: Harvard University Press. pp. 139–140.

The History of the Caucasian Albanians by Movses Dasxuanci. Translated by Charles Dowsett. London: Oxford University Press, 1961, pp. 3–4, 7, 24

Jennifer Rankin, *Council of Europe Members Suspected of Corruption, Inquiry Reveals*, The Guardian, April 22, 2018

Jesse Chase-Lubitz, *Council of Europe Body Expels 13 in Azerbaijan Bribe Case*, OCCRP, July 3, 2018

Edita G. Gzoyan: *Nagorno-Karabakh in the Context of Admitting Azerbaijan and Armenia to the League of Nations*. The Armenian Review Journal, Spring Summer 2017, vol 55 issue 3-4

Edita G. Gzoyan (2017): *The admission of the Caucasus states to the League of Nations: the role of Soviet Russia, Caucasus Survey*, DOI: 10.1080/23761199.2017.1342412, pg 6

Rouben Galichian, *Clash of Histories in the South Caucasus: Redrawing the Map of Azerbaijan, Armenia and Iran*. Nov 5, 2012, Bennett & Bloom

Richard G. Hovannisian, preface to Bedross Der Matossian, *The First Republic of Armenia (1918–1920): On Its Centenary: Politics, Gender, and Diplomacy* (Fresno, CA: Press at California State University, 2020).

"7000 Year Old DNA Found," Asbarez.

Armenica.org and Union of Armenian Associations in Sweden, *The Conflict of Nagorno-Karabakh*, website, accessed April 10, 2021, http://www.mountainous-karabakh.org/book_02.html#. X9jhN9QrLs0.

Armenian Institute, "Artsakh / Nagorno-Karabakh: A Brief History, Part 1," October 2, 2020, https://www.armenianinstitute. org.uk/viewstext/artsakh-part1.

Existed from the second century BC to the eighth century AD.

Hewsen, *Armenia*, 40–41.

Armenica.org and Union of Armenian Associations in Sweden, *Conflict of Nagorno-Karabakh*.

Nagorno-Karabakh: History. Defeating Genocide: Index. http:// www.cilicia.com/History.htm

"The third Caucasian people, the Albanians, also received an alphabet from Mesrop, to supply scripture for their Christian church. This church did not survive beyond the conquests of Islam, and all but few traces of the script have been lost, and there are no remains of the version known." Peter R. Ackroyd, *The Cambridge History of the Bible*, vol. 2 (Cambridge, UK: Cambridge University Press, 1963), 368.

Karabekir, Istiklâl Harbimiz/n.2/, p. 631

Emil Sanamyan, "Armenian, Azerbaijani Forces Tussle for High Ground on Tavush Border," USC Dornsife Institute of Armenian Studies, July 13, 2020, https://armenian.usc.edu/armenian-azer-baijani-forces-tussle-for-high-ground-on-tavush-border/.

Robert H. Hewsen, "Ethno-History and the Armenian Influence upon the Caucasian Albanians," in *Classical Armenian Culture: Influences and Creativity*, ed. Thomas J. Samuelian (Chico, CA: Scholars Press, 1982), 27–40.

George Bournoutian, "The Politics of Demography: Misuse of Sources on the Armenian Population of Mountainous Karabakh," *Journal of the Society for Armenian Studies* 9 (1996–1997): 99–103.

Richard G. Hovannisian, *Armenia on the Road to Independence, 1918* (Berkeley: University of California Press, 1967), 227.

Bournoutian, "Politics of Demography," 99–103.

Hovannisian, *Road to Independence*, 227.

Richard G. Hovannisian, *From London to Sèvres, February–August 1920*, vol. 3 in *The Republic of Armenia* (Berkeley: University of California Press, 1996), 152.

"Nurses Stuck to Post," *New York Times*, September 4, 1919, https://en.wikisource.org/wiki/The_New_York_Times/Nurses_stuck_to_post.

Kalli Raptis, *Nagorno-Karabakh and the Eurasian Transport* (Athens, Greece: Hellenic Foundation for European and Foreign Policy, 1998), 5–6.

Richard G. Hovannisian. The Republic of Armenia, Vol. III: From London to Sèvres, February–August 1920 p. 152

Robert Service, *Stalin: A Biography* (Cambridge, MA: Harvard University Press, 2006), 204.

Thomas De Waal (2003). *Black Garden: Armenia and Azerbaijan Through Peace and War.* New York: New York University Press. pp. 51–25. ISBN 9780814719459.

"Aliyev Admits Azerbaijan Worked to Boost Number of Azeris in Artsakh," *Horizon,* December 16, 2020, https://horizonweekly.ca/en/aliyev-admits-azerbaijan-worked-to-boost-number-of-azeris-in-artsakh/.

Law on Secession from the USSR, *Seventeen Moments in Soviet History: An On-Line Archive of Primary Sources,* accessed April 10, 2021, http://soviethistory.msu.edu/1991–2/shevarnadze-resigns/shevarnadze-resigns-texts/law-on-secession-from-the-ussr/

Law on Secession from the USSR.

Baroness Caroline Cox, to Tahir Taghizade, Ambassador of Azerbaijan in the UK, September 10, 2020, accessed April 10, 2021, https://www.hart-uk.org/wp-content/uploads/2020/09/Letter-from-Baroness-Cox-to-the-Ambassador-of-Azerbaijan_10-Sept-2020.pdf.

Dale Berning Sawa, "Monumental Loss: Azerbaijan and 'the Worst Cultural Genocide of the 21st Century,'" *Guardian,* March 1, 2019, https://www.theguardian.com/artanddesign/2019/mar/01/monumental-loss-azerbaijan-cultural-genocide-khachkars.

C Onur Ant. "Son of Murdered Armenian Journalist Convicted." *Guardian,* October 12, 2007, https://www.theguardian.com/world/2007/oct/12/pressandpublishing.turkey.

Sawa, "Monumental Loss."

"By analogy, other tragic events or threatening processes are designated today by Armenians as 'cultural genocide' (for example, the destruction by Azerbaijanis of the Armenian cemetery in Julfa)." Yulia Antonyan and Konrad Siekierski, "A Neopagan Movement in Armenia: The Children of Ara," chap. 17 in *Modern Pagan and Native Faith Movements in Central and Eastern Europe,* ed. Kaarina Aitamurto and Scott Simpson (London: Routledge, 2014), 280n17.

Caroline Cox and John Eibner, "Ethnic Cleansing in Progress: War in Nagorno Karabakh," Sumgait.Info, accessed April 10, 2021, http://sumgait.info/caroline-cox/ethnic-cleansing-in-progress/contents.htm.

Taner Akcam, *Killing Orders: Talat Pasha's Telegrams and the Armenian Genocide,* Palgrave Studies in the History of Genocide (Cham, Switzerland: Palgrave Macmillan, 2018).

John S. Kirakossian, *The Armenian Genocide: The Young Turks Before the Judgment of History* (Madison, CT: Sphinx Press, 1992), 169.

Orhan Kemal Cengiz, "1915: Heroes and Murderers," Cihan News Agency, November 2, 2012, http://www.armeniapedia.org/wiki/Orhan_Cengiz#1915:_Heroes_And_Murderers.

Matt O'Brien, Spencer Raley, and Casey Ryan, *How Many Illegal Aliens Live in the United States?*, fact sheet, Federation for American Immigration Reform (FAIR), September 2019, https://www.fairus.org/sites/default/files/2019-09/IssueBrief_How-Many-Illegal-Aliens-in-the-US_2019_1.pdf.

Ian Shwartz, "Trump: Mexico Not Sending Us Their Best; Criminals, Drug Dealers and Rapists Are Crossing Border," RealClear Politics, June 16, 2015, https://www.realclearpolitics. com/video/2015/06/16/trump_mexico_not_sending_us_their_ best_criminals_drug_dealers_and_rapists_are_crossing_border. html.

Bryan Ross, Alex Hosenball, Cho Park, and Lee Ferran, "Isis 2 Years Later: From 'JV Team' to International Killers," ABC News, June 29, 2016, https://abcnews.go.com/International/ isis-years-jv-team-international-killers/story?id=40214844.

"IS Said to Destroy Armenian Genocide Memorial," *Times of Israel*, September 22, 2014, https://www.timesofisrael.com/ is-reportedly-destroys-armenian-genocide-memorial/.

World Bank, "GDP Growth (Annual %)—Armenia | Data," accessed May 6, 2020, https://data.worldbank.org/indicator/ NY.GDP.MKTP.KD.ZG?locations=AM.

Charles Sykes, "The Humiliation of Lindsay Graham," *Politico*, October 7, 2019, https:// www.politico.com/magazine/story/2019/10/07/ trump-lindsey-graham-syria-kurds-turkey-229541/.

Natasha Turak, "Trump Defends Allowing Turkish Offensive Against Kurds: 'They Didn't Help Us in the Second World War,'" CNBC, October 10, 2019, https://www.cnbc.com/2019/10/10/ trump-defends-allowing-turkish-offensive-on-kurds-in-syria-they-didnt-help-us-in-ww2.html.

Ishaan Tharoor, "Trump's Perplexing Insistence on 'Keeping' Middle Eastern Oil," *Washington Post*, November 14, 2019, https://www.washingtonpost.com/world/2019/11/15/trumps-perplexing-insistence-keeping-middle-eastern-oil/.

Lindsay Wise, "House to Vote on Resolution, Opposed by Turkey, to Mark Armenian Genocide," *Wall Street Journal*, October 25, 2019, https://www.wsj.com/articles/house-to-vote-on-resolution-opposed-by-turkey-to-mark-armenian-genocide-11572039927.

The Nagorno-Karabakh Conflict: A Visual Explainer. International Crisis Group. Retrieved 15 April 2021

Emil Sanamyan, "US Allocates $100 Million in Security Aid to Azerbaijan 2018–2019," USC Dornsife Institute of Armenian Studies, July 17, 2019, https://armenian.usc.edu/us-allocates-100-million-in-security-aid-to-azerbaijan/.

Human Rights Watch, "Azerbaijan: Events of 2019," in *World Report 2020*, https://www.hrw.org/world-report/2020/country-chapters/azerbaijan.

Wise, "House to Vote."

Sanamyan, "US Allocates $100 Million."

Mushvig Mehdiyev, "Azerbaijan President Criticizes OSCE Minsk Group Inaction on Armenia's Illegal Activities," Caspian News, July 9, 2020, https://caspiannews.com/news-detail/azerbaijan-president-criticizes-osce-minsk-group-inaction-on-armenias-illegal-activities-2020-7-7-39/.

Genocide Watch, *Turkey: Erdogan uses "Leftovers of the Sword" anti-Christian hate speech*, May 11, 2020

Ara Khachatourian, "How Do You Prepare 'Populations for Peace'?: You Kill and Maim Them," Asbarez, May 23, 2020, https://asbarez.com/194322/how-do-you-prepare-populations-for-peace-you-kill-and-maim-them/.

Federal Register. 2022. Extension of Waiver of Section 907 of the Freedom Support Act With Respect to Assistance to the Government of Azerbaijan, https://www.federalregister.gov/documents/2021/05/04/2021-09259/extension-of-waiver-of-section-907-of-the-freedom-support-act-with-respect-to-assistance-to-the

Pierre Balanian, *Turkey sends 4,000 Syrian ISIS mercenaries to fight against the Armenians,* Asia News, Sept. 28, 2020

Elizabeth Owen, "Azerbaijan: Papal PR Pays Off," Eurasianet, October 3, 2016, https://eurasianet.org/azerbaijan-papal-pr-pays-off.

Joe Nersessian, "The Mixed Messaging of Ilham Aliyev," EVN Report, October 22, 2020, https://www.evnreport.com/politics/the-mixed-messaging-of-ilham-aliyev.

Ewelina U. Ochab, "Shortly Before Ceasefire, Experts Issue a Genocide Warning for the Situation in Nagorno-Karabak," *Forbes,* November 11, 2020, https://www.forbes.com/sites/ewelinaochab/2020/11/11/shortly-before-ceasefire-experts-issue-a-genocide-warning-for-the-situation-in-nagorno-karabakh/?sh=4dc502e9d005.

Paul Antonopoulos, "Captured Syrian Terrorist in Artsakh Gives Shocking Testimony, Bonus $100 for Chopping Armenian Heads," *Greek City Times,* November 6, 2020, https://greekcitytimes.com/2020/11/06/syrian-artsakh-armenian/.

"At Baku Victory Parade, Aliyev Calls Yerevan, Zangezur, Sevan Historical Azerbaijani Lands and Erdogan Praises Enver Pasha," *Armenian Mirror-Spectator,* December 11, 2020, https://mirror-spectator.com/2020/12/11/at-baku-victory-parade-with-erdogan-aliyev-calls-yerevan-zangezur-sevan-historical-azerbaijani-lands-erdogan-praises-enver-pasha/.

Alison Tahmizian Meuse, "Azerbaijan's Victory Carves Path to a Gold Mine," *Asia Times,* November 9, 2020, https://asiatimes.com/2020/11/azerbaijans-victory-carves-path-to-a-gold-mine/.

Gregory Pappas, "U.S. Groups Blast Outgoing Trump Administration for Last Minute Deal with Turkey," Pappas Post, January 21, 2021, https://www.pappaspost.com/u-s-groups-blast-outgoing-trump-administration-for-last-minute-deal-with-turkey/.

"At Baku Victory Parade," *Armenian Mirror-Spectator.*

Michael Sosikian, "Summary of Events Leading Up to the Establishment of Wilsonian Armenia," Asbarez, August 14, 2020, https://asbarez.com/196202/summary-of-events-leading-up-to-the-establishment-of-wilsonian-armenia/.

Sibel Ekin, "DNA-Based Tests Shake Turks' Beliefs in Their 'Turkishness,'" *Ahval,* October 10, 2019, https://ahvalnews.com/turks/dna-based-tests-shake-turks-beliefs-their-turkishness.

Yerevanci, CC BY-SA 3.0 <https://creativecommons.org/licenses/by-sa/3.0>, via Wikimedia Commons. No changes made.

Ambartsumian, Yelena. "Why Armenian Cultural Heritage Threatens Azerbaijan's Claims to Nagorno-Karabakh." Hyperallergic, May 12, 2021. https://hyperallergic.com/614619/why-armenian-cultural-heritage-threatens-azerbaijans-claims-to-nagorno-karabakh/

Daniel Larison, *Biden arms waiver is 'slap in the face' of Armenian-Americans, Responsible* Statecraft. May 20, 2021

Made in the USA
Monee, IL
04 March 2024

54148611R00213